CW00696462

# THE GREAT EASTERN RAILWAY IN SOUTH ESSEX

BOOK COVER PHOTOS

LNER built N7 No 69630 at Southminster on a Wickford train in the last days of steam working. Author's collection (Front cover)

B17 No 61611 *Raynham Hall* double heads another member of the class on a train at Wickford during the period of single line working the station whilst the Southend line was being electrified. Kidderminster Railway Museum (Back cover top)

Southend (Victoria) station in 1970 with a Liverpool Street train awaiting departure headed by rebuilt class 307 emu No 107. R.F. Roberts/SLS Collection (Back cover centre).

Southend Airport station with class 321 emu No 321 354 heading an 8 car train. Dr Ian Scotchman (Back cover bottom)

# THE GREAT EASTERN RAILWAY IN RAILWAY IN SOUTH ESSEX

## A Definitive History

Charles Phillips

PEN & SWORD
TRANSPORT

AN IMPRINT OF PEN & SWORD BOOKS LTD.
YORKSHIRE – PHILADELPHIA

First published in Great Britain in 2019 by
Pen and Sword Transport
An imprint of
Pen & Sword Books Ltd
Yorkshire - Philadelphia

Copyright © Charles Phillips, 2019

ISBN 978 1 52672 057 3

The right of Charles Phillips to be identified as Author of this work has been asserted by
him in accordance with the Copyright, Designs and Patents Act 1988.

A CIP catalogue record for this book is available from the British Library.

All rights reserved. No part of this book may be reproduced or transmitted in any form
or by any means, electronic or mechanical including photocopying, recording or by any
information storage and retrieval system, without permission from the Publisher in
writing.

Typeset in 10.5/13.5 pt Palatino
Typeset by Aura Technology and Software Services, India

Printed and bound in India by Replika Press Pvt. Ltd.

Pen & Sword Books Ltd incorporates the Imprints of Pen & Sword Books Archaeology,
Atlas, Aviation, Battleground, Discovery, Family History, History, Maritime, Military,
Naval, Politics, Railways, Select, Transport, True Crime, Fiction, Frontline Books, Leo
Cooper, Praetorian Press, Seaforth Publishing, Wharncliffe and White Owl.

For a complete list of Pen & Sword titles please contact

PEN & SWORD BOOKS LIMITED
47 Church Street, Barnsley, South Yorkshire, S70 2AS, England
E-mail: enquiries@pen-and-sword.co.uk
Website: www.pen-and-sword.co.uk

or
PEN AND SWORD BOOKS
1950 Lawrence Rd, Havertown, PA 19083, USA
E-mail: Uspen-and-sword@casematepublishers.com
Website: www.penandswordbooks.com

# Contents

|  |  |  |
| --- | --- | --- |
|  | Foreword | 7 |
|  | Introduction | 8 |
| **Chapter One** | Ancestry of the Lines | 10 |
| **Chapter Two** | The Building of the Lines | 16 |
| **Chapter Three** | Great Eastern Years | 58 |
| **Chapter Four** | London and North Eastern Years | 88 |
| **Chapter Five** | The British Railways Years | 117 |
| **Chapter Six** | From Privatisation to the Present Day | 177 |
| **Chapter Seven** | The Lines Described | 183 |
| **Chapter Eight** | Motive Power | 206 |
| **Chapter Nine** | Dates of Opening and Closing and Distances | 244 |
|  | Sources and Acknowledgements | 250 |
|  | Index | 254 |

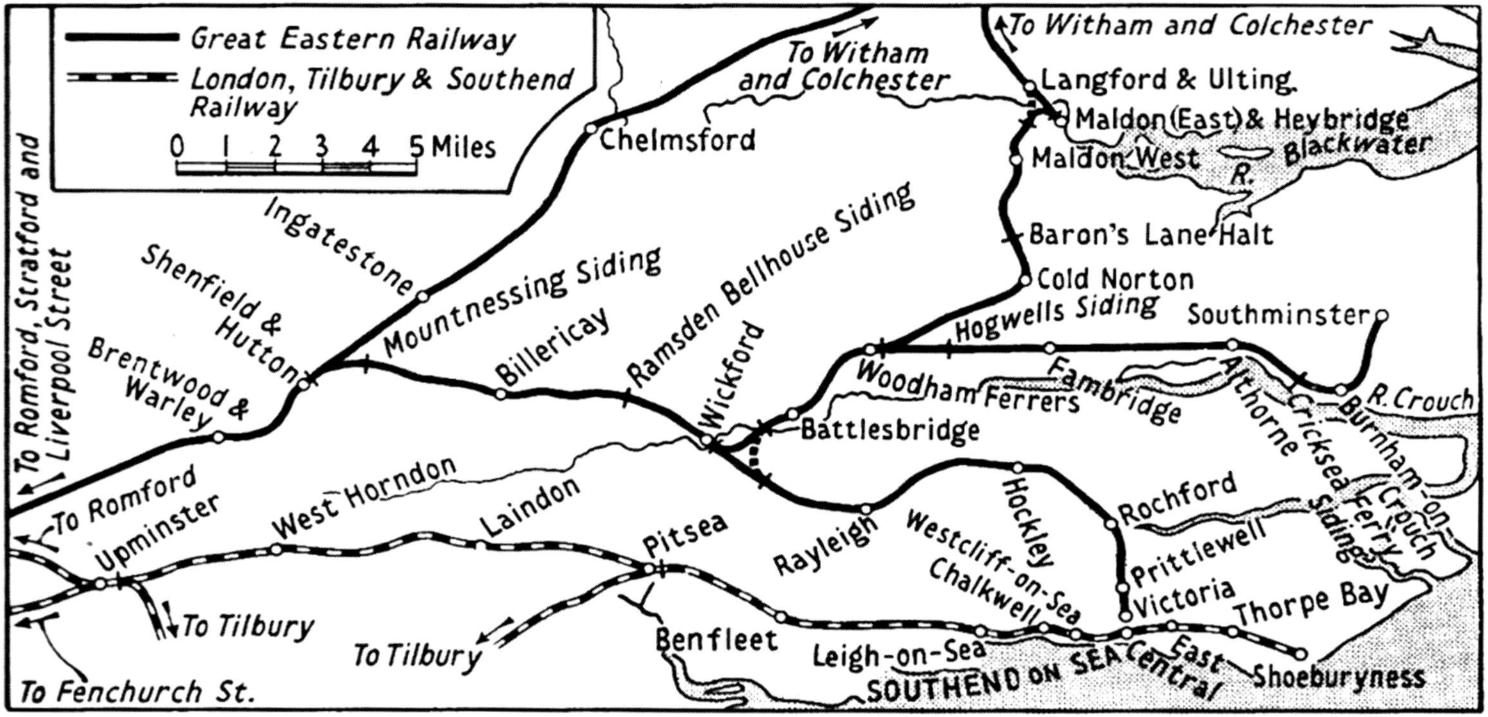


**The New** Essex Lines as at 1 January 1923. (Author's collection)

# Foreword

'You won't find much about this line; the posh enthusiasts and photographers seldom came down here!'

So I was told, many years ago, by a Southminster railwayman and of course, he was right. Yet why is it so? The network which the Great Eastern Railway was pleased to call the 'New Essex Lines' is, in terms of its history, operations and effect on the area it traverses, as interesting as any in the country and more so than many. As a result of its author's painstaking research, this book brings to light a host of fascinating facts. For example, who would guess, whilst travelling through the attractive village of Canewdon, that the flat marshland between it and the River Crouch was proposed, in 1811, as the route of the South Essex Iron Railway? This route would have been a direct connection between London and the coast that would have pre-dated the celebrated Stockton and Darlington Railway by more than a decade. Do any of the thousands of passengers who are whisked daily from Southend to Liverpool Street realise that for a few years around 1890 they could have travelled direct to Colchester, by way of long forgotten connections between Wickford, Maldon and Witham? In fact, the Woodham Ferrers-Maldon line, which enabled this journey, is the only part of the GER's original scheme which has disappeared from the railway map. The rest survives, providing a level and type of service to the local communities which would have surprised and, no doubt, gratified the nineteenth century promoters of lines both actual and proposed. In writing this book, Charles Phillips has done a great and long overdue service to all who are interested in the history, development and operation of the railways of South Essex and filled a major gap in the written history of Britain's railways.

*John Jolly*

# Introduction

This is a history of the New Essex Lines of the Great Eastern Railway which comprise Shenfield to Southend, Wickford to Southminster and Woodham Ferrers to Maldon. I have tried to cover the full history. The book should not only be seen as a work of railway history but also as a work of local history, because local history and railway history were unavoidably intertwined. Whilst I have attempted to include as much information as possible, sadly there has been information that I have not been able to find. Firstly, it is regretable that many of the files of the Great Eastern and London and North Eastern railways were destroyed. Whilst they would have been of great use to researchers, they were not regarded as worthy of keeping by the railways after their useful life had expired. The damage was offset, by the minute books of both companies having survived in the National Archives.

However, even these omit certain things. Furthermore what would have been deemed worthy of bringing to the attention of the board of the Great Eastern Railway (e.g. the provision of a halt at Barons Lane), would not have been deemed worthy of bringing to the attention of the board of the London and North Eastern Railway (e.g. the requests for the reopening of passenger services on the Woodham Ferrers to Maldon line). Also it would have been nice to have looked more fully at local newspapers. Unfortunately, there is only so much time that one can spend looking at microfilm copies of newspapers, so dates are selective. While one can now look at eighteenth to twenty-first century newspapers on the internet (courtesy of Essex County Libraries and the British Newspaper Library), there are more that one wishes were available. Equally, local newspapers did not report everything. For example I have not found anything on the openings of Barons Lane and Stow St Mary's halts. I have tried within this book to include illustrations and photographs that have not appeared elsewhere. It is inevitable though that because of the sparseness of photographs of some subjects or locations or a particular period, it has been necessary to include photographs that have appeared elsewhere. For example, it would have been nice to have found another photograph of

Stow St Mary's Halt either when the Halt was open or before the line through it was formerly closed. Neither have I been able to find a photograph of Billericay station in its original condition and featuring the station forecourt. Sometimes though I have not been able to find photographs of suitable quality that are available to me for reproduction. If you have information on the subjects covered by this book please feel free to contact me via the publisher.

All efforts have been made to trace the copyright holders. Where it has not been possible the author and the publishers apologise for the ommission.

I wish to thank all those who have helped me with the book and in particular John Jolly for writing the Foreword.

My part in the history of the lines was that of a season ticket holder from Billericay to central London via Liverpool Street between June 1972 and March 2005. As a child I started making use of the lines from 1953 onwards. I can vaguely remember steam and when very little recall travelling once on the line behind steam. In my days as a season ticket holder I once, and only once, had a ride in the cab from Liverpool Street to Billericay. This was in the mid-1980s. Rides in the guard's van were rather more frequent if the trains got very full.

*Charles Phillips*

# CHAPTER ONE

# Ancestry of the Lines

Although the lines from Shenfield to Southend, Wickford to Southminster and Woodham Ferrers to Maldon were not opened until 1888 to 1889, their ancestry can be traced back to the earliest proposal for a railway in Essex.

In 1811, there was a proposal deposited with the Clerk of the Peace for Essex for an Iron Railway from Islington to Wallsea Island with a branch to Mucking Creek on the Thames. In Essex the main line of the railway would have passed through (amongst other parishes) Little and Great Ilford, Hornchurch, Upminster, Great and Little Warley, Little Burstead, Ramsden Crays, Ramsden Bellhouse, Wickford, Rawreth, Hockley and South Fambridge. The branch line would have passed through Bulphan and Horndon on the Hill. From the places served, the proposed railway could be held to be the ancestor of both the Shenfield to Southend Railway Line and the London, Tilbury and Southend Railway. It would seem that the reason for the promotion of the proposed Iron Railway was the successful Surrey Iron Railway. The Surrey Iron Railway opened in July 1803 and linked Wandsworth and Croydon via Mitcham. The Croydon, Merstham and Godstone Railway opened in 1805 from a junction with the Surrey Iron Railway at Croydon to a quarry near Merstham. These two railways used horses as their motive power.

In 1836, the Eastern Counties Railway (ECR) was incorporated to build a railway from Shoreditch in London to Yarmouth via Colchester, Ipswich and Norwich. In 1839 the railway was opened from London to Romford, being extended to Brentwood in 1840 followed by Colchester via Chelmsford and Witham in 1843. Unfortunately the ECR got no further than Colchester and the line beyond to Norwich was completed by the Eastern Union Railway (EUR). The EUR, which was incorporated in 1845, opened to Ipswich/Bury St. Edmunds in 1846 and Norwich in 1849. There was at one time some acrimony between the ECR and the EUR. In order to make sense of everything in this history it is necessary to explain that at the end of 1843, the ECR had taken a lease of the Northern and Eastern Railway (NER) which had been incorporated in 1836 to build a railway from Islington in

London to Cambridge with a branch from just short of Cambridge to Yarmouth via Norwich. However it only obtained an act to build as far as Cambridge. In 1839 the railway obtained an act to introduce a deviation from Tottenham to Stratford on the ECR. By the end of 1843, the railway had only reached Bishop's Stortford. On 1 January 1844, the ECR took over the working of the NE Railway and then extended the line via Cambridge to Norwich in 1845 where it linked up with the Yarmouth and Norwich Railway which had been opened in 1844.

At the dawn of the railway age, the two principal towns that would be served by the New Essex Lines were Maldon and Southend. Maldon was an ancient port and market town whose origins go back to Roman times. In Saxon times the battle of Maldon was fought near the town between the Saxons and the Danes. In 1797, it had been linked to Chelmsford by the Chelmer and Blackwater Navigation. By 1831 it was connected to London by several daily stagecoaches and by sailing ships several times a week.

Southend had grown up as a small village on the north bank of the Thames at the south end of Prittlewell. In the latter part of the eighteenth century, it had developed as a bathing resort. At the beginning of the nineteenth century, it had been visited by royalty in the form of Princesses Caroline and Charlotte of Wales. By 1831, it boasted not only daily stage coaches to and from London via Rochford, Rayleigh and Billericay, but also during the season, daily steam packets from London.

Of the two towns, Maldon was the first to receive a railway when in 1848 the Maldon, Witham and Braintree Railway (which had obtained its act in 1846) was opened to goods traffic on 15 August 1848 and passenger traffic on 2 October 1848. Before it was built, it had been taken over by the ECR. From 1845, there were a number of proposals for railways to Southend. Whilst some of these could be considered to be the ancestors of the LTSR, the following could be considered to be the ancestor of the Great Eastern Railway's line to Southend. In 1845, there was proposed a London and Southend Railway and Dock Company which was to run from Shenfield east of Brentwood to Southend via Billericay, Wickford, Rayleigh, Rochford and Prittlewell. The railway would have terminated at the lower end of Southend i.e. on the foreshore at the low water mark, at which point construction of a dock was proposed. Apparently the reason for the failure of the scheme was that the board of the

ECR told the promoters that they could not support the scheme that year. Possibly this was because of a lack of funds.

Southend had received its railway in 1856 when the final section of the London, Tilbury and Southend Railway (LTSR) was opened there on 1 March. The LTSR grew out of an unsuccessful proposal of 1851 by the London and Blackwall Railway (LBR) for a railway from the LBR to Tilbury Fort with a branch from Barking to Forest Gate. The LBR had been opened from Minories to Blackwall in 1840 and extended east from Minories to Fenchurch Street in 1841. In 1849, the Blackwall Extension Railway of the LBR had been opened from Stepney to the ECR at Bow. The London, Tilbury and Southend Extension Railway was promoted in 1852 by the LBR and ECR. The proposed railway ran from a junction with the ECR at Forest Gate to a terminus at Tilbury Fort and then from there to a terminus at Southend. The railway was leased by the promoters to the contractors Peto, Brassey and Betts. There were a few independent shareholders. The engines, carriages and wagons were provided by the ECR. Therefore, you had the position where the railway was jointly owned by two companies (plus the few independent shareholders), leased to contractors, but with one of the owning companies running the train services as agents to the lessees.

The railway was ceremonially opened to Tilbury on 11 April 1854, which was the Tuesday before Easter. The public opening took place on Thursday 13 April – Maundy Thursday. On Monday 14 August 1854 the railway was extended to Stanford-le-Hope. On Sunday 1 July 1855 the railway was opened to Leigh and on Saturday 1 March 1856 the railway reached Southend. Whilst the route from London to Southend was flat, it was somewhat circuitous. The distance from Bishopsgate station in London to Southend via Stratford, Barking and Tilbury was forty-one and a quarter miles. From Fenchurch Street station in London to Southend via Stepney, Stratford, Barking and Tilbury was forty-two and a quarter miles. All trains had portions from and to Bishopsgate and Fenchurch Street which joined and divided at Stratford. In order to shorten the distance from London to Southend, a cut off railway was promoted in 1856 for a line from Gas Factory Junction on the LBR to Barking. The line was opened on 31 March 1858 and shortened the distance from Fenchurch Street to Southend to forty-one and three quarter miles. This represented a saving of precisely half a mile. To briefly complete the early history of the LTSR, a curve avoiding the terminus at Tilbury was opened in 1855. Although the exact date is not known, from the information available it appears to have been by 1 July of that year. Also on 7 June of the same year, a line was opened from just south of Stanford-le-Hope to Thames Haven. Thames Haven is now known as Coryton, but in those days was a rather unsuccessful port, which did not live up to its expectations. Prior to the oil terminal being built, its main traffic was cattle. There was briefly some excursion traffic in connection with paddle steamers plying the Thames.

Following the opening of the LTSR, there were a number of proposals for railways in the area covered by the New Essex Lines. In 1856, Peto, Brassey and Betts, the contractors of the LTSR, backed a railway from Pitsea to Colchester via Maldon with a branch from Cold Norton to Burnham-on-Crouch –The Tilbury, Maldon and Colchester Railway. Peto, Brassey and Betts were also the contractors for the East Suffolk Railway (ESR), which was ultimately intended to run from Lowestoft and Yarmouth to join an authorised but not yet constructed EUR line from Ipswich to Woodbridge at Woodbridge itself. The proposal was to obtain running powers over the EUR from Colchester to Woodbridge and so have a line from London to Lowestoft and Yarmouth independent of the ECR. The ECR responded, as a blocking move, by proposing lines from Shenfield to Pitsea, Maldon to Pitsea, Maldon to the Chelmer Navigation Basin and Rayleigh to the River Crouch near Burnham-on-Crouch. The Shenfield to Pitsea line would have passed through Great Burstead, Wickford, Rayleigh, Hockley and Rochford. The Tilbury, Maldon and Colchester was abandoned at the end of May in consequence of an agreement being reached by Peto, Brassey and Betts and the ECR for the latter to work the ESR. Nothing further then came of the ECR's proposed lines.

In 1857 there was a proposal for a Southend and Burnham Railway to run from Southend to a pier on the Crouch opposite Burnham-on-Crouch.

By the end of the 1850s, the ECR had either taken over or absorbed the working of practically all the existing railways north of the Thames and east of the Great Northern Railway to the Wash. In 1862 the Great Eastern Railway (GER) was incorporated by the amalgamation of the ECR and most of the other smaller existing companies although the NER was not absorbed until 1902.

In the same year of 1862, the lessees of the LTSR (with the aim of making it easier for them to escape from the lease on which they were making a loss), obtained an act of parliament constituting the London, Tilbury and Southend Railway as a separate company. This pleased the shareholders as they at last had a chance to have a partial say in the direction of the railway. However the engines, carriages and goods wagons were provided by the GER.

In 1864 there were some more plans for railways: one was for the East Essex Railway which was to run from Shenfield via Billericay, Wickford, Woodham Ferrers, Cold Norton, North Fambridge, Athorne, Southminster and Tillingham to Bradwell. At Shenfield there would have been curves both west facing and east facing. Only the plan of the section of line from Shenfield to Billericay was deposited with the Clerk of the Peace for Essex. Or to be more precise, only the plan of the section from Shenfield to Billericay survived to reach the Essex Record Office. Nothing came of this.

Another proposal was for the South Essex Railway. This was promoted in 1864 to build a line from Great Warley to Southminster, with a branch from Rettendon to Heybridge. This got as far as having its act passed. In 1866 it obtained powers to build a line from Rettendon to Pitsea. Despite having got its act passed, the railway was unable to raise sufficient funds to start construction. The company was formally wound up in 1874.

Apparently in 1868-71 a Billericay Railway was floated for a line from Brentwood to Billericay and Pitsea, to supplant the moribund South Essex Railway, but the GER would not become involved and no plans were ever drawn up.

In 1866 there was a Rochford Hundred Railway, which was planned to run from the already authorised South Essex Railway at Battlesbridge via Rayleigh and Rochford to Southend. There would have been a connection from the LTSR west of Southend to the railway, which would have had a separate station in Southend to the LTSR and would then have proceeded to a junction at which two lines would have divided. One was directed towards a terminus on the riverfront at Camper House and the other proceeding east to South Shoebury. Again nothing came of this.

In 1871 the Southend and Maldon Railway deposited plans with the Clerk of the Peace for Essex for a railway to run from the LTSR at Southend to Maldon via Rochford and Fambridge. The railway would have started on the LTSR to the west of Southend and run via Rochford, South Fambridge, North Fambridge, Mundon, Maldon Wall to a junction with the GER Witham to Maldon line at Langford facing in the direction of Witham. The scheme was revived in 1877 as the Southend, Latchingdon and Maldon Railway and plans were deposited with the Clerk of the Peace for Essex in 1878. This would have run from a junction with the terminus of the LTSR at Southend via Prittlewell, Rochford, Landsend Point and over the Crouch and then west of Latchingdon, west of Mundon and thence to Carves Kitchen. Just north of this point, the railway would have divided. One line curving round the north of Maldon to a junction with the Witham to Maldon line 350 yards north of the goods shed and the other going straight to the Hythe at Maldon.

According to the *Ipswich Journal* of 11 August 1877, the proposal was for the railway to run from Southend via Rochford, crossing the Crouch by an opening bridge (to avoid impeding navigation), and from there proceed to Latchingdon and Maldon. Stations proposed were at Prittlewell, Rochford, Fambridge, Latchingdon and Maldon. There was also a proposal within the scheme for a branch line from Latchingdon to Southminster. The plan in the Essex Record Office does not show this. According to the *Essex Standard* of 5 October 1878, the station for Southminster and Burnham-on-Crouch would have been at a point between the two places serving both towns. The line would have connected with the LTSR at Southend and with the GER at Maldon. There was also another project – the Dengie Hundred Railway. This railway was an extension of the Witham to Maldon line and was planned to run from a point near Maldon station crossing the Blackwater by means of a swing bridge. From there it would have taken the following route: for some distance parallel with the salting and (sea) wall east of Mundon church it was projected to a point in Latchingdon near the residence of a Mr Pulley near Latchingdon church. Then it would have followed a course over land occupied by Messrs Attenborough and Clarke to the bottom of Mayland Hill, past the residence of Mr J. Page and on to Southminster to a terminus in what was known as the Pantile Allotment Ground. Once again this proposal expired.

In 1880, there was an East and South Essex Railway. The plan in the Essex Record Office shows a line going from the LTSR at Southend via Prittlewell, Rochford, Little Stambridge but no further - this was yet another abortive plan.

In 1875, the LTSR acquired its own carriages and goods wagons. In 1880 it acquired its own engines.

Let us now turn our attention to the lines that were actually built.

# Chapter Two

# The Building of the Lines

At this point it will do no harm to explain the position of those towns in the area served by the New Essex Lines in the nineteenth century before the advent of the railway compared with towns in the area that were served by railways subsequently.

In the 1851 census the largest town in the area (if one excludes Prittlewell, which at that time included Southend and had a population of 3,603, and Maldon which had a population of 4,558) was Burnham-on-Crouch. Burnham had a population of 1,860 followed by Rochford which boasted a population of 1,701. Billericay was the third largest town with a population of 1,533 followed by Southminster with a population of 1,482 and Rayleigh with a population of 1,463. Billericay, Rochford and Rayleigh all had weekly markets.

The main roads of Essex did not serve the towns that later became intermediate stations on the new lines. Burnham-on-Crouch, Battlesbridge and Rochford all lay close to the Crouch estuary whereas Billericay had been the subject of an abortive proposal in 1825 to build a canal to the town. This did not progress beyond the depositing of the plan with the Clerk of the Peace for Essex.

Billericay, Burnham-on-Crouch, Rayleigh and Rochford were served by stage coaches from London in the days before the coming of the railways to Essex. Between 1851 and 1881 Billericay and Rayleigh suffered a population decline. In the case of Billericay it reduced from 1,533 to 1,418. In the case of Rayleigh it dropped from 1,463 to 1,326. Rochford suffered a decline and then a rise in the same period. It declined from 1,701 in 1851 to 1,589 in 1871 and rose to 1,665 in 1881. Southminster's population rose to 1,482 in 1851, to 1,552 in 1871 and then declined to 1,311 in 1881. Only Burnham-on-Crouch's population had a steady increase from 1,860 in 1851 to 2,032 in 1871 and 2,058 in 1881.

Those towns in southern Essex which had been served by the LTSR since its opening between 1854 and 1856 had experienced an increase in population between 1851 and 1881. To give a couple of examples, Leigh's population rose from 1,370 to 1,697 and South Benfleet's population rose from 570 to 679. Most dramatic of all was Southend whose population rose from 1,154 in 1851 to 8,064 in 1881.

The population of Maldon which was served by the GER and had received its railway in 1848 rose from 4,558 in 1851 to 5,458 in 1881.

As mentioned earlier, the LTSR's line from London to Southend as built, was not very direct. At the beginning of the 1880s there were outline plans for the Tilbury Docks. The LTSR could see that when the Tilbury Docks were built there would be a lot more traffic on the line to Tilbury from London and it also saw a need to shorten the distance from London to Southend. In 1881 consideration was given to building a cut off route from Barking to Pitsea to shorten the distance. This fairly soon developed into a firm proposal and in 1882 an act authorising the construction of the line was passed.

There is some confusion regarding the original idea for building of the line from Shenfield to Southend. At a meeting in Billericay on 20 March 1883 in support of the proposed railway from Shenfield to Southend, Mr H. J. Emerson (who was a linen and woollen draper in Billericay) had said that twelve months previously, he was thinking what steps could be taken for the improvement of the town and he came to the conclusion that nothing but a railway would have that effect. So he wrote to the (General) Manager of the GER and he received a reply back asking him for the route that he proposed. He replied that the line should commence midway between Brentwood and Ingatestone passing through Billericay, Ramsden Crays, Wickford, Rayleigh and Rochford to Southend. He forwarded his correspondence to the editor of the *Essex Chronicle* which was published in the edition of 24 February 1882. There, it came to the attention of the Rev Beresford Harris who was the Rector of Runwell near Wickford and the Rural Dean of Danbury who then took up the gauntlet. According to Peter Kay in Volume One of his *History of the London, Tilbury and Southend Railway*, the GER having 'lost' the LTSR wanted a line to Southend and decided on the Shenfield–Billericay–Wickford–Rayleigh–Rochford route. The company's Chief Engineer, Alfred Langley, had been asked late in 1881 to do a survey for the line for a bill to be promoted in time for the 1882 Parliamentary session, but owing to the difficulty of surveying the terrain, was unable to put the bill forward in time.

According to the *Essex Standard* for 14 December 1878, a crowded meeting was held in the Town Hall in Billericay in the evening of 10 December presided over by Mr. J. H. Price to discuss railway accommodation to the town, following which a committee was formed.

At the Directors' meeting of the GER on 1 January 1879 there was a letter from Mr J. H. Price asking the directors of the GER to receive a committee appointed at a meeting of the inhabitants of Billericay and vicinity for increased [railway] accommodation. It was resolved that arrangements were made for the Chairman of the GER (Charles Parkes) to meet the committee.

There were also letters to the GER in this period asking for increased railway accommodation for Shenfield. A previous station at Shenfield had been opened in 1847. Truscott's timetable for 1848 shows a service of two trains in each direction on Mondays to Saturdays, but on Sundays there were three trains in the up direction and four in the down direction. *Bradshaw's Railway Guide* for May 1849 shows a service of two trains in each direction on Mondays to Saturdays, but on Sundays there were three trains in the up direction and four in the down direction. The *Guide* for March 1850, (the year that the station was closed) shows two trains in the down direction on Mondays to Saturdays with three trains in the down direction on Sundays. In the up direction, the service was three trains on Mondays to Saturdays and two trains on Sundays.

Although the GER was not yet committed to building a line from Shenfield to Southend, it does seem that it was considering a new station there as the *Essex Chronicle* of 15 July 1881 carried a report of a meeting held at the Spread Eagle Hotel in Ingatestone the previous Wednesday on a proposal to remove the town's goods station from there to Shenfield. Understandably, those attending the meeting were less than happy with the proposal and angry scenes developed during which one person was assaulted. The proposal to close Ingatestone's goods station was not carried out by the GER and the station did not lose its goods facilities until October 1965 under British Railways.

At the meeting of the GER Directors on 18 August 1880, the Chairman reported that the parties behind the abortive Dengie Hundred Railway were reviving the proposal again and mentioned that the previous year he had had some sections taken of another route in the district. The one proposed between Brentwood and Ingatestone would not do. If the line was ever built, then it should be routed from Romford Factory (near where Gidea Park electric train sidings are now) or Harold Wood and should circumvent the hills towards Battlesbridge. This was for the future and he did not propose any action at present, but if the LTSR took up the matter the GER should confer with the LTSR so as not to oppose each other.

At the meeting of the Special Board of the GER on 25 July 1882, there was submitted a letter from Charles Andrews CE and others, relating to a new line from Shenfield to Southend and also submitted with the letter was a plan of the proposed line. The Special Board resolved that it [the letter and plan] be referred to the General Manager to arrange for the district to be prospected and report the result to the directors.

At the meeting of the Special Board of 5 September 1882 it was reported that the subject having been considered, it was resolved to request that the Board [of the GER] give instruction to the Chief Engineer to survey the line and prepare working plans and report before notices be served for land.

At the meeting of the Special Board of 29 August 1882, representations and letters were submitted from W.J. Beadel of Chelmsford, asking the directors to receive a deputation regarding a proposed South Essex Railway. It was resolved that Mr Beadel be informed that the directors would receive the deputation on Tuesday 5 September at 2.30pm.

According to the minutes of the GER Board of 3 October 1882, regarding the minutes of the Special Board of 29 August 1882, the Chairman reported back with regard to the interview with the deputation on 19 September 1882 on the subject. (Either more than one meeting had taken place or the date of the original meeting had been changed.) The minutes do not say. It was resolved that the matter again be discussed at the Special Board meeting on 24 October 1882 and that E. Wilson make trial sections and estimates for the proposed line as instructed.

At the meeting of the Special Board of 24 October 1882 a letter from Major W.V. Rutlidge was submitted, inquiring if there was any likelihood of a railway being constructed from Chelmsford to Southend. A letter was also submitted from Messrs Rice and Co, pointing out the advantages to agriculture of the existing line to Maldon being extended to either Rayleigh or Rochford in connection with the contemplated line from Shenfield to Rayleigh. The meeting of the board also submitted Messrs E. Wilson and Co's trial section and estimates for the line. It was resolved that notices be given and plans deposited for a line built in sections from Shenfield to Billericay, Rayleigh and Southend with branches to Burnham-on-Crouch and Southminster and also Maldon.

According to the minutes of the GER board of 7 November 1882, the minutes of the Special Board of 24 October 1882 were submitted. The Chairman reported on a visit he had made to the district on 4 November. It was resolved that notices be given and the required deposit made of the plans and book of reference of the following new lines: Romford to Tilbury; Shenfield to Southend; and branches to Maldon and Southminster and that these be included in the General Powers Bill. The GER decided to build a line from Romford to Tilbury because as a result of the LTSR Company taking over the working of its railway, the GER had lost access to Tilbury. It was just at this time that Tilbury docks were being developed. There had also been an independent Romford and Tilbury Railway which had been designed to give the GER access to Tilbury Dock and which secured the GER's support. This Company's bill of 1882 had failed. According to a contemporary newspaper account, it would seem that the lines to Maldon and Southminster were afterthoughts. The reason for the proposed lines to Southminster and Maldon was to keep any competitors such as the LTSR from building lines to these places.

Meanwhile, the LTSR which could not avoid learning about the GER's proposed lines, itself proposed new lines from Romford to Tilbury and from Pitsea to Southend via North Benfleet, Rayleigh, Hockley, Rochford and Prittlewell. The junction at Southend would have been east of Southend station facing the direction of London. The LTSR also backed an independent Mid-Essex Junction Railway from Ingatestone to Pitsea via Mountnessing, Buttsbury, Great Burstead, Laindon and Basildon. The junction with the GER at Ingatestone would have been just south-west of the station. At Pitsea there would have been a Y-shaped junction with the LTSR. One side of the Y would have been to the west of Pitsea station and would have been facing in the direction of Stanford-le-Hope and Tilbury and the other side of the junction would have been at a point 325 yards east of Pitsea station facing in the direction of Benfleet and Southend.

Although the railway is described as serving Great Burstead, it would have served Billericay as for many years Billericay and Great Burstead were intertwined; what is modern Billericay started off as a hamlet of Great Burstead. At Billericay, the railway would have crossed the Hutton to Wickford road to the south and east of the town, and would also have crossed the road going round the back of the north-western part of the town. The railway would have passed over the recently authorised line from Barking to Pitsea via Upminster at Laindon. At Ingatestone, the railway would have passed near Ingatestone Hall; undoubtedly, Lord Petre the owner, would not have been happy.

According to the *London Gazette* of 28 November 1882, the LTSR and the GER would have worked the Mid Essex Junction Railway jointly under a joint committee. The bill, if passed, would have authorised the formation of such a committee. The two companies would have been authorised to run over some parts or all parts of the railway.

The *Essex Chronicle* of 24 November 1882 under the headline 'Proposed Public Works in Essex' said that powers were sought to construct a railway from Ingatestone to Southend by Hutton, Great Burstead, Ramsden, Vange, Pitesa 'and other parishes'. The railway was to be called the Mid Essex Junction Railway. However the *Chronicle* of 30 March 1883 reported that it was one of forty-one Parliamentary Bills that were 'either withdrawn, not proceeded with or thrown out'. The *Leeds Mercury* of the same day reported that:

> 'of the 276 private bills which were deposited at the Private Bill Office on or before the 21 December 1882, forty-one have to the present time been either withdrawn, not proceeded with, or thrown out on second reading or standing orders. Of this number, the following twenty-one relate to London and its suburbs ....Mid Essex Railway ....'

However the minutes of the GER's Board meeting of 6 February 1883 is the only GER reference I can find to the Mid Essex Junction Railway, where it notes that the bill has been withdrawn.

According to Peter Kay in his history of the LTSR, the GER and the LTSR did not want a parliamentary conflict. In the latter part of 1882 and the early part of 1883, the two companies' General Managers and Chairmen met to see if a mutual understanding could be reached to avoid such a conflict. In late September or early October, the two companies' General Managers had come to an agreement that the GER would build the sections of line from Romford to Upminster and Shenfield to Rayleigh whilst the LTSR would build sections of line from Upminster to Tilbury and Rayleigh to Southend. However, at this point the GER's Chairman approached the LTSR's Chairman with the proposition that the former company might take over the latter company. This was something that happened periodically throughout the existence of the LTSR. The LTSR considered the offer and rejected it. Apparently whilst the GER was definitely enthusiastic about the Shenfield to Southend line, it was not enthusiastic about the Wickford to Southminster and Woodham Ferrers to Maldon lines. The LTSR was not particularly enthusiastic about the Romford to Tilbury line, which as finalised joined the existing line to Tilbury just west of Grays.

References to these meetings were mentioned in the minutes of the GER Board of 3 October 1882 when the General Manager reported an interview with Mr Stride the General Manager of the LTSR but not what was discussed. In the GER's Board minutes of 6 February 1883, it was resolved that the General Manager should see Mr Stride the General Manager of the LTSR, with respect to the projected lines and report at the next Board meeting. In the minutes of the GER Board on 6 March 1883, the Chairman reported on an informal meeting that had taken place on 1 March between the Directors of the GER and the LTSR.

At this point I will mention a number of stories that have grown up about the origin of the lines for which I can find no proven evidence, either contemporary or otherwise. According to one story, the GER intended to build a railway from Ingatestone to Southend via Stock, Wickford, Rayleigh, Hockley, and Rochford. I was told the story by the late Donald Jarvis who was one of the historians of Stock. Mr Jarvis apparently obtained it from certain residents of Stock. I have found no evidence whatsoever to support this claim. There are no plans or even a newspaper report of it. Whilst such a line would have avoided the deep cutting at Billericay, it would have been considerably longer at forty-six miles than the line as built at forty-one and a half miles or the thirty-five and three quarters miles of the LTSR line via the new cut off from Barking to Pitsea. One wonders if there were several sources for the legend. Firstly did the GER actually do a survey of such a route but decided that it would be unviable when competing against the LTSR? Secondly, was the Mid Essex Junction Railway proposal the source of the legend? In the parish of Buttbury the line would have passed west of Perry Street and Gooseberry Green; in those days Perry Street and Gooseberry Green were part of Buttsbury and the parish boundaries of Stock and Buttsbury were very intertwined. Did some people in Stock get the idea that the line would have gone near Stock and somehow things got twisted even in a short passage of time so that it was claimed that the Southend line was going to run from Ingatestone to Wickford?

In the report in the *Essex Chronicle* of 24 March 1883 referring to the meeting of 20 March in support of the proposed railway from Shenfield to Southend, there is no mention of the Stock scheme. There is however reference to the Pitsea to Southend scheme. The meeting was attended by some prominent Stock people including the Rector the Rev E.P. Gibson and William Gillow, who was the leading Catholic layman in Stock.

Another suggestion is the inclusion in the lines as eventually built of the curves at Wickford, Maldon and Witham on the Maldon to Witham line for strategic purposes. I haven't found any information on this. It would probably only make sense if the Southend line had been linked to the LTSR at Southend to enable through running between the garrison towns of Colchester and Shoeburyness.

I have not been able to find anything contemporary about proposals for extending the Southminster line to Bradwell-on-Sea despite the fact that the terminus at Southminster is clearly built as a through station. The answer to this question might well have been found in what has not survived. Logic says that there were a lot of files of the GER that have not survived. As to when they were destroyed is unknown. I would suggest that Southminster was built as a through station to make it easier to construct an extension to Bradwell should that ever have been considered.

It was not only the LTSR that was opposed to the new lines. The *Essex Chronicle* of Friday 17 November 1882 reported that the previous Friday a deputation of the inhabitants of Maldon and the Crouch and Blackwater country met with the directors of the GER to propose a line from the GER at Maldon to Southminster in preference to the GER's line from Wickford to Southminster. This was a revival of the Dengie Hundred Railway proposal of 1877. According to the *Chronicle*, the project proposed by the deputation which, whilst it was well meant, would have had the effect of postponing the time when railway accommodation would be provided for the Dengie area. The plan proposed had cropped up at various intervals since the opening of the Witham to Maldon line in 1848. Either because of the sparseness of the population of the Dengie district, or the difficulties of making a junction with the existing line, no one had had much courage to go beyond talking about it. Whilst most people wanted a direct line to Maldon, there were some who believed that the line to Brentwood via Wickford would be just as well, and the difference of opinion was calculated to make the GER withhold their hands from the Dengie area for another year. The point that the deputation urged, was that the people of Dengie wanted direct communication with Chelmsford and Colchester rather than London. The line to Brentwood would to some extent serve both purposes, but would keep the Dengie area as far as ever from its natural metropolis on the banks of the Blackwater – i.e. Maldon. A unanimous opinion in favour of one or the other would help the area, but the smallest doubt or division implied delay. The *Chronicle* hoped that the fact that there were two schemes afoot for railways to Dengie, would not delay the Brentwood to Southend line, as the Southminster branch was an afterthought and it made little difference to the railway company where the line to the Dengie area ran from. Note that the line to Southend is said to be running from Brentwood and not Shenfield.

At this point, one should also observe that besides the aforementioned, there were proposals in 1882 for auxiliary railways or tramways in Southend under the title 'The Southend on Sea and District Auxiliary Railways or Tramways' and in 1883 there was a proposal by the Essex (South East) Tramways for a line from Prittlewell to Paglesham. This would have been a steam tramway and would have run to a point opposite Burnham-on-Crouch. Roadside steam tramways were cheaper than ordinary railways, but in this country were not necessarily quicker. Unlike the continent and in particular the Low Countries, there were very few roadside steam tramways in this country.

According to a report in the *Essex Chronicle* of 9 March 1883, a contemporary newspaper had reported an erroneous statement to the effect that the GER had made an agreement with the directors of the LTSR. This statement contended that the latter company had agreed to construct the line from Southend to Rochford and the GER would construct the line from Rochford to Shenfield. The *Chronicle* said that it had the best grounds for saying that the statement was unauthorised and that no such agreement had been formalised or ever would be. The statement had caused great surprise and annoyance to those interested in the scheme for the railway (from Shenfield to Southend). This would suggest that somehow details of the proposed agreement of late 1882 had got out and been slightly twisted.

THE BUILDING OF THE LINES · 25

The bills for the rival railways were prepared for presentation to Parliament. The GER's proposals were: Romford to Tilbury via Hornchurch; Shenfield to Southend via Wickford; Wickford to Southminster via Woodham Ferrers; and Woodham Ferrers to Maldon.

The LTSR's proposals: were for lines from Romford to Grays via Upminster and from Pitsea to Southend via Rayleigh and Hockley.

The Mid Essex Junction Railway proposal was not proceeded with. Had the LTSR's bills been passed in full and the GER's been rejected in full, it might have been proceeded with later.

Deposited with parliament but not proceeded with was a revived bill for the Romford and Tilbury Railway. According to the *Essex Chronicle* of 9 March 1883, a committee had been formed in Billericay to promote the construction of the new railway. A meeting of the committee had been held in the Town Hall presided over by the Rev S.S. Maguth of Norsey Place, Billericay. It had been the unanimous feeling of the committee that every exertion should be made to promote the scheme and to that effect, a public meeting would be held in the Town Hall in Billericay on Tuesday 20 March.

This meeting was chaired by Sir John Johnson JP, who was one of the principle landowners of St Osyth in the Tendring Hundred. It was held in the Town Hall in Billericay to take into consideration the GER's proposals. The time of the meeting was three o'clock in the afternoon. According to the report of the meeting in the *Essex Chronicle* of 24 March, most people supported the GER's proposals. It was at this meeting that Mr H.J. Emerson said that the idea for the railway was his.

The meeting held at Billericay was not the only meeting held about the railway proposals. On 17 February, a meeting arranged by the Rev Beresford Harris in support of the proposed railway was held at Rayleigh. A petition signed by more than 200 inhabitants of Rochford and its neighbourhood in support of the railway was sent to the directors of the GER. On 28 March, a meeting was held at Southminster in support of the building of the branch line from Wickford to Burnham-on-Crouch and Southminster. At Rochford on 21 March, a meeting was held in the Corn Exchange at which Mr Stride, the General Manager of the LTSR, explained the company's scheme to build a railway from Pitsea to Rayleigh and Rochford to Southend. He said that he had heard that the proposal was a block proposal put forward in opposition to the other (GER) scheme and that if the powers were obtained for the making of

**Poster announcing** the meeting in Billericay to discuss the railway scheme. (*GERS*)

# IMPORTANT MEETING

## South Essex Railway

A

# MEETING

OF THE

Landowners, Occupiers, and Inhabitants of the Town of Billericay and Neighbourhood will be held in the

# TOWN HALL

## BILLERICAY

On TUESDAY, MARCH 20th, 1883

AT THREE O'CLOCK

To take into consideration the above Railway Scheme that is now before Parliament

THE CHAIR WILL BE TAKEN BY

# SIR JOHN JOHNSON

All persons interested are earnestly requested to attend

it, the last thing the company would do would be to build it. He was instructed by his directors to say that if the act was obtained it would be constructed as quickly as possible.

The *Essex Chronicle* of 30 March contained amongst other letters, one from F. Wood, who pointed out the advantages that would accrue from building the railway from Brentwood (Shenfield) to Southend and one from 'Unis e Mulis' who criticised Mr Stride's speech at Rochford.

The GER Board minutes of 3 April 1883 included details of a letter submitted from the Rev Harris enclosing a resolution passed at the meeting held in Billericay Town Hall on 20 March about the railway. The Chairman reported what had taken place in relation to the LTSR and the subject would continue to receive his attention.

On 24 April a House of Commons Committee under the chairmanship of Sir John Ramsden started considering the bills. This lasted until 4 May. The GER's bill was heard first. The Committee made it clear that they were unfavourable to the GER's Romford to Tilbury line. The GER's counsel pointed out that the LTSR's line from Romford to Grays was only being promoted for blocking purposes. The LTSR got the Committee to approve the Romford to Grays line, but the Committee hinted that they were not impressed by the Company's Pitsea to Southend line via Rayleigh. A lot of the Committee's time was taken up with another aspect of the LTSR's bill, which was the seeking of running powers into Liverpool Street. Having access to the underground railway, Liverpool Street was more beneficial than Fenchurch Street which did not. At the time of the bill, the GER ran a service of four trains a day in each direction between Liverpool Street and Barking. This did not provide an adequate means of getting LTSR passengers to Liverpool Street and the Underground. The Chairman of the LTSR offered the GER running powers over the already authorised direct line from Barking to Pitsea in exchange for running powers for the LTSR into Liverpool Street. This offer may have been two-edged in the hope that the Committee would reject the GER's Shenfield to Southend line on grounds that it could run to Southend via Upminster.

On 1 May, the Committee proposed a compromise. Under this, the GER would give the LTSR access into Liverpool Street and the latter would withdraw their Pitsea to Southend line via Rayleigh. The GER rejected this. It is worth noting at this point that the LTSR did gain access of a sort to the Underground in 1884, when the Inner Circle was completed through Mark Lane (later Tower Hill), which was near to Fenchurch Street station. Eventually after further consideration the Committee reported in favour of the GER's lines except for the Romford to Tilbury line and against the LTSR on the Pitsea to Southend via Rayleigh line.

Whilst the LTSR's application to obtain running powers into Liverpool Street was rejected, the GER was obliged to run eight trains a day between Liverpool Street and Barking in each direction and these were mandated to include through carriages to and from Southend (LTSR). The approval for the GER's lines was given under the proviso that the section of the line from Wickford to Southend could not be opened until the lines to Southminster and Maldon had been.

The bills then went before the House of Lords Committee, which did not alter them. However the Counsel for the LTSR proposed that the company should be given running powers over the GER's line via a connection to be built between the two stations at Southend under a future bill, so that passengers from the GER's line would have convenient access to the LTSR system. This was rejected. On 8 July 1883 the GER's Act was passed. The LTSR's Act was passed on 20 August.

On 4 September, John Wilson was appointed Chief Engineer of the GER. The special Board meeting of the GER of 5 November resolved to recommend to the Board to give instruction to the Chief Engineer to survey the lines and prepare working plans and report before notices were given for land. This was resolved and approved.

According to the Board meeting of 2 September 1884 there was a letter before it from John Wilson the Chief Engineer, in which he said that as soon as the crops were off the ground, he had started staking out the line and making a five chain plan and section of the same. The work was in hand and in the course of a fortnight or three weeks he hoped to be able to have the plans in the hands of Mr Adams for the purchase of the necessary land from Shenfield to Wickford. It was resolved by the Board that the same be approved. In obtaining the land that the new railway would pass through, it was inevitable that in many cases that the owners would have a difference of opinion between what they wanted for it and what it was really worth. According to the *Essex Standard* of 14 August 1886 in an article on the commencement of the work on the railway connecting Maldon to the Rochford and Dengie Hundreds, it was understood that the landowners and occupiers had nearly all been compensated, in many cases very liberally, whilst practically all of the route was in the hands of the contractors. To give an example from the Southminster line, the Drapers Company extracted over £1,000 from the GER for three acres of land that the railway needed at Salcoats Farm near Woodham Ferrers when the normal agricultural land value at that time was below £10 for an acre.

Regarding the section of line from Shenfield to Wickford, it was decided by the Board of the GER that only the section from Shenfield to Billericay be laid as double track, but that the section from Billericay to Wickford be laid as a single line with provision for an extra pair of rails at a later date.

The *Essex Standard* of 4 October 1884 reported that on 26 September the Chairman and the General Manager of the GER inspected the route of the new railway from Shenfield to Billericay, on which work was to begin shortly.

Construction of the new station at Shenfield started in April 1885 according to reports in the *Essex Chronicle*. The original contractor for constructing the section from Shenfield to Wickford was Mr T.D. Ridley of Harwich and Middlesbrough, but a dispute arose in mid-1885 between the GER and Mr Ridley as to the terms of the contract. In consequence, the contract was abandoned and a new one awarded to Messrs Holme and King of London and Liverpool except for building the stations which were the responsibility of Mr T.L. Bennett. The plans, gradients, sections, etc were prepared by the GER's Chief Engineer John Wilson. The work was carried out under the superintendence of Frederick King, who was the son of one of the contractors. The engineer on the site for the Great Eastern Railway was Mr H. Jones and for the contractors Mr J.H. Davis. According to the *Chronicle* the contract price for the section from Shenfield to Wickford was £100,000. The contractors for the section from Wickford to Southend were Walter Scott and J.T. Middleton, except for Southend station which was the responsibility of Messrs Bennett Brothers. The contractors' engineers were Messrs Gray and G. Arthur. Signalling was the responsibility of the firm of Mackenzie and Holland. The plans, gradients, sections, etc were again prepared by the GER's Chief Engineer John Wilson. The engineers on site for the GER were Messrs H. Jones and H. Wilmer. Mr G.K. Waghorn was in charge of the Rochford section. The resident engineer was Mr W.T. Foxlee. Walter Scott and J.T. Middleton were also the contractors for the Wickford to Southminster and Woodham Ferrers to Maldon sections. The plans, gradients, sections, etc were once again prepared by John Wilson. On the Southminster line, Mr G.K. Waghorn was the engineer in charge. Mr T. Middleton was the engineer in charge for the contractors of the Burnham section. On the Maldon line, Mr W.T. Foxlee was the resident engineer.

According to the *Essex Chronicle* of January 1889 and the *Essex Standard* of 26 January 1889 construction of the section of the line (from Shenfield to Wickford) started in June 1885. This is open to question and newspaper reports from that year suggest a start date of July or even early August. According to the *Essex Newsman* of 29 August 1885:

> 'Messrs Holme and King, the contractors for the Great Eastern new line of railway from through Billericay to Wickford commenced operations at Shenfield, near Arnold's Wood some time since, and last week a number of navvies were employed near the Union-house, (i.e. workhouse) Billericay, in clearing the ground at the site of the proposed station. The ground is being fenced in with hurdles.'

According to a contemporary press report, the contractors engineer for the section of line from Shenfield to Wickford, Mr J.H. Davis, had endeared himself to the people of Billericay. From the *Essex Chronicle* of 15 July 1887, there is a report of a cricket match played on the 12th of the month at Billericay between the town and those building the railway. The score was Railway Works 45 runs and 17 runs and Billericay 125 runs, Billericay winning by an innings and 63 runs.

The *Essex Standard* of 19 September 1885 reported that several truck loads of stakes had recently arrived at Maldon station and had been distributed on the proposed route for the purpose of marking out the course of the new railway from Wickford to Southminster.

The *Essex Standard* of 14 August 1886 said that work on the railway connecting Maldon to the Rochford and Dengie Hundreds had commenced. The newspaper said that the contract for the sections of line from Wickford to Southend, Wickford to Southminster and Woodham Ferrers to Maldon, which amounted to £450,000, had been let to Messrs Walter Scott and Co of Newcastle, whose principal representatives had already taken up residence in and about Maldon. Mr Middleton, the partner in charge of the contract, had taken up his residence in Purleigh, where Mr Gray, the resident engineer for the Maldon to Woodham Ferrers section, would also reside. Mr Forbes, the General Manager for the works for the same section, had opened his offices near the site of the Spital Road station in Maldon and Mr W.T. Foxlee who was the GER's representative had taken Shrublands in Maldon. The first sod of the Maldon section had been turned the previous week and fencing and the bringing in of the working machinery was being briskly carried on.

The Rev Frederick Williams, the Rector of Cold Norton from 1877 to 1890, recorded in his diary for 11 August 1886 'was told that men had already begun the railway in Maldon'.

In building the section of line from Shenfield to Wickford, the contractors had had to contend with tremendous difficulties owing to the treacherous character of the soil and shifting sands. This not only seriously impeded the work, but also caused the contractors to spend a lot of money for which they had not budgeted. At several points large slips took place in the embankments and at Billericay it was necessary to erect a stout retaining wall.

Not all the work on building the line was done by hand. In digging the cuttings, a steam excavator was used. Another name for this was a steam navvy. Local people called it a Devil Digger. My maternal grandfather, Frederick Such, was taken to Billericay to see the construction of the railway. The *Essex Chronicle* of 13 August 1886 in a report on the building of the new railway at Maldon said that three steam navvies were expected to arrive by ship there and

**Engineers building** the railway near Wickford using a steam navvy. (*Christopher Corbin*)

that each was capable of turning over a ton of earth in five minutes which would take over fifty men to do.

A couple of photographs exist of the building of the line. One shows a steam navvy in use building the line near Wickford and the other some navvies, contractors' men and a contractor's locomotive and wagons at Cold Norton. A photograph taken at Billericay purporting to show the railway under construction was taken after the railway had been completed to Billericay. The station and running lines and a siding are clearly completed. Some of those in the photograph are wearing the uniform of the GER. As to who the rest are I do not know. It may show the first staff of Billericay station and the contractors' foremen.

In building the lines, the contractors used various forms of transport to move the material needed in the construction to the working sites. At Maldon, some items of equipment were brought in by ship. Horses and carts were used before a temporary railway had been laid by the contractors. The railways had their own engines and wagons. From information in *Industrial Railways and Locomotives of Essex* by Robin Waywell and Frank Jux (Industrial Railway Society 2011) it is known that there were at least fifteen locomotives used by Holme and King in building the section of line from Shenfield to Wickford. However there is only information for two locomotives being used by Walter Scott and Middleton on the sections from Wickford to Southend, Wickford to Southminster and Woodham Ferrers to Maldon. In addition, photographic evidence exists of a third locomotive. There were without question more locomotives used. Where there was a navigable river nearby, i.e. the Crouch, sailing barges were used to transport material and equipment. Some use would also be made of existing railways where the working sites were in the immediate vicinity of them as at Shenfield and Maldon. At Maldon, a temporary connection to the contractor's railway was made from the existing line. Although I have not found any evidence in the company's minutes one must assume that a temporary connection was put in at Shenfield.

The *Essex Chronicle* of 26 November 1886 recorded that a locomotive was delivered to the contractors at Cold Norton using temporary rails laid on public roads, whilst the edition of 10 December said that the same method was used to deliver a locomotive to Stokes Hall near Althorne.

The *Essex Herald* of 23 May 1887 recorded that eight locomotives, three steam excavators and about 600 men were employed in building the section of line from Shenfield to Wickford. It said that the platform at Billericay was in the process of construction and that the station buildings on one side were in a forward state and that on the other side operations had started. A commodious goods shed had also been erected near the railway line. According to the *Essex Chronicle* of 16 December 1887, during the previous summer upwards of a thousand men, three steam navvies and seven steam locomotives had been employed in building the railway between Billericay and Wickford. Close to the Gooseberry Green Bridge a navvy camp had been erected for the men and their families. On the Dengie and Rochford hundreds sections of the railway (east of Wickford) between 1,600 and 1,700 navvies had been employed together with a large number of horses and five steam navvies (or according to the newspaper 'American devils' as they were more commonly called). At Southminster, according to the newspaper, there would only be one platform and the next point for the GER to consider was whether it should continue the line to Tillingham and Bradwell.

According to the *Essex Standard* of 28 August 1886, Maldon Town Council had held a special meeting on 24 August. The Town Clerk Mr J.C. Freeman submitted and explained the deed of grant from the Corporation to the GER over an easement over the river Chelmer. The Council approved this and the common seal was affixed to it. On the proposition of Councillor Mr W. Humphrey and seconded by Councillor Mr W. Strutt, it was resolved that the Council write to the GER to suggest that an arch not less than ten feet wide be erected over the footway leading from the Union Lane across the Hillyfield to Beeleigh. Plans had been submitted to the Sanitary Committee as to the temporary diversion of the London Road by the GER and the committee suggested that the new road should not be less than twenty feet wide at the top. The Council adopted the suggestion with a further one to the GER that two lights be placed on the bridge. Plans for the proposed railway bridge over the Chelmer had been submitted to the Committee and had been approved.

The *Essex Standard* of 4 September 1886 said that a number of men had been employed in the last few days at Stoke's Hall (landing) stage at Althorne in unloading vessels containing railway plant intended for the new line and in making preliminary arrangements for the construction of the railway which would pass through several parishes in the Dengie Hundred. In short, still more active steps would be taken as several other vessels were shortly expected.

For some reason unknown, Herepath's Journal of 18 September 1886 reported that the LTSR were about to connect Rochford with their railway and that work had started the previous week at Hawkwell and Hockley. Clearly the Journal had got it wrong and this refers to the start of work by the GER's contractors on the section of line from Wickford to Southend.

The Rev Frederick Williams of Cold Norton recorded in his diary for 11 December 1886 'had to go over temporary bridge by Leeches Lane for first time!'

The navvies building the railway tended to have something of a bad name. Rough men doing a dirty job which had to be done was a popular thought. There were those who attempted to make the navvies a little more civilised. The *Essex Standard* of 30 October 1886 recorded that on 27 October about seventy of the navvies employed in building the railway were entertained to a tea of hot roast beef, potatoes, bread and butter, cake, tea and coffee by Mr A.G. Sadd at the Temperance Hall in Maldon. It had been arranged to hold mission services for the railway builders every Sunday in the Temperance Hall.

At Wickford, James Ruffhead the landlord of the Castle Inn obtained a late licence to provide supper for the workmen. Navvies did have a reputation for fighting as in this case reported in the *Ipswich Journal* of 8 July 1887. On 4 July 1887, a coroner's jury at Wickford committed for trial James Locock, a navvy working on building the railway from Shenfield to the Rochford and Dengie Hundreds. The charge was causing the death of Henry Francis, (another navvy) on 28 June. The two men were fighting at Wickford when Francis, who was described as a well known boxer, received a blow on the left ear and fell. He died within five minutes. Locock was described as a quiet inoffensive man and evidence was given to the effect that Francis had started the row. On 2 July, Locock was brought before the Billericay magistrates and was committed for trial at the next assizes. According to the *Essex Standard* of 6 August, Locock was acquitted at the Essex Summer Assize, evidence having been given of the exemplary character the prisoner had previously borne.

Secondly the *Essex Standard* of 12 May 1888 reported a case of assault before the Chelmsford Petty Session on 4 May. Messrs William Taylor and George Smith, who were navvies employed on building the railway, were charged with assaulting at Rettendon Charles Poor, a ganger in charge of a steam navvy at Battlesbridge on 30 April. On the day in question, the two navvies went to lunch at the usual time and returned at three the worse for drink. The two stripped (to the waist) and wanted to fight Poor, who asked them to go away, but they refused to do so, therefore Smith went up to Poor and knocked him down. When he got up, Taylor knocked him down an eighteen foot embankment slope. The two navvies followed Poor down and kicked him about the head and rendered him insensible. Poor used his stick to defend himself and knocked the two navvies down. The assault caused the steam navvy and thirty men to be delayed from working that afternoon. The navvies were given six weeks hard labour without the option of a fine.

And thirdly, the *Essex Standard* of 18 February 1888 reported that on the afternoon of Sunday 12 January 1888, four navvies went to the front door of the Eagle Inn in Woodham Ferrers and finding that they were not immediately answered started halloaing and kicking at both doors. The landlord, Mr S. Cooper, went out of the back door and round to the front when the navvies said that they wanted some beer and did not care if it was prohibited hours or not. The landlord refused, so two of the navvies went to the house of PC Hailstone, who advised them to move on, whereupon one of them hit him in the face, knocking him down. He soon regained consciousness and after a short but sharp tussle overcame his assailant and handcuffed him. The other navvies stood insolently in the middle of the road and, seeing the constable change the position of his truncheon to apparently relieve his bruises and bleeding, told him that if he touched the other navvy he was a dead man. A conveyance was quickly procured and the handcuffed navvy bundled in it and taken to Chelmsford. According to the *Essex Standard* of 25 February, at the Chelmsford Petty Sessions on 17 February the navvy (Robert Fiddler) pleaded guilty and was sentenced to three weeks imprisonment.

Some of the navvies were either interested in supplementing their diet from the property of others or possibly trying to enhance their income from the sale of the property of others. According to the *Essex Standard* of 20 August 1887, Thomas Smith, a railway navvy, was charged at the Chelmsford Petty Session on 12 August with trespassing in search of game on the land in the occupation of Henry Waller at Woodham Ferrers on 22 July. He was fined five shillings with eight shillings cost in default of seven days imprisonment.

Elopement in its literal sense means to run away and not come back to the point of origin and the *Ipswich Journal* of 22 March 1889 reported a case of theft combined with this. On Saturday 16 March, Sarah Emma Johnson and George Drury were before the Latchingdon Petty Sessions for stealing £40 and sundry articles from Pettit Johnson, the husband of Sarah, on 4 February. Mr Johnson had said that his wife had gone off with the money with which she was going to pay two years' rent which was due and to do some shopping, but that she might not return very early. When she did not return that day he went to Maldon and found that she had eloped with Mr Drury, who was a ganger employed on the new railway works at Maldon. One William Hall said that Mrs Johnson had asked him to drive her to Witham, as she did not know the way. He complied and saw her at the (Albert) Railway Hotel with Mr Drury. James Mace, the landlord of the hotel, confirmed this. Mrs Johnson and Mr Drury took the 1.8pm. train to London. A warrant was issued for their apprehension and a description of them was circulated. They were arrested at Dronfield in Derbyshire and handed over to the authorities at Latchingdon. The bench committed them for trial at the Quarter Sessions at Chelmsford. Mr Drury applied for bail, but was refused. This was not the only case of elopement. The *Essex Standard* of 17 March 1888 mentions one at Southminster on 10 March and one the previous year at Burnham.

The work was inevitably dangerous. During the building of the difficult section of line from Shenfield to Wickford one man and a boy had been killed. The contractors reckoned this to be light as the general rule was the loss of one man per mile. The *Essex Standard* of 20 November 1886 reported a number of recent accidents. At Maldon on 13 November a navvy named Griffiths was hit on the head by a heavy iron mallet flying off its handle. On the same day, a navvy named Parker was working on the cutting at Cold Norton when a wagon load of earth tilted on him and buried him up to his chest. On 15 November at Maldon, a wagon tilted on the right hand of a navvy named Dingfield splitting it in two between the thumb and finger and crushing the hand generally. The thumb was nearly severed. All three men survived. The *Essex Standard* of 29 January 1887 recorded that on 22 January, Mr J. Whitehead, a 'tipper' at the Cold Norton cutting on the railway, was uncoupling a wagon with his right hand when he inadvertently placed his left hand on the buffer of the wagon. With the engine sending on another wagon his hand received the full force of the collision and received dreadful injuries. It was necessary for him to have part of a finger amputated, but it was hoped that the hand would be saved. The

*Essex Standard* of 20 August 1887 mentions that a man by the name of Rose (who the previous week had fallen from the bridge under construction over the Blackwater without injury) did the same thing later that week and sustained a serious scalp wound. Another man, by the name of Smith, had his hand crushed almost out of shape between two buffers of wagons. Both the *Ipswich Journal* and the *Essex Standard* of 7 July 1888 reported that the previous day a navvy by the name of Atkinson was working on the line near the viaduct at Maldon when a train of wagons filled with earth came up and as he endeavoured to get out of the way, his clothes got caught by the train and he was severely bruised about the arms and legs, but no bones were broken. The *Ipswich Journal* said that it was lucky that he wasn't killed.

Not so lucky was Frederick Cable, who was employed on the new works at Purleigh. According to the *Essex Standard* of 13 April 1889 he was returning home from work on a train and when he reached his destination he jumped off, but alighted on a piece of loose earth, which crumbled beneath his weight and he was thrown forward and run over by the train, which at the time was going very slowly. The engine was at once reversed so that only one wheel passed over the unfortunate man. He was removed to his home. Mr E.P. Gutteridge, the surgeon at Maldon, was at once summoned. Mr Gutteridge's assistant Mr Sanderson was soon in attendance, but Mr Cable was dead before his arrival.

An unfortunate boy was Edward Collis aged fourteen, who was employed on night work on the building of the railway between Shenfield and Wickford and whose job was greasing wagons and greasing points. His death on 24 June 1887 from a cause unknown was recorded in the *Essex Newsman* for 28 June 1887 and *Essex Chronicle* for 1 July 1887. He was last seen alive between 1am and 2am in the morning. Shortly afterwards, he was found badly injured a few yards from the side of the line by John Pike. He was taken to Billericay Union but died shortly after 8am. The newspapers mention that his father was Robert Collis who was from Ramsden Crays, a labourer employed in building the railway. Another unfortunate was Walter Phillips aged 28, who was employed in the building of the railway south of Wickford. His death on 13 December 1888 was reported in the *Essex Chronicle* of 21 December 1888 and the *Essex Newsman* of 22 December 1888. He was run over by an engine having slipped when getting off the engine. He was taken to Billericay Union and later died.

As mentioned earlier, it was originally intended that on the section from Shenfield to Wickford only the stretch from Shenfield to Billericay be laid as double track but that the stretch from Billericay to Wickford be built for double track, but only a single track laid. At the meeting of the GER Board in November 1887, on the recommendation of the Chief Engineer it was decided that the section from Billericay to Wickford would also be laid as double track. Also to help agricultural development, public agricultural sidings were to be provided at Ramsden Bellhouse and Hawkwell (near Rochford).

It would appear that the railway may have been substantially completed as far as Billericay by early November 1887 as the *Contract Journal* for 9 November that year announced that there were ten contractors' locomotives for sale by Holme and King, Billericay. This is further borne out by a report in the *Essex Chronicle* of 16 December 1887 which states that all the buildings of the stations and public sidings on the section of line between Shenfield and Wickford were complete. As no evidence has been found in the records of the GER it would be idle to speculate if the railway company considered opening to Billericay from Shenfield either solely for goods traffic or for passenger and goods traffic in late 1887 or early 1888.

During the construction of the railway, Roman remains were found at Billericay when the cutting was being dug. Near Barons Lane near Purleigh on the Maldon branch, Iron Age urns are reputed to have been found when ballast was being dug out and burnt.

The construction of the railway also had implications for religion in Billericay. This came about because a large number of the navvies building the railway to Wickford and Southend were Irish Catholics. The navvies were accommodated in a wooden hut on the site of what later became the goods shed, which was demolished in the 1960s when the goods yard was closed. The site is now part of the station car park. On Sundays, Mass was celebrated in the hut to which Catholics in Billericay had free access. Sometimes Father (later Monsigneur) William Cologan, the Catholic parish priest of Stock, said Mass, and sometimes a priest came from Romford (on horseback). The hut was not though the place where the first Mass was said in Billericay since the Reformation as in 1884 Father Cologan had celebrated a Mass at 108 the High Street, the home of Mr and Mrs Cole. Shortly after his appointment as Catholic parish priest of Stock in 1877, Father Cologan had been given responsibility for the Catholics in Billericay. When the navvies left, the Catholics of Billericay naturally started looking around for ways of carrying on where they left off. From 1888 to 1909, Father Cologan said Mass at regular intervals in Billericay at a variety of places.

The first part of the line to be opened was the new station at Shenfield on 1 January 1887. The *Daily News* of Monday 3 January 1887 reported that:

> 'A new station on the Great Eastern Colchester main line was opened on Saturday. It is situated between Brentwood and Ingatestone and is to be called Shenfield and Hutton Junction. The junction is to connect Billericay by rail with Brentwood and the line will become connected with the Rochford Hundred District.'

The *Ipswich Journal* of Monday 3 January 1887 used exactly the same words in reporting the opening of the station.

Work on building the other stations seems to have started in 1887. Judith Williams in her history of Wickford reproduces a photograph of the foundation stone of Wickford station which was laid by the Rev Beresford Harris on 24 June 1887.

The *Essex Standard* of 12 May 1888 recorded that a satisfactory settlement had been arrived between the GER and Mr Thomas Dowsett and other owners of the land on which the new station at Southend was to be built. The land to be taken by the GER covered fourteen acres and the price to be paid for it had been mutually settled at £8,800 or £628 per acre.

Either in late October or early November, the GER was of the opinion the section of line from Shenfield to Wickford was now ready to be opened for public service and informed the Board of Trade in writing that it was ready for inspection by the Board's Inspector, Major General C.S. Hutchinson. Unfortunately, the Board's file containing the GER's request has not survived, but from the information that has survived we know that the Board's Inspector was concerned about slippage of earth in the cuttings. He would not, therefore, allow passenger trains to run on safety grounds, but would allow the running of goods, sheep and cattle trains. Apparently the running of these trains were of no concern. On Monday 19 November 1888, the section of line from Shenfield to Wickford was duly opened to goods traffic. According to the *Essex Chronicle* of 23 November 1888, the first goods train left Shenfield for Wickford at about 9 am. The train consisted of thirty- three trucks, some of which were laden with manure, coal and other goods. The journey was accomplished without a hitch. On the engine were Mr Denning, the Inspector of the Goods Department of the GER, and other officials. The train returned from Wickford at about 11 am. The initial service was two trains a day from and to Temple Mills in East London. The *Chronicle* reported that it was expected that the line would be open to passenger traffic the following January.

Following a further inspection, the Board of Trade's Inspector authorised the opening of the line to passenger trains to Wickford. On or just after 29 December 1888, a poster appeared, announcing the opening of the line to passenger traffic to Wickford on 1 January 1889. One has to be careful about this as the poster says 'Corrected'. Presumably copies of the poster were displayed not only in Shenfield, Billericay, Wickford and surrounding area but also all over the GER's system. At this distance in time it is not known whether an earlier poster was printed and displayed but was then cancelled. Perhaps the poster promulgated an opening date for passenger services of 19 November 1888. Either that, or the train times originally given were amended. But I am speculating with no evidence other than a rather fragmented copy of the poster in the Essex Record Office. *Contract Journal* for 21 November 1888 and *The Engineer* for 23 November announced that A.T. Crow was to auction, on 29 November, plant, including five locomotives belonging to Holme and King at Mountnessing yard, which I take to mean Mountnessing public siding.

Ken Butcher writing, about Billericay station in *Great Eastern Journal* No.127, gave some interesting information about the building of the section of line from Shenfield to Wickford. According to Ken, this section would have opened earlier, but problems had arisen with the earthworks. According to the Board of Trade Inspector's report dated 24 December 1888, serious slips had occurred at several places. In the deep cutting on the Wickford side of Billericay station, very great difficulty had been encountered in dealing with the slip there. The problem was overcome with the help of a substantial drainage system and elaborate retaining walls. The cost of dealing with the problems had increased the cost of building the section of line from the tendered price of £104,996 to £140,580. The largest difference in terms of percentage between the tendered price and the actual price had been for drain pipes, etc, which in the tender had been quoted at £912 but actually cost £4,096 which was a percentage increase of 349 per cent. Other substantial increases had been for earthworks from £54,247 to £75,430 and brickwork from £19,227 to £26,638, both an increase of thirty-nine per cent. Of the other increases, that for stations, buildings and platforms was from £14,700 to £18,118 which was an increase of twenty-three per cent, for the laying of permanent way from £1,922 to £2,003 which was an increase of six per cent and for all other trades plus extras from £6,802 to £8,200, an increase of twenty-two per cent. However, the cost of fencing decreased from £7,186 to £6,065, a reduction of sixteen per cent. The overall increase for the section of line from Shenfield to Wickford was thirty-four per cent. Regarding the earth slip between Billericay and Wickford, the *Essex Chronicle* in its report on the works in its edition of 16 December 1887 stated that 'The contractors have experienced the greatest difficulty owing to the many serious slips, and this has been the cause of serious expense and delay'.

The section of line from Shenfield to Wickford duly opened to passenger traffic on Tuesday 1 January 1889. The first train was the 7.37am from Wickford. There were three passengers; two women and a policeman. The train was late. The reason for the lateness was that the train had run empty from Stratford (where the GER had its main engine shed and carriage sidings in the district) to Wickford and there had been fog in the Stratford area. The *Essex Chronicle* noted that the driver of the first train was a Mr Pollock and the guard a Mr Sparrow. The name of the fireman was not given. Nor was the number of the engine. A lot of people joined the train at Billericay for the journey to Shenfield. The first train from Shenfield to Wickford was due to leave Shenfield at 8.10am. The 10.15am train from Liverpool Street which normally terminated at Brentwood, that morning was run as a special from Brentwood to Wickford. The train conveyed the local MP, directors of the GER and the contractors' representatives. At Billericay, the Maldon town band played 'See the Conquering Hero Comes' as the train steamed into the station. The train returned from Wickford to Billericay where there was a public lunch in the Town Hall at 1.30pm. A committee had been formed to mark the opening of the railway. At the lunch, which was attended by prominent people from Billericay and the surrounding area, as well as people from the GER and the contractors, speeches were made about such things as how the area had suffered from the lack of a railway, the building of the railway and the benefits the new railway would bring to the area. Mr H.J. Emerson, mentioned earlier, read out a poem he had composed in celebration, which included some verses praising himself. A shuttle service was run all day between Shenfield and Wickford. The newly constructed Railway Hotel and the High Street were bedecked with flags. Billericay's station boasted two platforms and a goods yard. At Wickford a celebration was held in the Castle Inn. According to the *Essex Chronicle*, the first stationmaster at Billericay was Mr G.C.Taverner and the first stationmaster at Wickford was Mr Lucking. The *Daily News* in its report of the event said that the opening of the line for passenger traffic was celebrated with a public lunch in the Town Hall at Billericay presided over by Mr W.J. Beadel MP. There were about 200 guests. The section just opened was the first part of a very important system of lines designed to open up the Rochford and Dengie Hundreds, also bringing Rochford, Southend, Burnham and Southminster into direct communication with the centre of the county and better links with London. It was expected that the Southminster and Southend lines would be opened in July. The Maldon line was not mentioned. Mr Beadel mentioned in his speech at the lunch that on the previous Friday, 28 December, he and Mr Wilson, the GER's Chief Engineer, had gone over the line from Shenfield to Wickford and on to Southend. This suggests that by the end of 1888, construction of the railway was complete to Southend, although obviously the line was not ready for traffic beyond Wickford.

The line from Shenfield to Wickford was double track with a conventional up and a down line, up being to London and down to the country. There were stations at Billericay and Wickford with public goods sidings at Mountnessing (between Shenfield and Billericay) and Ramsden Bellhouse between Billericay and Wickford. The *Chronicle* does not describe the stations. Thus no mention is made that Billericay, unlike Wickford and Shenfield stations, was in a cutting with the ticket office at the top of the cutting and the platforms in the cutting.

After this, things settled down. Initially there were six passenger trains a day to and from Shenfield on Mondays to Saturdays. According to the GER's notice for the opening of the section of line from Shenfield to Wickford for passenger traffic in January 1889, motive power for the service was provided from Brentwood shed. There was a light engine working each morning from Brentwood to Wickford and return working each evening. Carriages were stationed at Wickford, as the note states that on 1 January the light engine would work carriages from Stratford to Wickford. There was a speed limit of 25 miles per hour over the whole of the line from Shenfield to Wickford. The initial goods service of two goods trains a day was replaced by one a day, but the first down passenger train was allowed to work six trucks of important goods and cattle. The daily goods train was a Temple Mills to Wickford return working. Passenger services were five trains a day in each direction between Shenfield and Wickford with an additional train in each direction on Wednesdays, Fridays and Saturdays. There was also one train in each direction a day from Shenfield to Billericay. There were no trains of any description on Sundays.

The GER public timetable for November and December 1888 and January 1889 had a notice inserted for February 1889 as a February 1889 timetable was not issued. This announced that the first section of the Essex Lines from Shenfield to Wickford had been opened and gave details of the service. As to what happened about giving information on the train service from the beginning of January to the publication of the notice is not clear. The service was shown in the March 1889 timetable. When the March timetable appeared, the railway company made its first alteration to the timetable by amending the time of the down train to Billericay by one minute and one of the down trains to Wickford by two minutes. The timetable also showed all the stations on the uncompleted sections of the lines. Interestingly, Cold Norton station on the Woodham Ferrers to Maldon branch was shown as Purleigh, whilst Woodham Ferrers was called Woodham Fen.

Construction of course was still continuing on the unopened parts of the lines. The *Essex Standard* of 30 March 1889 reported that at Witham, some fifty men were busily engaged in extending the Maldon line by constructing a line of rails so that trains from Maldon could run direct to Colchester avoiding Witham via a south to east curve.

The *Essex Standard* of 25 May said that a special meeting of Maldon Borough Council had been held on 21 May where Councillor Mr L. Bentall had called the attention of the Council to the opening of the railway to Southminster on 1 July, and asked if something could be done to induce the GER to open at the same time the section of line to Maldon. Councillor Mr C. Handley proposed the motion and Councillor Robert Blaxall seconded a motion that the Mayor, Councillor Joseph Sadler, Alderman Mr A.P. Clear and Councillors Mr A.P. Float and Mr L. Bentall with the Town Clerk John Crick

Freeman, should wait on the Directors of the GER with reference to the matter. Nothing further is recorded about this. However it is obvious that the line to Maldon was not yet complete as a report in the *Essex Standard* of 21 September 1889 records an accident at Maldon to a fireman on one of the contractors' engines used in the building of the railway.

The *Essex Standard* for 6 July 1889, in its report of the opening of the railway to Southminster mentions that Southminster station was laid out for an extension to Bradwell. Earlier, in the *Essex Standard* in 1887, there had been correspondence calling for the extension of the railway from Southminster to Bradwell-on-Sea. Whilst in an article in the edition for 26 January 1889, about the new line from Shenfield to Wickford it was stated that when Bradwell was brought within reach (by the opening of the line to Southminster), London would have another accessible seaside resort beside Southend. Bradwell was only five miles from Southminster. Bradwell differed in features and climate from other east and south coast resorts. Whilst one is not supposed to use hindsight, I would make the following observations. From personal experience, having visited the sea front at Bradwell on a nice warm sunny afternoon, it is a beautiful place, but it is still remote and very rural. The main feature of the place is the barn-like chapel of St Peter on the Wall, which in the twentieth century developed into a pilgrimage site. It is its remote situation which makes it an attractive place. Depending on how one looks at things, is it a good or a bad thing that the expectations did not materialise?

On Saturday 1 June 1889, the line was extended to Southminster for goods trains. According to the report in the *Essex Chronicle* of 7 June 1889, the progress of the first train was watched with very great interest by the inhabitants of the district. The *Chronicle* said that the line was a few chains in length over 16 miles and had been constructed by Messrs Walter Scott and Co of Newcastle upon Tyne. The line was provided with passing places at the various stations, which were Wickford, Battles Bridge (Battlesbridge), Woodham Fen, North Fambridge, Althorne and Burnham. For some reason at this point, the *Chronicle* did not mention the terminus at Southminster. In building the line, the contractors did not have any formidable difficulties to contend with. For some distance the line passed along the marshes and it was not until Althorne that cuttings and embankment became more pronounced. The only point at which the River Crouch was crossed was between Wickford and Battlesbridge. The country through which the railway passed was on the whole very thinly populated. The most important places were Burnham, the population of which in 1881 was 2,180, and Southminster with a population of 1,311. Burnham was noted for its oysters and it was anticipated that when the railway was opened for passenger traffic that the Crouch would be developed for yachting purposes. Burnham was also the centre of a market gardening industry.

The very first train had passed along the railway on 30 May carrying the stationmasters, porters and signalmen who were on duty at the new stations. The names of the stationmasters were: Mr F.R. Lilley at Battlesbridge, Mr F.W. Avery at Woodham Ferrers, Mr H. Pallent at Fambridge, Mr S. W. Pryke at Althorne, Mr F. B. Thain at Burnham-on-Crouch and Mr C. Leather at Southminster.

The train left Wickford at midday and the various passengers were safely deposited at their stations. The arrangements were supervised by Mr J. Flower the District Superintendent from Ipswich, with whom were Mr J. Hunt the telegraph inspector of Ipswich, Mr Hyde the signal inspector of London and Inspector Norman of Ipswich.

On the afternoon of Friday 31 May, several tradesmen of Southminster were busy carting empties to the station ready for the arrival of the first goods train, which was timed to arrive at Southminster at 3.20pm on Saturday afternoon, departing at 4pm. A large number of the inhabitants of Southminster were at the station to witness the arrival of the first train. After a considerable time, steam was seen in the distance and amid a scene of great excitement, into the station came one of the contractors' engines with two ballast wagons. Naturally this came as a big disappointment to the onlookers, most of whom walked off in disgust! Those who stayed, however, were rewarded with the arrival of a very respectable engine and some cattle trucks eighty minutes after the train was due. No time was lost in disposing of the cargo and in making arrangements to load again ready to depart. The first person to get anything on board was Mr James Gale of Bradwell-on-Sea who sent down a consignment of seventy Oford Down shearlings (sheep that had been shorn once). Mr Charles Croxon of Reddings also sent thirty shearlings making one hundred in all. There was also a consignment of wool for Wales. After pulling up at the goods station to take in parcels and empties sent by Messrs J.S. Prior, W. Harvey and Son, Samuel Pipe and Son and others, the first goods train steamed out of Southminster at 5.25 pm.

The *Chronicle* commented that there would have been a great deal
more sheep sent, but some of the farmers got the impression that
there would have been a Sunday service, which was not the railway
company's intention. At Burnham, a large number of people had
assembled to witness the arrival of the first train. There was a good
display of bunting and much cheering to greet the train. The freight
consisted of fruit empties for Messrs W. Newman, J. Camping, etc.
and goods for Messrs W. Carter, A. Newman and other tradesmen.
Mr H.J. Cooke of the Star Hotel had been appointed agent for
the collection and delivery of goods. The *Chronicle* said that the
station was replete with every accommodation. There was also
a goods shed forty-two yards by fifteen yards and four cottages
for porters and signalmen. It is now that one discovers a puzzle.
The *Chronicle,* in one paragraph, said that the service (at any rate
for one month) would be one luggage train per day to be run by
the contractors' engines as far as Wickford. The train would leave
Southminster at 4.30pm. However in the following paragraph, the
paper said that during that month (June) there would be one train
only for goods, which would leave Wickford at 1.25pm arriving
at Burnham at 3pm and returning to Burnham from Southminster
at 4.10pm and leaving at 4.20pm. One can assume that a luggage
train and a goods train are the same thing. This suggests that the
correspondent at Southminster somehow got different information
from the correspondent at Burnham. Further, GER Special Order
No R2870 of 27 May 1889 states that the train was worked by the
railway company and not the contractors. All that one can say is that
there was one goods train a day. According to the aforementioned
Special Order there was also a goods siding at Creeksea, between
Althorn(e) and Burnham. From a mention in the same Special
Order, that a temporary junction for the use of the contractor had
been laid at Stoke's Hall Wharf, about midway between Althorn (e)
and Creeksea Siding, it is clear that the contractors had continued
access to the line in connection with uncompleted works. The
Special Order makes clear that the line was to be worked under
the Train Staff System over the following sections: Wickford
to Belchamp Junction (between Wickford and Battlesbridge);
Belchamp Junction to Woodham Fen; Woodham Fen to Fambridge;
Fambridge to Burnham; and Burnham to Southminster. According
to the Special Order, Creeksea Siding was only to be called at by
trains shown in the working timetable as noted to call at it. As to
how contractors' trains to and from Stoke's Hall Wharf were to be

worked is not stated. For Creeksea Siding, the lever working the points was secured by Annett's Patent Lock. The lock could only be opened and the lever released by a key attached to the Fambridge and Burnham train staff and the key could not be withdrawn until the points had been replaced in their proper position and the lever relocked. Note that according to the notice, Woodham Ferrers was still called Woodham Fen.

Concerning passenger traffic, the *Chronicle* said that according to the latest reliable reports, the passenger services would exceed expectations. It was said that there would be as many as six trains run each way per day.

When the Wickford to Southminster section opened, Hogwell Public Goods Siding between Woodham Ferrers and Fambridge was not completed and the Board of Trade's Inspector, Major-General Hutchinson, in his report on the inspection of the line, refused to give permission for the siding to be opened. On 12 September 1889, he again inspected the line and found that the siding had been completed and that he had no objections to it being opened to traffic. The exact date of opening has not yet been established. All one can say is that it was sometime between 12 September to 1 October 1889.

Following an official inspection of the railway on Thursday 28 and Friday 29 June by officers of the Board of Trade and finding that the work had been carried out satisfactorily, Major-General Hutchinson issued a certificate allowing the railway to be opened for passenger traffic.

The railway opened for passenger traffic on Monday 1 July. According to the *Essex Chronicle*, the cost of the line together with the as yet unopened Maldon and Southend lines (and presumably the already opened section from Shenfield to Wickford) had cost nearly half a million pounds. Incidentally, by this time, the *Chronicle* was calling Woodham Fen Woodham Ferrers, as was the Great Eastern in its timetable. The reason for the change of name was the result of requests from residents in the neighbourhood. The explanation was that there was no such place as Woodham Fen in the neighbourhood of the station, (which was odd considering that Woodham Fen had been marked on the maps as such for some time) whilst the village of Woodham Ferrers was one mile to the north.

The opening of the railway was of deep interest to the people of the district. Burnham and Southminster were decorated with bunting and evergreens and part of the day was given over to holiday making, with the shops closing at 1pm. At Southminster, a complementary banquet was given to the leading officials of the railway together with the contractors and others and there was also a flower show and in the evening a grand display of fireworks. The trains, particularly in the afternoon, were crowded with many people making their first journey by train. One has to remember that even at that late date in the nineteenth century, a lot of country people did not move very far during their life. So as to make the day a memorable one in the lives of the children of Burnham, Messrs A.B. and W.A. Croxon treated those aged between 5 and 12 to a free trip to Wickford and back. Mr J.S. Prior did the same for those in Southminster. The train conveying the children consisted of seventeen carriages and was hauled by two engines. There were nearly 700 children on the train, 500 of whom came from Burnham and 200 from Southminster. At Burnham, there was not sufficient room in the carriages for all the children, and some had to ride in the guard's van. One or two of those in charge of the children rode on one or possibly both of the engines. The Burnham Temperance Band under Mr G. Trussell accompanied the excursion. One old lady named Courtman, aged 91, had never seen a train before and was carried on to the bridge at Burnham station to see the train depart. The first passenger train to travel over the line was timed to leave Southminster at 8.15am and reach Wickford at 9.4am. A crowd of people assembled at Southminster to see it depart and about fifty bought tickets, being anxious to have a ride on the first train. At Burnham, about twenty people got on. The journey was accomplished without mishap.

The first train for Southminster left Wickford at 9.30am. It seems though that there were about one hundred passengers on it from Wickford, with more getting on at other stations, particularly Battlesbridge and Burnham. The next down train brought the officials of the railway company, who travelled down in a special saloon carriage, which was an object of great interest. The train was crowded. At Southminster the schoolchildren, who were all carrying flags, formed an avenue through which the passengers leaving the station had to pass. The invited guests, which included the local MP Major Rasch, proceeded to Southminster Hall, which was the residence of Mr William Page. Meanwhile the schoolchildren, headed by the Southminster Brass Band, marched in procession through the principal street of Southminster. The public lunch, which was well attended, was held in a marquee in a field owned by Mr William Ely near the railway station. Spanning the entrance to the meadow was an arch, on one side of which was the inscription 'Success to the Railway' and on the other side the inscription 'C.H. Parkes', who was the Chairman of the GER.

At the lunch, a number of speeches were made including one from the chairman of the organising committee for the lunch (possibly Mr W. Page), Mr J. Wilson, the Chief Engineer of the GER, the contractors' resident engineer Mr J.T. Foxlee, Mr J.T. Middleton of the contractors and Major Rasch MP. One speaker, the Rev J. W. Mills in his speech, hoped that Bradwell (on-Sea) would soon get its railway.

The Rev Frederick Williams of Cold Norton recorded in his diary for 1 July 1889:

'Railway opened to Southminster.' We all went to Fambridge station and by train to Southminster.

Good speeches made, especially one from Mills who said that GER meant:
1. Great Expectations Realised
2. Go by it, Enjoy yourselves, Return
3. Gives Extraordinary Returns
4. Toast of the (?) Guard Engineer Gumption Experience Reliability - then This Railway will Gradually Eradicate Rubbish.'

The contractors still had some work to do as according to GER Special Order No R2897, the temporary junction for the use of the contractor (which had been laid at Stoke's Hall Wharf) about mid way between Althorn and Creeksea Siding was still in place and there was now another one about 600 yards on the Burnham side of Southminster station.

The GER's timetable for July 1889, shows the service for both the section of line between Shenfield and Wickford and Wickford and Southminster as follows. Seven trains between Shenfield and Wickford on weekdays. Of these five went through to Southminster. There was an additional train between Shenfield and Wickford on Fridays and an additional train between Shenfield and Southminster on Saturdays. In the reverse direction, there were seven trains between Wickford and Shenfield on weekdays. Of these, five started at Southminster on Monday to Friday with one only starting from Wickford on Saturday. There was an additional train from Southminster to Shenfield on Saturdays and an additional train from Wickford to Shenfield on Fridays. The July timetable said that the opening of the lines to Southend and Maldon was expected to take place in August, the service would be revised and a special notice would be given of the revision. The idea for the August opening was to catch the summer traffic to Southend and also to take some traffic away from the LTSR. In this edition of the timetable, Cold Norton had been given its correct name.

The effect of the new railway in the district was soon felt. The *Ipswich Journal* of 26 July 1889 reported that whereas as previously the agricultural produce of the district had to go by wagon to Maldon station, (which in some cases involved a long journey) it now only had to go to Burnham or Southminster for example. Vehicular traffic had diminished. Unfortunately this did not suit everyone as some of the roadside inns had lost trade.

Shortly after the opening the minutes of the 8 August 1889 meeting of the Traffic Committee of the GER record that the General Manager of the Railway had a petition that he had received from owner occupiers and residents of the northern part of the Dengie Hundred, requesting that the Company would make a railway from Southminster via Tillingham to Bradwell. The General Manager was asked to write a letter to them saying that the Company had no intention of promoting a bill for such a railway in the next session of parliament. They would take the matter under consideration the following year and probably visit the spot. Nothing further was heard about this.

After the first sections of the railway were opened, excursions appeared on the lines. The *Essex Chronicle* of Friday 7 June reported that the previous Saturday an excursion had been run to Billericay from Silvertown, North Woolwich, Canning Town, Stratford and Forest Gate. The newspaper said that the excursionists, who were respectable artisans, conducted themselves to the satisfaction of the inhabitants, who had feared that the town would suffer from the invasion and it was said that some inhabitants had even tried to induce the directors of the company to abandon the excursion. One is tempted to wonder if they were fearful of a repetition of an incident which happened on a Saturday in July 1881, when nearly 200 men who were the employees of several London firms, had gone to the town by horse drawn brakes and after dinner went for a walk during the course of which they vandalised people's gardens and the town's Reading Room. Some had walked around the town carrying stinging nettles and drawing them across the face of anyone who happened to be in the way. After a few fights among themselves in the Brentwood Road the men 'got clear away'. The same newspaper on Friday 19 July reported that three special trains had been run the previous Saturday from North Woolwich, Silvertown, and Canning Town, etc to Billericay, Burnham and Southminster. Two of the trains took nearly 900 visitors to Billericay and about 400 visitors were conveyed by the third train to Burnham and Southminster.

The expected opening to Maldon and Southend in August did not take place until 1 October 1889. It will be noted that this was slightly at variance to the proviso in parliament's approval for the lines that the Southminster and Maldon should be open before the Southend line. The *Daily News* of 17 August reported that the opening of the railway from Wickford to Southend had been officially fixed for 1 October. The same newspaper on 21 September 1889 reported that the lines to Maldon and Southend would be officially opened for traffic on 1 October. A demonstration of some kind was also expected to take place at Maldon. On Tuesday 1 October, the *Daily News* reported that the GER would that day commence running passenger trains to Southend. The event would be marked by a series of festivities at Southend and that the Mayor and Corporation of Maldon had arranged to assist.

The *Essex Chronicle* of 4 October 1889 reported the opening of the lines to Southend and Maldon. According to the newspaper there were celebrations at Southend and Rochford for the opening. At Rayleigh and other places, there were signs of unwanted animation. It had been hoped at one time that the line to Southend would be opened before the close of the excursion season, but the work was of a heavier nature than expected and there were slips between Rayleigh and Hockley which caused a serious delay.

The total length of the new system including the already opened sections was about fifty miles. There were sixteen stations and in addition six goods sidings. The work had involved the construction of two viaducts, sixty-seven bridges and 126 culverts. There were 2,865,000 yards of excavation. The distance from Southend to Shenfield was nearly twenty-one miles and from Southend to Maldon East station nearly twenty-five. A fairly good train service had been arranged. There were seven trains a day except Sunday on the line to Southend. The first down train from Liverpool Street would reach Southend at 9.2am and the last 8.58pm. The first up train from Southend would reach Liverpool Street at 8.58am and the last up train from Southend would reach Liverpool Street at 8.48pm. On Sunday there would be two trains in each direction. This would mean that the Southend line would have the advantage over the Southminster line, which had no trains on Sundays. On the Maldon branch there were five trains a day plus an additional one on Saturday which would run from Southend to Colchester via Rayleigh, Battlesbridge, Woodham Ferrers and Maldon West.

One has to say at this point that the *Chronicle,* which published the timetable of the new lines, had got things slightly wrong. For a start, on Monday to Friday there were only six trains a day between Shenfield and Southend. On a Saturday, there was a seventh train. Further, there was also one train a day which only ran from Shenfield to Billericay. Also, not all of the down trains on weekdays stopped at all of the stations. There was one that went non-stop from Wickford to Rochford and another that went non-stop from Billericay to Rochford. The *Chronicle,* despite its lack of accuracy over the timetable, went on to describe the lines. The line from Wickford to Southend was described as rather picturesque. The scenery between Wickford and Hockley was particularly striking. From Wickford to Prittlewell the line was single track and from Prittlewell to Southend the line was double track. There were stations at Rayleigh, Hockley, Rochford, Prittlewell and Southend, with a goods siding at Hawkwell. At Rayleigh, Rochford and Southend, there were very commodious goods sheds for dealing with the usual goods traffic and extensive yards for coal and general produce. At Prittlewell, there was only a small goods yard, but no goods shed. At Rayleigh, Hockley and Rochford stations, there were passing loops. Provision had been made to enable the line between Wickford and Prittlewell to be doubled. The station at Southend was described as of a special design and of an imposing character. There were two island platforms, the greater part of the length of which was covered with an umbrella awning. There was a large concourse with an iron and glass roof plus an engine shed. The signal box had no less than 110 levers. The line from Woodham Ferrers to Maldon, which connected with the line from Witham to Maldon, was nearly nine miles long and the construction work was described by the *Chronicle* as of a much heavier description and was attended with more serious engineering difficulties.

There were two new stations. One at Cold Norton (for Purleigh and Stow Maries) and one at Maldon West. There was also a goods depot at Barons Lane. There was an imposing viaduct over the River Blackwater between the original Maldon station (Maldon East) and the new Maldon station (Maldon West). The viaduct comprised of one opening span of eighty feet length and eight brick arches of eighty-five feet in length for the floodwaters. There was also a bridge wholly of brickwork over the Chelmer and Blackwater Navigation with three forty-five foot openings, one being for the Navigation and the other two for floodwaters. Maldon West station was described as a very fine building. There was a large and well-lighted booking office from which grand staircases led down to the platform. The *Chronicle* goes on to mention the spur from new line to the old line avoiding Maldon (East) and at Witham from the old line to the main line in the direction of Colchester avoiding Witham station. The *Chronicle* does not mention the spur between the Southend line and the Southminster line avoiding Wickford. The Maldon branch was single track, but the spur avoiding Maldon (East) station was double track and the section of the old branch from its bridge over the Chelmer and Blackwater Navigation was doubled. The *Chronicle* chose not to mention the fact that the old Maldon line had originally been built as double track, but had been singled in about 1850.

The first train to reach Southend was an excursion which left Colchester at 7.45am for Southend and called at Marks Tey, Kelvedon, Maldon (West), Cold Norton, Woodham Ferris, Battlesbridge and Rayleigh. As the day went on, the ordinary trains (which were of an extraordinary length) became crowded. Sadly the weather that day was a bit wet which interfered with outdoor proceedings.

At Southend, except for a few lines of streamers across the High Street at the GER station, there was not much in the way of decoration. The first train left Southend at 7.13am by which time a large number of people had assembled at the station. Mr A. Harrington of Rochford was the first person to buy a ticket. A total of ninety-two people bought tickets for the first train. Of these thirty-seven were for Rochford, thirty-four for Prittlewell, nine for Wickford, three for Rayleigh, three for Chelmsford, two for Shenfield, two for Hockley, one for Brentwood and one for Liverpool Street. Many of those returned to Southend by the next train. Their only object was to be amongst the first travellers on the line.

One passenger on that first train was a Mr Duncan McBryer, a harness maker of Rochford. Each year on the anniversary of the opening of the line, he displayed a poster advertising the opening in his shop window.

At Southend, there was a public lunch to which the members of Southend Local Board, the Celebration Committee, Maldon Corporation, the officials of the GER and the contractors had been invited. Some of the members of the Celebration Committee were also members of Southend Local Board including Mr F. Wood who was both the Chairman of the Local Board of Health and of the Celebration Committee.

One source says members of the Southend Local Board, the Celebration Committee and the contractors departed Southend by the 11.52am train to meet members of Maldon Corporation and the officials of the GER at Wickford, but there is a dispute over the timing of this. The party from Maldon left on the 11.34am train and travelled in a saloon carriage. At Woodham Ferrers the special carriage was attached to the train from Southminster to Wickford which left Southminster at 11.29am and arrived at Woodham Ferrers at 12.2pm. When the train got to Wickford, things went awry. Drawn up in one platform was a train full of happy children from Rochford who had been treated to a free trip over the new line. The Southminster train steamed up to the other platform and as soon as it had left, its place was taken by a Southend train. The platforms were crowded with people, most of whom were travelling to and from Southend. It had been hoped that the saloon carriage would be attached to the 12.48pm from Shenfield which was due in Wickford at 1.4pm and which conveyed officials of the GER, but so heavily laden was that train that it was delayed at Shenfield whilst a second engine was telegraphed for. The Maldon and Southend parties waited nearly an hour at Wickford. The time was spent mostly in introductions and pleasant chat. Amongst those who turned up during this time were Major Rasch MP and Mrs Rasch, who had driven over from Danbury, and Mr William Page JP, of Southminster Hall. Eventually a special train for Southend was made up at Wickford to which was attached the saloon carriage in which the parties from Southend, Maldon and the contractors travelled. When the special train reached Southend, a hearty reception awaited it. Hundreds of people had assembled at the station to cheer the visitors, whilst the pier band under Mr J. Soloman played 'See the conquering hero comes' One presumes this means not only the special train, but also the scheduled train. Immediately after the arrival of the train, a public lunch was served in a large marquee which had been erected on the west side of Victoria Avenue. It would be deemed to be rather ill-mannered to start the lunch without the officials of the GER present. I have to say that contemporary press accounts are somewhat unclear on this, though. Those attending included people from the Celebration Committee, whose chairman was Mr F. Wood, the Chairman of the local Board of Health, the visitors from Maldon, various other people, officials from the GER and representatives from the contractors, Major and Mrs Rasch. Besides Mrs Rasch, there were other women present. Speeches were given by (amongst others) Major Rasch, Mr J. Wilson, Mr W. Lloyd Wise of the Celebration Committee, Mr T. Middleton for the contractors and Councillor J. Sadler, the Mayor of Maldon.

At Rochford, the celebrations took a different turn. There were no elaborate decorations, but there was a liberal display of flags and lines of streamers which were strung across the roads. The proceedings started with a procession of the various tradesmen of the town. Included in this was a stagecoach. After this, about 600 children accompanied by about 400 adults were treated by the Celebration Committee to a trip by train to Wickford and back. The children did not have to pay anything, but the adults had to pay one shilling. The long train was very heavily laden. After an hour had been spent in Wickford, the party returned to Rochford where a tea was provided for the children in the goods shed, which the GER had placed at the service of the Celebration Committee. In the evening, there was a public dinner in the Corn Exchange, followed by an entertainment at the County Court office and a smoking concert at the Corn Exchange. About one hundred people attended the public dinner. It was presided over by Major Tawke. Major Rasch was present for a short time. Determined to be amongst the passengers on both the first up and down trains, a party of about twenty of the principal tradesmen of Rochford took a trip by the first up train to Rayleigh, breakfasted at the Crown Inn and returned to Rochford by the first down train. Throughout the day, Rochford station was crowded and the arrival of each train was the signal for hearty cheering. About 645 tickets were sold and 720 collected. The reason for this discrepancy is that some tickets were bought at stations other than on the new lines.

However not all went well on the opening day. On the first up train from Southend to Shenfield the guard lost his temper at Rayleigh because a porter was not quick enough in his work. Also, as a goods train was being shunted at Rayleigh a pointsman shut the points too soon and two trucks left the rails. This suggests that the first trains that day on the line were goods trains. It seems that platelayers had to be called in to repair the damage to the track caused by the derailment. This delayed the first down passenger train by forty-five minutes. The Mayor of Maldon got in trouble; there being considerable dissatisfaction in the town over the alleged apathy of the authorities in moving until it was too late to do anything to celebrate the opening of the new railway to Maldon. According to the *Daily News* of 2 October, when the Mayor and Corporation of Maldon returned to Maldon they were met at Maldon West station by about 1,000 people. As the Mayor was walking home alone he was followed by a mob of about 200 people who hooted and hissed and pelted him with mud. The *Essex Standard* of 5 October 1889 said that the Mayoress was hit on the shoulder by a missile when she opened the front door of the house to receive her husband. The *Standard* was very critical of the people who carried out the outrage and regretted that they could not be punished. It said that they were the hypocrites who had opposed the new railway to Maldon but had been the first to use it to go elsewhere after complaining about the authorities for not having celebrations in the town to mark its opening.

According to the *Essex Standard* for 5 October 1889, excursions were run from places including Colchester, Harwich, Brightlingsea, Clacton and Walton to Southend (via Maldon) during the first week of operation from Woodham Ferrers to Maldon and Wickford to Southend. They do not appear to have been well patronised according to the newspaper. There were also other occasions prior to their closure when the curves were used by special trains.

The identities of the locomotives hauling the first trains are not known. The late E.L. Ahrons, who wrote a series of articles on locomotive and train working in the British Isles at the latter part of the nineteenth century, mentions in the articles on the GER that some of the No 1 class 2-4-0 engines were allocated to the line in 1889 and 1890. The No 1 class had originally been built by Messrs Sharp, Stewart and the GER between 1867 and 1872 to the design of the then locomotive superintendent of the railway Samuel W. Johnson. In 1889 to 1893, one of Samuel Johnson's successors, James Holden, rebuilt the engines with larger cabs, modified boilers and larger driving wheels. According to Chris Hawkins and George Reeve in volume one of their books on Great Eastern Railway engine sheds, No 28 of the class was recorded as being on the Southminster branch in the afternoon of 12 October 1887. I assume this to mean 1889 rather than 1887. It is idle to speculate as to what engines were used at the start, for as far as I know no records of locomotive allocations have survived from the period but it would suggest that from the opening of the line to Southend and Maldon, the class was in operation on the lines.

Apart from the existing engine shed at Maldon, which gained a new fifty foot Ransomes Rapier turntable in 1889, new engine sheds were constructed at Southminster and Southend. At Wickford, which had an allocation of locomotives, in the absence of an engine shed there was an engine siding. At some time a fifty foot turntable was installed at Shenfield. It is not absolutely clear when this was. Possibly, this was when the station was built in 1887 or perhaps towards the end of 1888. Certainly it was there by 1891 as it is mentioned in the appendix to the working timetable for that year. There was also a fifty foot turntable provided at Woodham Ferrers, as it is shown in the appendix also. Of the engine sheds, the accommodation provided was varied. Southend consisted of a two-road building with shelter for four tender engines or six tank engines. At Southminster, the accommodation was quite generous being a two-road building providing shelter for two tender engines or four tank engines. In *Great Eastern Engine Sheds Volume 1*, mention is made of the GER board authorising £900 on 5 August 1890 for a new 'New Engine House, Pump and Tank' at Wickford. It is known that by 1895 turntables were located at Wickford and Southminster.

# CHAPTER THREE

# Great Eastern Years

The GER was determined to lure some traffic away from the LTSR. The LTSR did however have two advantages over the GER. Firstly, its route to Southend via Upminster was shorter by thirty-three and three quarter miles from Fenchurch Street compared with forty-one and a half miles by the GER's from Liverpool Street. Secondly, whereas the LTSR's line was double track throughout, the GER's was only double track as far as Wickford – twenty-one miles from Liverpool Street, plus the half mile from Prittlewell to Southend. The twelve miles of single track with passing loops between Wickford and Prittlewell restricted the number of trains that could be run. Whilst the LTSR was the GER's only competitor for the business traffic from Southend, it was not its only competitor for the excursion traffic. The other competitor or competitors were the Thames paddle steamers. These offered something which neither of the two railways could offer, for example, bars and toilets. The paddle steamers may not have been as fast as the trains, but the accommodation was superior. Assuming that the weather wasn't too bad, being able to stroll or sit on the deck of a paddle steamer in the open air was preferable to sitting in a compartment of a railway carriage.

The GER having built the lines to Burnham-on-Crouch, Southminster and Maldon did however have a market there for both business and leisure traffic which neither the LTSR or the paddle steamers could reach. During the first ten years from the opening of the lines, traffic to Southend increased by forty-three per cent.

Until 1911, the main source of traffic for Southend was excursion traffic. Burnham-on-Crouch on the Southminster line also provided some excursion traffic both in the form of day trippers and weekenders. Any business traffic on the Southend line came mostly from places either not served or not within easy reach of the LTSR. This is not to say that the GER (in the early days of the New Essex Lines existence) did not attempt to try and build up some business traffic from Southend.

Initially, Sunday services on the Southminster line were provided only in the summer. However, with the start of the winter 1897 timetable, a service was provided on the line on Sundays during the winter. In GER days there were no Sunday services on the Woodham Ferrers to Maldon line.

Until May 1911, the GER made some use of slip coaches at Shenfield as a means of providing a through service to Southend. Briefly, a slip carriage was a carriage detached from a train at a station without the train stopping. These were quite common at one time in this country. Indeed, on the lines of the former Great Western Railway they lasted until 1960. However, no one ever devised a method whereby a carriage could be attached to a train at a station without the train stopping.

The GER in the early days tried a variety of termini in the London area in addition to Liverpool Street in an attempt to lure excursionists away from the LTSR and the Thames paddle steamers. The first attempt seems to have been aimed principally at the Thames paddle steamers, as from July to September 1890 a Sunday through service was tried out from North Woolwich to Southend and Southminster. This train joined with a through train from Liverpool Street to Southend and Southminster at Shenfield. The train then ran to Wickford where it divided with one portion going to Southend and the other to Southminster. In the evening the whole thing was done in reverse.

The LTSR were understandably concerned that the GER would take away some of its Southend traffic, particularly as it did have a direct connection to the Underground at Liverpool Street as opposed to Mark Lane for Fenchurch Street. In May 1890, Arthur Lewis Stride, the Managing Director of the LTSR, drew up plans for a service of LTSR trains from Liverpool Street to supplant the existing service of through carriages on the GER's Liverpool Street to Barking service. The GER objected on the grounds that the LTSR had no running powers into Liverpool Street and the trains had to be deleted from the draft timetable. The through carriages from Liverpool Street to Southend (LTSR) and Shoeburyness in some form remained until at least 1908 or even later. After 1897, there was only one service a day from and to Liverpool Street conveying the through carriages.

Peter Kay, in his history of the LTSR, stated that the GER started excursion trains from Fenchurch Street to Southend (GER) in August 1890. As the earliest reference I can find is in the timetable is October, this would suggest that from August to September the trains were advertised by a separate handbill. The ticket clerks at Fenchurch Street station were employees of the GER and could be instructed to influence traffic to the company's trains. The LTSR's Managing Director suggested to the company's board that the railway should appoint its own ticket clerks there, which it was entitled to do so under an agreement of 1876.

On August Bank Holiday Monday, which in those days was the first Monday of the month, the GER suspended the Liverpool Street to Barking service for most of the day. This was allegedly due to a mistake by an Inspector. This meant that anyone wanting to go from Liverpool Street to Southend had to use the trains via Shenfield to Southend (GER). The LTSR did not believe that a mistake had been made.

In October the through train from North Woolwich and Liverpool Street to Southend and Southminster was taken off and replaced by a scheduled through train from and to Fenchurch Street and Blackwall. The train both joined and divided at Wickford. This targetted the Thames paddle steamer trade at Blackwall and at the LTSR custom at Fenchurch Street. The line between Fenchurch Street and Gas Factory Junction just beyond Stepney was owned by the London and Blackwall Railway (LBR) which had been leased by the GER in 1866 for 999 years and used by both the GE and the LTS railways. Before the starting of through services from Fenchurch Street to Southend via the GER's route, railway passengers from intermediate stations between Fenchurch Street and Blackwall would have taken a local GER train to Stepney or Fenchurch Street and changed to an LTSR train to Southend.

At the end of October, all Sunday services ceased apart from on the line to Southend. In 1891, the LTSR again sought running powers into Liverpool Street. Powers were only sought for eight trains a day, in order that the GER could not claim problems with line capacity. The idea behind this was to replace the then existing GER service from Liverpool Street to Barking with a new LTSR service. The GER, of course, opposed this and it was thrown out. The only sop to the LTSR was that in the future, the GER should charge the same fare from Liverpool Street to Southend as the LTSR did to Southend. Naturally the GER had been charging a slightly lower fare (around 2d cheaper) to its station than to the LTSR's station.

In the summer of 1891, in order to build up business traffic, the GER started a sixty-five minute service to and from Southend. The morning service left Southend at 8.45am. At that time, most people used to work on Saturday mornings. The Monday to Friday service left Liverpool Street at 5.25pm and the Saturday service at 1.57pm. William Birt, the GER's General Manager, had said in March 1891 that the company had only one Southend season ticket holder. The same year saw summer services again on the Southminster branch including the through trains from Blackwall and Fenchurch Street (and return) on Sundays restarted for the summer. The year also saw the start of a summer Sundays only service between Gospel Oak and Southend and return. At the end of the summer there was a change in the Southend to Colchester through service. The train to Southend from Colchester now called on request at Wickham and Langford on the Witham to Maldon branch, ran into Maldon East and then ran from there to Southend via Rayleigh. In June that same year the Essex Agricultural Society had held its annual show at Maldon in the grounds of Maldon Hall and Hill House which was within a few hundred yards of Maldon West station.

In the summer of 1892, the GER put on two daily through trains on weekdays to and from Fenchurch Street to Southend,

**Adams Class**
61 0-4-4T crossing the viaduct at Maldon. (*Author's collection*)

Fred Spalding Photo Chelmsford Copyright

RAILWAY STATION WOODHAM FERRERS

**An R24** 0-6-0T at Woodham Ferrers. (*Author's collection*)

the purpose being an attempt to gain passengers from the LTSR. In the same summer, the service from Blackwall was withdrawn and replaced by one to and from Gospel Oak to Southend. The Sunday service showed two trains to and from Fenchurch Street. One of these in each direction divided and joined at Wickford for Southminster.

The timetable for the summer of 1893 shows two trains a day in each direction between Southend and Fenchurch Street in addition to the trains to and from Liverpool Street. On Saturdays, there was a through train from Fenchurch Street to Southminster. The return working was to Liverpool Street. The Sunday service showed two trains to and from Fenchurch Street. One of these in each direction divided and joined at Wickford for Southminster and Southend.

In July 1894, the GER found itself faced with competition for Southend traffic from the Midland Railway (MR) following the opening of the Tottenham and Forest Gate Railway. This was a joint railway owned by the LTSR and the MR. The railway was opened for through goods traffic on 2 July, passenger services on 9 July and local goods services on 1 September. Initially, there was only one through train a day from St Pancras to Southend and return, but in September, an additional through train in both directions commenced running on Saturdays. The through services ceased on 15 October, but were resumed the following year and thenceforth were run through throughout the year. The through services from the Midland line lasted into British Railways days in various forms and finally ended with the electrification of the LTSR line in June 1962.

On the night of Sunday 23-Monday 24 September 1894, there was a severe storm accompanied by torrential rain in Essex which caused great damage in the Maldon area. The first train of the day from Maldon to Woodham Ferrers on 24 September was unable to get through and had to return to Maldon. The passengers were forced to continue their journey on a later train. At Woodham Ferrers, the line was blocked by the floods and trains on the Southminster line that Monday consequently ran between half an hour and an hour late. At Woodham Ferrers station, the water was one foot seven inches deep over the level crossing and between two feet six inches and three feet deep between the up and down platforms. The stationmaster was forced to wade up to his knees in water from his house to the booking office which, along with his office and the waiting room, was under water. He promptly telegraphed to all other stations and stopped the trains until the railway was fit for traffic to pass through the station. According to the report in the *Essex Chronicle* of 28 September, large pieces of timber were floating away and the wooden boxes over the points were carried away and the points got blocked.

One may be mistaken with hindsight, but one gets the impression that the GER didn't really care about the Woodham Ferrers to Maldon branch. At the end of February 1895, the Southend to Colchester through service was taken off and the curves avoiding Wickford, Maldon East and Witham were disconnected. The last day of the service running was Saturday 23 February. Authority for the closure of the curves and their associated signal boxes was granted on 5 June 1895. The removal of the curves appears to have been completed by the end of 1895. Passengers then had either to change at Shenfield for Colchester or change at Wickford, Woodham Ferrers, Maldon East and Witham. One feels that the line could have been developed. The distance from London to Maldon via Shenfield, Wickford and Woodham Ferrers was forty-two miles compared with forty-four miles via Witham. Maldon still is a pleasant place. There is a promenade, a quayside and some rather attractive buildings which existed when the railway was extant. People visited Maldon for the sake of it and still do. One feels that the GER was more interested in Southend with its pier and river front and also to some extent the Dengie area featuring Burnham-on-Crouch.

The *Ipswich Journal* of 29 August 1896 mentioned the announcement made that week, of a projected railway from the Great Northern Railway at Holloway via Stoke Newington, Walthamstow, Chigwell, Ongar, Dunmow, Bury St Edmunds and Wymondham to Norwich, with a branch from Ongar through Chelmsford and Maldon to the mouth of the River Colne. Here, it was proposed to construct a deep water harbour. Nothing came of this. The railway was one of many proposed in the latter part of the nineteenth century by Mr J.F. Errington Barnes, a civil engineer of Dorchester. All came to nothing.

An interesting special train ran on the Southend line in 1899. On 23 July, Barnum and Bailey's Greatest Show on Earth circus visited Southend. The train carrying the circus comprised American-style rolling stock adapted to the British loading gauge and travelled from Chatham to Southend. After performing at Southend the circus moved to Colchester on 24 July.

In order to permit more trains on the Southend line, the single-track section was progressively doubled. The section between Prittlewell and Rochford was doubled in 1896. That from Rayleigh from Wickford in May 1900, with Rayleigh to Hockley following sometime between October 1900 and January 1901. The final section to Rochford was doubled in 1901, some time after February. Hawkwell Siding closed from 1 March 1901 as Goods Manager Liverpool Street Circular CR194 dated 1 March 1901 states; 'Hawkwell Siding permanently closed for traffic after today'.

With regards to passenger services, the summer timetable for 1900 still shows through trains to and from Southend and Fenchurch Street daily, but only to and from Gospel Oak on Sundays. Southminster on Sundays had a through service to and from Liverpool Street taking just over an hour and a half. The summer timetable for 1901 shows only a service from Gospel Oak to Southend, but no return service. A connecting service was run from Stratford to Gospel Oak. For the summer of 1903 the Gospel Oak train ran in both directions before reverting to the previous working pattern.

In 1899 came the first threat of competition, when Southend Corporation obtained a light railway order for a number of light railways within its boundaries and just beyond. These light railways were in fact tramways. The light railway system was opened on 19 July 1901. Routes ran from the High Street terminus to Leigh, Southchurch, the Beach and Prittlewell. Whilst only one of these was in competition with the GER ( and that was between the only two stations on the line which were within walking distance of one another), there were proposals for other routes that would have presented serious competition to the Southend line. One was for a line from Southend to Rochford and another was to Rayleigh via Chalkwell and Hadleigh. Whilst the latter would not have probably presented too much of a problem, the former would have. By their very nature, circuitous routes are not very popular for through journeys. In 1901, there came another threat of competition in the form of a proposal for a Southend, Burnham and Bradwell-on-Sea Light Railway. This was to have run from the LTSR station at Southend via Prittlewell, Rochford, to the west of Great Stambridge, to the east of Canewdon, Burnham, Southminster, Asheldham, and Tillingham to Bradwell. The railway would run partially along streets and partially through fields. It would have crossed the Crouch via a flying or other sort of ferry, which suggests that it would have been necessary perhaps for through traffic to be transported across the Crouch by boat. At no point was there any connection with the GER. The GER was opposed to the proposed light railway and was concerned that it might fall into the hands of the LTSR which would then mean competition between Southend and Rochford, Burnham and Southminster. However nothing came of this. Shortly afterwards, there was a proposal for a Southend and District, Bradwell-on-Sea and Colchester Light Railways. This would have connected not with the LTSR, but with the Southend Corporation Light Railways at Prittlewell and as originally proposed, would have run via Rochford, Burnham-on-Crouch and Southminster to Bradwell-on-Sea. The Crouch would have been crossed by a bridge and the light railway would have terminated at a point just east of the hamlet of Bradwell Waterside. At Southminster, there would have been a connection with the GER. From Southminster the railway would have followed the route of the previous proposed light railway to Bradwell. From Bradwell there would have been a ferry crossing to West Mersea. From there the railway would have continued to a point just south of Colchester where it would have split into three branches. Two would have gone to Stanway, three miles west of Colchester and one of these would have joined the GER. The other branch would have terminated in Drury Lane (now Drury Road) in the town, about a mile away from Colchester's own tramway system pointing in the direction of the latter, so that it would have been possible at a later date to extend the line to meet up with and join the Colchester system. Whilst the first two were rejected, the third branch was approved. However, this branch would have been isolated, as the main line south from its junction to Abberton via Berechurch was also rejected. In 1902, a revised route from the point of the junction to Abberton via Black Heath was approved.

There was a further alteration to the Light Railway's plans in 1907, when the crossing of the Crouch was amended from a bridge to a ferry. The proposed light railway would have had a few problems. One problem was the proposed gauge of four feet eight and a half inches, whereas both the Southend and Colchester tram networks, had the light railway ever extended to connect with them, were three feet six inches gauge. However that was not an insolvable problem as prior to the First World War, Bradford and Leeds, whose tramways were of different gauges, were able to operate through services using trams whose axles were able to run on both systems via a tapered section of line. In 1907, the gauge of the light railway was altered to three feet six inches to connect with the Southend trams. The GER was opposed to the proposed railway as it would obviously be in competition with it and the Board instructed its solicitor to oppose all applications. In 1908, the Light Railway Company applied for an extension of time for the construction of the railway. The Light Railway Commissioners were not satisfied that the capital could be raised for the whole undertaking and therefore withheld sanction for the central portion – namely the Burnham and the River Blackwater section. Sanction was allowed in regard of the southern and northern portions. The sanction applied to either or both and was subject to the deposit of capital within twelve months and the works being substantially in hand within eighteen months. The GER however did not oppose this application. The order was confirmed by the Board of Trade in December 1910 (*The Times* 23 December 1910). The powers expired unexercised in 1912. By the end of January 1913, the Railway was in the Chancery Division of the High Court (*The Times* 23 January 1913). *The Times* of 22 March and 2 December had notices regarding those who had claims to make against the Company in respect of land or money.

In April 1906, another form of competition emerged in the form of the Southend on Sea and District Motor Omnibus Company which started operations with three Dennis double decker buses from Southend to Hadleigh, Rochford and Shoebury /Wakering. The venture was short lived, but it aroused interest in motor transport.

Whilst the competition was not there except between Southend and London in the form of the LTSR, the opportunity for it was. For example, in 1903, the chairman of Wickford Parish Council, the Rev Dormer Pierce, proposed that the GER be asked to make the return fare from Wickford to Southend the same as the return fare from Southend to Wickford as the latter was cheaper than the former.

The timetable for July 1906 shows amongst other things two through trains from Fenchurch Street to Southend on weekdays and one train in the reverse direction. One of the down trains and the solitary up train are shown as not running after 15 September, the other down train running until the end of the summer timetable. On Sundays, there were two trains from Fenchurch Street to Southend and one train to Fenchurch Street from Southend. There was also a daily train from Gospel Oak to Southend, but in the reverse direction there was no through train. A change had to be made at Stratford.

The daily service from Fenchurch Street to Southend and return and the daily train from Gospel Oak were withdrawn after 1908 and in 1909 only ran on Sundays. After 1909, there was a summer Sundays only train from Fenchurch Street to Southend, but there was no return working. The service ceased after the 1913 summer timetable.

During the 1900s, the GER put newer and better locomotives on some of the trains on the Southend service so that whilst some trains may have been hauled by T26 class locomotives of the 2-4-0 wheel arrangement, others might be hauled by S46 and D56 express locomotives of the 4-4-0 wheel arrangement. These were collectively members of the famous Claud Hamilton Class. Briefly, the difference between an S46 and a D56 was that an S46 had a round topped firebox whilst a D56 had a firebox of the raised Belpaire type.

Southend locomotive shed in the 1900s and beyond was a source of trouble to the GER. The water supply was awful. The water at Southend was very hard with the resultant bad effects on the locomotives' tubes that even water softening couldn't cure. The water was so bad for engine boilers that those hauling express trains could not use it and it was necessary to send them to Rochford for watering, a round trip of about six miles. The problem was to some extent solved in 1913 by pumping water from Rochford where, under plans which been developed since 1903, a large concrete reservoir was built. The pump at Rochford was manned by two attendants who were part of Southend shed's staff.

By the beginning of 1910, the services on the Woodham Ferrers to Maldon line were giving concern to Cold Norton Parish Council. At the meeting of the Council of 14 March it was decided that a letter be sent to the General Manager of the GER asking that the same service of trains on the line that was provided in the summer timetable from the previous July be continued throughout the year. The General Manager of the GER, Walter Hyde, in a letter of 23 May in reply to the Council's letters of 22 April and 10 May, said that the question of running a connection off the 7.38pm train from Liverpool Street through to Cold Norton and Maldon all year round had been very carefully considered, but the traffic to those places was not sufficient to warrant the expense of the additional train. He regretted that he was unable to comply with the Council's request. Stow Maries Parish Council had also expressed a similar concern at its meeting of 9 May. However the Parish Council minutes contain no record of the GER's response.

Whilst the use of the GER's express locomotives on some of the trains may have been of interest to railway enthusiasts in the area, by the beginning of 1911 there was concern both by the shareholders of the GER and in the Southend area local newspapers about the service provided by the GER from Southend.

**S46 No** 1851 near Mountnessing on a Southend train in 1909. (*Ken Nunn*)

**N31 No** 993 at Mountnessing signal box in 1913. (*Ken Nunn*)

On 1 June 1910 the LTSR had started a through service from Southend to Ealing via the Metropolitan District Railway (MDR). The trains were hauled by the LTSR's steam locomotives to and from Barking or East Ham and from or to there by the MDR's electric locomotives. By running to central London on the Underground the new service had an advantage that the GER did not have in that it was possible to travel from the Southend area to a station right in the heart of the City of London, albeit only to a station on the southern part of the Circle Line. Admittedly there were only two trains a day in each direction on weekdays of which one in each direction was for day trippers from West London to Southend and of the other two, one was for the 'market traffic' and the other was for the 'theatre traffic'. The new service was mentioned by the *Southend Standard* in its edition of 26 May 1910. Nevertheless to a detached observer it showed initiative by the LTSR. However, there was no mention of it in the subsequent week's edition.

The concern about the service provided to and from Southend was raised by Walter Hyde at the meeting of the Traffic Committee on 16 March 1911. The General Manager said that the question of the Southend services had been raised more than once by shareholders at the half yearly meetings. The fact that the GER had done practically nothing to cater for the residential traffic to and from Southend was the subject of comment in local newspapers. The Company was constantly being urged to improve the service so as to afford an alternative route for business traffic in view of the overcrowding and discomfort of the travelling on the LTSR. After twenty-one years since the opening of the line, the number of season ticket holders from the Southend area using the GER route was thirty-three. The number using the LTSR from the Southend area including Westcliff was 6,000, to which figure it had risen from twenty-seven during the previous thirty-five years, according to a statement by the Chairman and Managing Director of the LTSR, Arthur Lewis Stride. In 1891, the population of Southend was 12,333. By 1901, it had more than doubled and was now approaching 70,000.

The population was not confined to the district adjacent to the LTSR but also to the GER. The GER did not secure the traffic from the district owing to the poor service provided. Receipts from bookings at Southend, whilst they had increased by forty-three per cent in the first decade after the opening of the line, had shown little expansion in the last ten years. Traffic returns had shown a serious and almost continuous decline. Thus, for a place that was growing by leaps and bounds, the LTSR was obtaining a greater share of the traffic than formerly. It was evident that unless the GER could secure some proportion of the Southend area season ticket traffic, it could not expect other members of the household of season ticket holders, nor their visitors to travel by the GER route. The time for action had come. The question of improvements to secure a fair proportion of the residential traffic had been examined by the Superintendent of the Line and proposals were submitted, providing the principal features of the proposed service, compared to the existing service and the service provided by the LTSR. On Mondays to Saturdays the GER's existing service was three trains from Southend to London between 8am and 11am. The proposed service would be five trains between those times. The number provided by the LTSR was nine during the same times. On Mondays to Fridays the number of down trains from London to Southend between 5pm and 9pm under the existing service was five. Under the proposed service, it would be seven. The LTSR ran eight trains during that period. There would be a corresponding increase during Saturday afternoons. There would be down trains at 9.45pm and

12 midnight and improvements to up evening trains. The scheme also took into account the requirements of season ticket holders from intermediate stations (Brentwood to Rochford) and the Southminster line (and obviously the Maldon West line). At that time these numbered about 400. An additional train was also proposed to and from Southminster. The cost of the scheme was about £7,500 p.a. This expenditure would be more than covered if the result was an additional 500 season ticket holders, which was less than ten per cent of the number travelling on the LTSR. It was recommended to initiate the improvements from 1 May 1911. The Committee resolved that this recommendation be approved by the Directors.

The GER's publicity machine soon got to work as an announcement appeared in the *Southend Standard* at the end of March advertising a 'New Service of Fast Trains for London Businessmen. Southend to Liverpool Street in 58 mins'. The *Essex Chronicle* of 24 March carried an article headed 'SOUTHEND AND LONDON. GER'S IMPROVED SERVICE' which began:

> 'Commencing on 1st May the Great Eastern Railway will greatly improve their train service between Southend and London'.

Meanwhile, on 7 April, a deputation from the recently formed South-East Essex Travellers Association met with the General Manager of the GER regarding the train service from Southend to London and vice versa. The whole question of a fast and frequent train service was thoroughly discussed. Walter Hyde assured the deputation that the suggestions put forward would receive his serious consideration and also gave his assurance that the new arrangements coming into force would be of a permanent nature. This was reported in the edition of the *Southend Standard* for 13 April.

The *Southend Standard* of 27 April said that it was understood that in connection with the new express service of trains between Southend and London it had been arranged to run a service of corridor restaurant car trains. The service would include breakfast up by the 8.16am from Southend, tea down by the 5.3pm train (5.37pm on Saturdays) and supper on the 12.0 midnight train (12.07 on Saturdays). The new vestibuled train would be open for public inspection at Southend (GER) station from 10am to 7pm on Saturday 29 April.

The *Southend Standard* of 4 May contained a glowing description of the new service, giving a description of the restaurant car trains including the engine (of the Claud Hamilton type according to the newspaper) and also the start of the service on Monday 1 May. Whilst the 7.17am departure from Southend did not have a large number of passengers, the 8.16am restaurant car train attracted at least one hundred, not to mention railway officials. The *Standard* said that at least some passengers had transferred from the LTSR, one man saying that he had done so as soon as the expresses were promised, as his season ticket had expired. Subsequent trains also did rather well. The returns for the other three trains were thirty, fifty and eighty passengers. The return trains were also well patronised. There was a genuine feeling of pleasure with the way that the GER was handling the service. A very small point was that whilst the First Class carriages were lit by electricity, the Third Class carriages were lit by gas.

*The Times* of 26 April reported that from 1 May the GER had arranged to improve their train service between London and Southend. Four express trains would leave Southend arriving at Liverpool Street before 10am and in the evening a similar number of expresses would run between 5pm and 6.30pm. The journey accomplished by the fastest train would be in fifty-eight minutes. A midnight train would leave Liverpool Street for Southend daily.

The newly established *Great Eastern Railway Magazine* had a short article devoted to the new services. According to the magazine the new services were to:

'meet the requirements of the public for a morning and evening express residential service to and from Liverpool Street at times convenient for those engaged in business in the City'.

At the same time the magazine also said that season tickets from suburban stations to London would be obtainable at the suburban station on demand so that passengers would no longer have to fill in a form and forward it to the Secretary of the Company each time that they wanted a season ticket. Excepting in the case of half rate tickets and those subject to a discount, in future a form would only be required on the first application. This could be filled up and handed in at once and the ticket obtained forthwith. Amongst those places to which the new arrangements would apply would be Southend.

Both the *Railway Magazine* in its June edition and the *Railway and Travel Monthly* in its May edition mentioned the improved service on the Southend line, devoting short articles to it, the former's being titled 'The Great Eastern Railway New Southend Service' and the latter 'The Great Eastern's Southend Accelerations'.

The LTSR responded to the GER's improved Southend service by improving its service to and from Southend including adding extra through trains to and from Ealing via the MDR. According to the minutes of the Traffic Committee for 20 July 1911, the improved service had brought in an additional 100 new season ticket holders from the Southend area. For the period ending 31 December 1911, the increase in the number of season ticket holders equalled 749 quarterly season tickets according to the minutes of the Traffic Committee meeting of 6 February 1912.

However, despite the improvement in the service in the mornings and evenings, the service between 10am and 4pm on Mondays to Fridays was still in need of improvement and was still the same as before the improvements were made. The minutes of the Traffic Committee of 6 March 1913 recorded that deputations of GER season ticket holders from the Southend and District Railway Travellers Association had waited upon the General Manager and the Superintendent of the Line urging a need for earlier and later trains and for an improved service between 10am and 4pm for family members travelling up to London. The service provided compared badly with that provided on the Midland Railway (which had taken over the LTSR in August 1912) from the Southend area between those hours. Various points were put forward by the deputations and were considered by the Traffic Committee. It was found that the deputations' principal requests could be met and that various other improvements could be made in the service including accelerating the up supper express train at a cost of approximately £176 per month. It was proposed to run additional trains from the start of the summer timetable, during which time they would be carefully monitored before a decision was made as to whether they should continue for the winter.

The increases in the number of season ticket holders continued. The minutes of the Traffic Committee of 19 June 1913 record that by the end of April 1913 there were now 800 season ticket holders using the GER service from the Southend area. The minutes of the Traffic Committee for 20 November 1913 reported that there were now 964 season ticket holders from the Southend area; whilst the minutes of 18 June 1914 record that there were 1,011 season ticket holders from the Southend area using the GER's service. At the same meeting the General Manager, Henry Worth Thornton, said that from the 1 June one of the early morning trains from London to Shenfield had been accelerated and extended to Southend to afford better facilities for newspaper and market traffic and he was arranging for several additional trains to and from Southend on Sundays during the summer with a view to further increasing the excursion traffic to Southend by the GER route.

Not all of the proposed alterations to the services initially lived up to their expectations. Those on the Southminster line initially did not meet their running costs and according to the minutes of the Traffic Committee in February 1912 had made a light loss. However by June 1914 this loss had been reversed.

The effect of the new railways on the population of the area is interesting.

**D56 No** 1790 approaching Southend in 1911. (*Ken Nunn*)

**T26 No** 1256 approaching Shenfield in 1913. (*Ken Nunn*)

| Year | Billericay | Wickford | Rayleigh | Hockley | Rochford | Woodham Ferrers | Burnham-on-Crouch | Southminster | Cold Norton |
|------|-----------|----------|----------|---------|----------|----------------|-------------------|--------------|-------------|
| 1881 | 1,418 | 491 | 1,326 | 605 | 1,665 | 673 | 2,180 | 1,311 | 185 |
| 1891 | 1,394 | 501 | 1,301 | 666 | 1,612 | 769 | 2,360 | 1,303 | 183 |
| 1901 | 1,319 | 638 | 1,773 | 902 | 1,826 | 877 | 2,918 | 1,430 | 173 |
| 1911 | 1,526 | 1,028 | 2,401 | 932 | 1,821 | 894 | 3,190 | 1,567 | 233 |

Looking at the figures, it can be seen that the arrival of the railway did not necessarily have an immediate effect in halting a decline in population. Billericay was a very good example of this. On the other hand, in the long term it did have an effect on halting the decline. As to what effect it had on local industry is another matter. One has to remember, though, that the railways arrived at the time of the great agricultural depression and undoubtedly did create new work.

From 17 to 19 August of 1911 there was a national railway strike. Neither the GER or the LTSR were greatly affected by the strike according to the *Southend Standard*. Only ten per cent of the GER's staff belonged to a union. One young man at Southend GER who was inclined to make a stand was dissuaded from doing so by others. The *Essex Chronicle* told a slightly different story. According to it, large numbers of drivers and firemen at the Stratford locomotive sheds in east London came out on strike on 18 August which caused considerable disruption to the GER's suburban service. According to the GER, the Stratford district of the Company was where most of the men who belonged to a trade union worked. Main line trains in which were included Southend as well as the Southminster and Maldon services were hardly affected.

In the early part of 1912 there was a national coal strike. Fortunately the GER had laid up a large stock of coal before the strike and was able to operate a normal service throughout the strike unlike other railways. According to *Railway and Travel Monthly* for April 1912, the LTSR maintained a full service for the first week of the strike but was then forced to curtail its service. According to the *Essex Chronicle* it made considerable alterations to its services.

In August 1912, the LTSR was taken over by the Midland Railway. The GER was aware that the MR wanted to take over the LTSR. News of the proposed takeover had appeared in both the national and the local press as early as the beginning of February 1911. The GER would have liked to have taken over the LTSR but hadn't got enough money to do so.

In the MR's Act of acquisition of the LTSR, it was required to electrify the direct line via Upminster from London to Southend and Shoeburyness. The electrification was dependent on the quadrupling of the section of line from Stepney to Bromley-by-Bow and the rebuilding of Fenchurch Street station. The GER agreed to allow the electrification of the line into Fenchurch Street. According to Peter Kay in volume 3 of his history of the LTSR, the suggestion was given to terminating trains using the Tilbury loop at Barking to keep Fenchurch Street clear for Southend via Upminster trains.

The GER's immediate reaction to the Midland take over was to ban a new class of 4-6-4 tank engines being built for the LTSR, from running over the London and Blackwall Railway (LBR) into Fenchurch Street station, as they were too heavy for the viaduct. This was regarded as an act of spite. According to the late Kenneth Leech, who was the last surviving former employee of the LTSR and the apprentice of their designer, Robert Harben Whitelegg, Whitelegg had been assured by the GER that there would be no problems. As the original design of the 4-6-4Ts was lighter than the locomotives as built, this is open to question. In February 1913, the GER served a notice on the MR prohibiting not only the 4-6-4Ts from running over the LBR but also two classes of 4-4-2Ts – the rebuilt 37 and the 79 class locomotives for which permission had not been sought. As the MR was not likely to stop using the two classes of 4-4-2T without a fight and brazened it out, they were allowed to continue to run over the LBR. The result was a draw. Kenneth Leech was of the opinion that possibly the GER would allow a small company, such as the LTSR, something it would not allow a large one, such as the MR.

It is interesting to speculate what would have happened had the LTSR not been taken over by the MR. By 1912, not only were 4-4-0 locomotives of the two Claud Hamilton classes running to Southend, but also the new 1500 class 4-6-0s. The use of large express locomotives on what was a very short run could be deemed to be wasteful. The London, Brighton and South Coast Railway used tank locomotives of the 4-4-2 wheel arrangement on the London to Brighton service and Brighton was fifty miles from London as opposed to just over forty-one for Southend from Liverpool Street. It is known that a design for a 4-6-2 tank locomotive was prepared by the GER. This would probably have been developed had the LTSR remained independent. Such a locomotive was obviously intended for the Southend run as no other destination warranted the use of a large tank locomotive.

How the GER would have competed with electric trains between London and Southend over the former LTSR line is something which is open to speculation. One cannot imagine the GER electrifying to Southend. The limits of its own proposals for electrification according to company minutes (of admittedly 1922) were Broxbourne, Ongar and Gidea Park.

In 1913, the GER toyed with the idea of introducing a push and pull service on the Southend line. In addition to serving the existing stations, halts were to be opened at Mountnessing, Ramsden Bellhouse, Down Hall between Rayleigh and Hockley and Hawkwell. The trains would have connected with the through trains to and from London at Shenfield. In April some trials were conducted with a small tank engine of class Y65 and a pair of coaches. Unfortunately the idea was abandoned. The trials were reported in the local newspapers and according to the memories of a resident of Ramsden Bellhouse, the prospect of a passenger station there influenced their parents' decision to move there. This suggests that other people moved there and possibly some of the other places for the same reason. By August 1914, the fastest trains to and from Southend did the journey in fifty-eight minutes.

On 4 August 1914 war was declared between Britain and Germany. The railways immediately came under the control of the government through the Railway Executive Committee. This was a committee of the general managers of the nine leading British railway companies, nominally presided over by the President of the Board of Trade, but its working president was elected from amongst its own members and was known as the

Acting Chairman. At first the war didn't have too much impact on the New Essex Lines. Troops arrived in the area, which bought in some extra traffic, and some of the male season ticket holders joined the forces. On 5 October of that year, the GER chose to unveil its radical timetable alterations. On the Southend line, the services were increased to thirty-five trains in each direction on weekdays, ten in each direction on the Southminster branch and five in each direction on the Maldon branch. On Sundays, the service was ten trains in each direction on the Southend line and three trains in each direction on the Southminster branch. The *Essex Chronicle* of 2 October reported that the 'entire timetable has been re-modelled, but the accomodation will be much better than before' and that three systems had been devised, 'slow', 'fast' and 'express' to allow for connected working which would be of the uttermost convenience to passengers.

It is not certain what troop trains and other military-related trains worked over the lines. Ken Nunn took a photograph in February 1915 of a Mountnessing to West Hampstead troop special, which indicates that Mountnessing Siding on at least one occasion was used for the entrainment of troops.

Plans were drawn up for the evacuation of civilians in the event of a German landing in Britain. From documents of the period I have seen, the evacuation of civilians was to be undertaken by road and not by rail. The railways would have been kept for the exclusive use of the military including the movement of troops. Railway locomotives were not left in the coastal area overnight but were shedded inland to prevent the enemy making use of the railway. The war also put an end to the MR's proposal to electrify the LTS's direct line to Southend.

On 1 January 1915, there was a collision at Ilford, in which unfortunately ten people lost their lives. Whilst the line was being cleared and repaired, all trains to and from London were diverted via Leyton, Woodford and the eastern curve off Chigwell Loop to Seven Kings on the main line. Prior to the extension of the London Underground Central Line after the Second World War over the Loughton, Epping and Chigwell lines and the building of the tunnel under Eastern Avenue, trains over the Chigwell Loop from London either joined or left the Loop via the western curve at Ilford.

One way that the war affected the area served by the New Essex Lines was air raids. On 19 January 1915, the first raids took place over Britain, when two airships, or Zeppelins, raided Great

Yarmouth killing two people and injuring sixteen. The first air raid against London took place on 31 May 1915, killing seven and injuring thirty-five. Southend was bombed in March and April 1915, fortunately without causing any deaths. A subsequent raid on Southend on 10 May 1915 caused the death of a woman. On 16 April 1915, in the early hours of the morning, Maldon was bombed. The only casualties were a young girl who received a minor injury and a speckled hen that was killed outright. A number of buildings were damaged including a workshop and shed in Spital Road which were completely destroyed and others including Maldon West station received superficial damage from shrapnel.

There were counter measures against the air raids. Blackout was instituted, anti-aircraft guns and searchlights were put in place and home defence airfields were built for use by fighter aeroplanes. On the New Essex Lines, airfields were established at Rochford (autumn 1915) on the Southend line and at Stow Maries near Cold Norton (August 1916) on the Maldon line. During its life as an operational airfield, RFC Stow Maries received its material via Maldon West goods yard and not Cold Norton. Both of these airfields were operational until 1919 after the end of the war. Emergency landing grounds were established for the fighter aeroplanes at Shenfield, Burnham, Mountnessing and Runwell near Wickford. Their period of operation varied. Burnham was operational from 1914, before the start of the air raids, to 1919, Mountnessing was only operational in 1916 and was replaced that year by Shenfield which lasted until 1919, whilst Runwell was operational from 1917 to 1918. There was a naval base at Osea Island near Maldon.

Probably the most spectacular impact (with regards to traffic) that the war had on the Southend line occurred in late September 1916, when in the early hours of the morning of 24 September, the Zeppelin L32 was shot down at Snail's Farm, Great Burstead, near Billericay by Second Lieutenant Frederick Sowrey of the Royal Flying Corps flying a BE2c aircraft on patrol from Suttons Farm, Hornchurch. It was said that when L32 was burning, a newspaper could be read from the glow within a distance of twenty miles and that the sky was lit up for sixty miles. News of the airship's crash had spread by various means –word of mouth and telegraph. By 4am, some hours before daylight, a large crowd had gathered from all around, especially from London. Six special trains were put on and the station staff at Billericay were kept exceedingly busy. In booking the large number of sightseers back home, the station ran out of tickets and the staff were obliged to issue substitutes. The idea of putting on special trains for such a thing cannot be imagined now. Indeed it would not have happened later in the war when things were tightened up rather more.

On 7 March 1918, two aeroplanes were returning from attacking one of the last air raids over London when they collided near the railway line, halfway between Rochford and Rayleigh. The two pilots were killed. Captain H.C. Stroud from 61 Squadron at Rochford dying that day and Captain A.B. Kynoch from 37 Squadron at Goldhanger, just north-east of Maldon, the next day.

On at least one occasion, Southend station suffered casualties during an air raid. The Rev Andrew Clark, the Rector of Great Leighs near Chelmsford, records in his diary of 16 August 1917 that one of his women parishioners had gone to Southend with a friend on 12 August and were sitting in a train at the station in the evening, waiting to return home when the raid began. According to the diary, at least two people died in the station during the raid. A sad thing about the raid, apart from the deaths, was that when the raid started the two women had run to shelter leaving their belongings in the compartment that they were sitting in. When they returned after the raid, their luggage was still there, but their handbags had been opened and all their money taken out of their purses. Both the casualties and the thieving were sad. Obviously the air raid had been an advantage to some unscrupulous person. *The Times* reports of 13 August 1917 of the bombing stated that the bombing raid was carried out by about a dozen aircraft. However, one of the reports stated that one bomb fell in Victoria Avenue killing seven people, five of whom were holidaymakers going back to the railway station. The other two were in a restaurant. The *Southend Standard*, reporting the incident, said that of those killed, fifteen were killed in the vicinity of the GER station. There was a bit of a stink in Southend about the raid as it was felt that no warning of it had been given to the public. The *Manchester Guardian* of 13 August 1917 said that a number of people making for the railway station and that some people at the station had been killed by the bomb that fell there. One of the dead was guard Charles Humphries, who was the oldest guard in the employ of the GER, and had been on his way to take charge of his train. He was the head passenger guard at Southend and had worked on the first passenger train to leave Southend on 1 October 1889. According to the *Daily Telegraph* of 14 August 1917, his body was mutilated beyond recognition and it was only by his uniform that he was identified. The *Manchester Guardian* of 13 August 1917 also reported that no warning had been given of the raid. What is equally horrible, is that quite a few of the casualties had gone to Southend for a day out. They clearly didn't expect to be slaughtered in the same manner as men were being killed on the Western Front in France and Belgium. According to Edwin A. Pratt's *British Railways and the Great War*, one bomb fell in the goods yard and the only material damage done at the station consisted mainly of broken windows.

At Rayleigh on 29 October 1917 bombs dropped in the roadway, smashed the water main and windows in the station buildings, and tiles on the stationmaster's house. The war had other impacts on the New Essex Lines. Visually, the Royal Blue livery of the passenger locomotives was replaced by a grey livery.

With staff either voluntarily joining the forces or being conscripted, the GER had to make economies. Several stations were closed, amongst them Maldon West which was closed to passenger traffic on 22 May 1916 and did not reopen until 1 August 1919. Train services were reduced. The restaurant cars on the Southend trains were withdrawn in January 1917. Women took the place of men in some jobs such as porters, engine cleaners and guards, but not shunters or footplate crew.

In 1917, the New Essex Lines caused the siting of a cathedral, when the Bishop elect of the proposed Roman Catholic diocese for Essex, Bernard Wall (who was a railway enthusiast), having rejected Chelmsford as the proposed cathedral site (as he preferred Ilford, which was then the south-western junction for the Chigwell loop), reached a compromise and settled on Brentwood.

From 20-27 September 1918, there had been a partial but unofficial railway strike. On the GER, only a few men came out but those who did caused a fair amount of disruption. The *Essex Chronicle* of 27 September reported that at Southend GER the NUR men turned up for work but there was only one man to drive and stoke the engines and that trains arrived from London and returned there. At Maldon, none of the footplatemen went on strike. The striking GER men went back to work on the 26th.

Following the armistice on 11 November 1918 and the signing of the peace treaty on 28 June 1919, things started to get back to normal. Maldon West station reopened to passengers on 1 August 1919. Sadly, the GER did not start repainting its engines Royal Blue, though it did repaint its carriages from varnished teak to maroon.

However it was not a time of peace. From 27 September to 5 October 1919, there was a general railway strike. According to the *Essex Chronicle* of 3 October the preceding Saturday, which was 27 September, visitors to Southend found initially that there were no trains running from the town. The GER station having been closed, but however at 8.45pm a train left the MR station calling at all stations to Plaistow, from where travellers would have had to make their way to their destination by bus or tram. Plaistow was where the former LTSR had its London area locomotive sheds. On the following Monday, the GER ran two trains from Southend to London and the following day the service was increased to three up and two down plus one to Shenfield. Also on 29 September, a collection was made amongst the passengers of a train that ran from Southend to London and nearly £100 was handed to the driver and fireman when the train reached the destination. The *Chronicle* also reported that Southend travellers used camp stools whilst waiting for their trains. During the strike, although a limited service of trains ran on both the Southend and Southminster lines, according to the *Chronicle* there were no trains on either of the lines running to Maldon. As well as giving information of the trains running during the strike, *The Times* reported that many businessmen cycled from Southend to London.

Between 31 March and 28 June 1921 there was a national coal strike which resulted in reductions in train services. Unfortunately, there are few exact details. From the information that is available from *The Times*, it is known that the entire GER Sunday suburban service and almost all of the Sunday main line services were suspended with effect from Sunday 24 April to minimise the withdrawal of business trains on weekdays. *The Times* of 28 May reported that fifty GER locomotives had been adapted to run on oil fuel and from Monday 30 May additional trains would be provided on main lines, branch line and suburban line services. From this one can deduce that there were considerable reductions in the services. However, even before the end of the strike, services were improving, but were not fully resumed until the strike was over.

Also, motorbuses were starting to become more competitive. According to contemporary newspaper reports, the National Steam Car Company started operating services from Chelmsford on 21 July 1913 when it took over the existing GER's bus services operated from there since 1905. There were three routes going to Writtle, Great Waltham and Danbury.

The National Steam Car Company used oil fired steam buses which in appearance did not look different from petrol buses. The National in 1917 had services which could loosely be held to be in competition with the GER's New Essex Lines. It ran from Chelmsford to Billericay, albeit on Tuesdays and Fridays only. This was a new route which had started to Galleywood in January 1914 and had been extended to Stock at some date between April 1914 and the beginning of July 1914. Later that year it extended to Billericay. There was also a direct service from Chelmsford to Maldon on Fridays which was an extension of the former GER route to Danbury. This service had also been started in 1914. After the end of the war, the National converted from steam buses to petrol buses. It expanded its services. The services from Chelmsford to Maldon and Chelmsford to Billericay became daily from 15 May 1920. Even so the services initially consisted of a couple of buses a day. In 1920 the National and the Westcliff-on-Sea Motor Charabanc Company Ltd applied to the Southend Light Railways Committee of Southend County Borough Council for licences to run buses from Chelmsford via Billericay, Wickford and Rayleigh to Southend. The Light Railways Committee gave its verdict in favour of the National. The start date of the service according to a contemporary newspaper report was 14 August 1920. As to whether it ran during the following winter is not known. However, there was a daily service in the summer of 1921, and on Mondays, Wednesdays, Fridays and Saturdays the rest of that year and early 1922. From the summer of 1922, the service returned to running daily and continued so through the winter of 1922-23. However, from the end of the summer of 1923, the service only ran in the summer and did not run throughout the year until 1928. The timetable of the National Omnibus Company dated 10 October 1921, besides showing the Maldon, Billericay and Southend services, also shows a Fridays only service from Chelmsford to Southminster and Burnham-on-Crouch and a Tuesdays, Fridays and Saturdays service from Chelmsford to Woodham Ferrers. In 1921, the National started another service from Chelmsford to Southend via Rettendon. Until 1928, this was summer only. The Westcliff Company whilst not getting approval for the route to Chelmsford was able in 1921 to start routes to Rayleigh via Hadleigh and via Eastwood and to Rochford. In January 1922 the company renamed itself Westcliff-on-Sea Motor Services Ltd.

However, all was not doom and gloom. The number of trains running over the lines had increased. Bradshaw for January 1921 shows thirty-one passenger trains over the section of line from Shenfield to Southend on Mondays to Fridays and thirty in the reverse direction. On Saturdays, there were twenty-eight down and twenty-nine up trains. On Sundays it was ten in both directions. On the Southminster line there were ten passenger trains to and nine passenger trains from Southminster on Mondays to Saturdays. On Sundays, there were three trains a day in each direction. On the Maldon line it was five trains a day in each direction on Mondays to Saturdays. On 11 November 1920, the GER introduced Pullman cars on some of its services. The *Great Eastern Railway Magazine* of December 1920 had an article about them. Southend was one of the lines on which they were used. According to *The Times* of 12 November 1920, the GER was running Pullman cars in a number of trains to Cambridge, Southend and Clacton. Bradshaw's Railway Guide for January 1921 shows 1st class Pullman cars in two trains in each direction between London and Southend on Mondays to Fridays and one train in each direction on Saturdays. These were the 4.48pm Liverpool Street to Southend (Saturdays excepted), 8.02pm, Liverpool Street to Southend (Saturdays only), 9.45pm Liverpool Street to Southend (Saturdays excepted), 8.44am Southend to Liverpool Street and 7.20 pm Southend to Liverpool Street (Saturdays excepted). The supplementary charge for using a Pullman between Liverpool Street and Southend and vice versa was 2 shillings. The supplementary tickets could be obtained from the ticket offices at Liverpool Street and Southend and from the attendants in the Pullman cars. By the end of 1921, the trains were only carrying 3rd class Pullmans. Bradshaw's Railway Guide for July 1922 and the GER's passenger timetable for the same month show that 3rd class Pullman cars were running in one train in each direction on Mondays to Saturdays.

On 10 July of 1922 a platform for passengers was opened at Barons Lane Siding on the Maldon branch. The GER's timetable calls it Barons Lane Halt. Barons Lane was about half a mile from Purleigh by a footpath. Trains called on request to pick up or set down passengers. According to the *Great Eastern Railway Magazine* for January 1923, the Halt consisted of a sixty foot platform and a waiting room. From the evidence available it would appear that part of the goods office was converted to provide passenger waiting accommodation. According to Peter Paye in *Branch Lines to Maldon* (Lightmoor 2016) this was only in inclement weather. Whilst the public timetable commencing 10 July 1922 states that tickets from Cold Norton, Barons Lane and Maldon West on the Woodham Ferrers line were issued on the train by conductor guards, the working timetable does not indicate that they were. The working timetable that commences in October 1922 indicates that conductor guard working was in operation. However, according to the minutes of the Traffic Committee of the GER dated 20 April 1922, conductor guard working on the line was already in operation. When conductor guards were introduced is not mentioned. The meeting had before it, a report from the General Manager of the Railway dated 29 March about a request from Purleigh Parish Council for a Halt at Barons Lane. Unfortunately, as the minutes of Purleigh Parish Council for 1922 are believed to have been destroyed along with the minutes for preceding and succeeding years prior to 1962, no record of the Council's discussions, etc about the Halt are known to have survived. The cost of building the Halt according to a minute of the GER Board of 17 March 1922 was £121. According to the *Great Eastern Railway Magazine* for January 1923, between 10 July and the end of December, about 3,300 passengers had used the Halt, which had therefore justified its existence. The earliest press account that I have found of the Halt is in the *Essex Chronicle* of 29 September 1922, which stated that on and after 2 October, parcels, milk, and fruit traffic, etc, also luggage in advance for dispatch from or consigned to Barons Lane Halt by passenger train would be dealt with at the Halt on weekdays between the hours of 9am and 5pm. The service of collection or delivery would not be undertaken at the Halt. Season tickets could also be obtained from Barons Lane Halt. Applications could be made to the Foreman at the Halt, to the Stationmaster at Maldon, or the Commercial Superintendent at Liverpool Street Station. It is difficult to draw too many conclusions from it other than that none of the services mentioned were available when the halt first opened.

Following the First World War, there were calls for the nationalisation of the railways. Railways had already been nationalised as in a number of countries before the war, such as Italy and Switzerland. What happened was a British compromise. The railways, with the exception of the Underground railways of London, were grouped into four large companies – the London, Midland and Scottish, the London and North Eastern, the Great Western and the Southern. The GER became part of the London and North Eastern and the LTS lines became part of the London,

**Barons Lane** Halt and Sidings about 1930. (*Stephen Potter collection*)

Midland and Scottish, thus ensuring competition on the Southend lines. The act authorising the Big Four as they came to be known was passed on 19 August 1921 – four days after the government relinquished control of them.

According to Peter Paye, just prior to the Grouping, the working of the Witham to Maldon and Woodham Ferrers to Maldon lines by push-pull trains was under consideration. Since this did not happen it is clear that the Grouping put an end to the proposal. On 1 May 1922, a halt was opened at Bridge 774 between Wickford and Rayleigh for workmen of Messrs Muirhead, Macdonald, Wilson and Company, builders of the Southend Arterial Road. The amendments to the working timetable show that an additional train was put on in each direction on Mondays to Saturdays. However the working timetable amendment for May does not show the halt but says that the trains were put on to convey Messrs Muirhead, Macdonald, Wilson and Company's workmen. The Halt appears as a note in the July 1922 working timetable. The Halt was provided at the request of the builders of the road, who had been asked by the Ministry of Transport to take on more men to build the road and the Halt would enable the men to get more easily to work.

There were even proposals for new railways. One idea that went back to 1911 was for a Deep Water Port on Canvey Island. Most of the proposals for railway connections merely involved the LTSR and later the MR. That for 1911, was for a line from Benfleet and that for 1917, was a line from Pitsea. The 1919 proposal put forward a line run from the site of Fanton Junction to join the MR at a point near Rookery Farm on Bowers Marsh, which would have then have proceeded to the proposed port which was near Deaman's Point on the south side of Canvey Island. The GER opposed the scheme because it preferred to build a flyover at Fanton Junction rather than a flat junction. The scheme was also opposed by the MR who did not want their line crossed on the flat and the Port of London Authority because it had invested £6,290,000 in the London Docks. Nothing came of the proposed port. Similar schemes in 1921 and 1922 were thwarted by the Port of London Authority and in 1924 by the Ministry of Transport.

In 1919 two proposals were deposited with the Clerk of the Peace for Essex. One was for an Ongar and Shenfield Light Railway to run from Ongar on the GER to Shenfield. At Ongar the railway would have commenced in the station yard alongside the existing line. One assumes that there would have been a trailing connection from the Ongar line to the light railway. The light railway would have run north of Chipping Ongar, west of Blackmore, east of Doddinghurst and west of Mountnessing. At Shenfield, there would have been a spur running alongside the main line without affecting the junction but there would have been a spur to the Southend line to the east of the station. The spur would have faced west rather than east so that it would not have been possible for there to be through running from the light railway to the Southend line. Nothing came of this. Equally unsuccessful was a Bradwell- on-Sea Light Railway to run from Southminster station to Bradwell-on-Sea. The railway would have run across fields via Asheldham, Dengie and Tillingham and would have cost an estimated £60,679. In the same year of 1919 the Special Committee of Essex County Council reported on schemes to be submitted to the Ministry of Reconstruction to facilitate rural development after the war. No fewer than nine schemes were put forward. Of these, two were connected with the New Essex Lines. There were proposals for lines from Southminster to Bradwell-on-Sea and Rochford to Paglesham. Nothing came of these proposals for railway connections.

# CHAPTER FOUR

# London and North Eastern Years

The Grouping of the railways took place between 1 January 1922 and 1 July 1924. Most of the railways in the Great Western group were absorbed by the Great Western Railway on 1 January 1922. The amalgamation of most of the railways in the London, Midland and Scottish (LMS), London and North Eastern (LNER) and Southern groups took place on 1 January 1923. None of the underground railways of London were absorbed into any of the groups.

Initially, not a great deal happened on the GER. The drab wartime grey livery which had survived beyond the war, was replaced by an apple green livery. After the winter 1923-24 timetable Pullman cars were withdrawn from most of the former GER's services, including the Southend line. Locomotives and rolling stock from some of the other constituents of the LNER started to make an appearance on the former GER lines. In the summer of 1923 the section of line from Maldon West to Maldon East was singled.

In January 1924 there was a strike by the footplatemen's union ASLEF which lasted from Monday 21 to Tuesday 29 January. The former GER line into Southend was very badly affected. There were no trains at all on the New Essex lines during the strike whereas on the former LTSR line according to reports in *The Times* quite a frequent service was maintained.

The 28 January edition of the paper, when mentioning the service provided to Southend by the former LTSR line, said that the town was cut off from London on the former GER line, whilst the edition of 30 January said that those who lived in Southend had been deprived for a week of any trains via the former GER line.

At the Cold Norton Parish Council meeting of 15 April 1924, it was proposed that the Clerk of the Council write to the LNER asking for the provision of a Sunday service on the line from Woodham Ferrers to Maldon. An early train from Maldon to connect with the 7.30am train from Woodham Ferrers, which the Council considered would be of benefit to the inhabitants of Cold Norton and the surrounding area, was also proposed. Whilst no record of the LNER's reply remains, and nothing has been found in the minutes of the company, it would seem that at least in the case of a Sunday train service, the views of the Parish Council were accepted, as from July 1924, a Sunday service was indeed provided on the line from Woodham Ferrers to Maldon. Stow Maries Parish Council had expressed similar concerns at its meeting of 3 April 1924. Again, no record of the LNER's response is recorded in the Council minutes. With effect from 1 May 1925 the Halt at Bridge 774 between Wickford and Rayleigh closed.

From 3 to 13 May 1926 there was a general strike of workers including railwaymen in Britain. The General Strike was called by the Trades Union Congress in an attempt to force the government to act to prevent wage reductions and worsening conditions in the coal mining industry. During the strike, some trains were run on both the former GER and LTSR lines into and out of Southend. All the trains were driven by amateurs, whose experience of driving a steam locomotive varied. Not everyone employed by the railway went on strike. Those in the ranks of management such as foremen and stationmasters tended not to strike. At Southend former GER station, the locomotive foreman and his assistant kept three or four engines warm. Only one platform was available for trains as the others were used for storing carriages during the strike. The first train to have run on the New Essex Lines was on 5 May. The situation was somewhat farcical. According to a report in the *Southend Standard* that week, a telegram arrived at Southend station to say that a train had left Liverpool Street at 10.45am. It was not known what time it would arrive. The stationmaster and other officials at Southend at intervals made attempts by telephone to find out where it was. Late in the afternoon it was announced that it had passed Romford at 4.30pm. Eventually a message was received that the train had no hope of reaching Southend and it was believed that it had been abandoned at Wickford. According to the following week's *Southend Standard*, forty-five minutes after arriving at Wickford the engine was reversed and returned to London. As the strike progressed, a service of sorts was introduced on both the Southend and Southminster lines. On the only Sunday during the strike (9 May) the LNER, unlike the other three main line companies, did not run any passenger trains, only goods, fish and milk trains. According to *The Times* of Saturday 8 May, from that day onwards until further notice there would be trains from Liverpool Street to Southend at 11am, 1pm, 4.15pm and 5.15pm and from Southend to Liverpool Street at 8.10am, 9.10am and 2.30pm. The trains would call at Stratford, Ilford, Harold Wood and all stations beyond. *The Times* of Tuesday 11 May reported that trains ran from Liverpool Street to Southend at 11am, 3.35pm, 4.45pm and 5.45pm calling at Stratford and Ilford to pick up and then all stations to Southend. From Southend there were trains to Liverpool Street at 8.10am, 9.10am, 10.10am and 2.30pm calling at all stations to Harold Wood and Ilford. From Liverpool Street to Southminster there was a train at 4.45pm and from Southminster to Liverpool Street via Wickford there were departures at 7.50am and 9.50am. As far as can be ascertained from contemporary newspapers, there were no services on the Maldon line.

During the strike, the National Omnibus Company's workers continued to work and whilst the service may not have been frequent, they were at least operating to a known timetable. The Westcliff-on-Sea Motor Services operated a reduced service during the strike, as some of the men withdrew their labour. Of all the services operated by volunteers during the General Strike, the railways came off worse as to operate them efficiently they needed skilled people. The skilled people tended to be on strike, as evidenced by the first attempt to run a train from Liverpool Street to Southend.

After the strike, the coal miners did not go back to work for some months. As a result there was a reduction in train services. The shortage of coal led to appalling engine performances and the virtual failure of stopping services on the Southend line.

In 1927, Nigel Gresley, the Chief Mechanical Engineer of the LNER, prepared a design for a 2-6-4 two cylinder tank locomotive specifically for the Liverpool Street to Southend service. Such a class of locomotive would have eliminated, or at least reduced, the use of the Claud Hamilton and 1500 classes of tender locomotives on the service. Unfortunately circumstances conspired against the proposed locomotive. That year there was a derailment at Sevenoaks on the Southern Railway (SR) of a River class 2-6-4 tank locomotive. This gave rise to grave doubts, which were later dispelled, of the wisdom of using large tank locomotives on fast passenger trains. Although press criticism after the accident was not justified, no-one on the LNER was prepared to risk public alarm by introducing the proposed tank locomotives whilst the accident was still fresh in the minds of the public. Instead, Gresley opted to build some more 1500s. Had the class been built, there is no reason to assume that it would not have been a success. The cause of the

Sevenoaks accident could be laid at the bad ballasting of the South Eastern section of the SR. On the former London, Brighton and South Coast section large tank locomotives had, and would, operate successfully for some years.

On the Maldon line on 3 September 1928, a Halt was opened at Stow Maries between Woodham Ferrers and Cold Norton. This halt however, was not called 'Stow Maries' but instead was named 'Stow St Mary'. This was apparently at the request of the incumbent of the Church of St Mary and St Margaret, the Rev Gordon F. Smythe, who had been instrumental in getting the Halt built. The minutes of Stow Maries Parish Council for 8 October 1928 record that 'Proposed by Mr F.H. Calderbank (the Chairman of the Parish Council) and seconded by Mr W.E. Crump that a letter be sent to the Rev Gordon F. Smythe thanking him for all he had done in connection with obtaining a railway station at Stow St Mary'. The Rev Smythe was the Rector of Stow Maries from 1918 to 1932 and was responsible for obtaining a number of things for the village besides the Halt. At the meeting of the Parish Council on 24 November 1932 following his death, the Council paid a tribute to him. The Halt does not appear in the minutes of the LNER. The *Railway Gazette* of 7 September 1928 stated that the station was now open. In other publications, a date of 24 September has been given as the date of opening. The reason for this discrepancy was the commencement date of the public timetable in which the Halt first appeared. A poster for the opening of the Halt survives. A wooden hut was provided there as passenger waiting accommodation. The evidence for this is confirmed from the minutes of Stow Maries Parish Council for 10 April 1934 when 'The Clerk was instructed to write to the London and North Eastern Railway drawing their attention to the disgraceful state of the waiting room at Stow St Mary Halt'. The Parish Council minutes do not record the LNER's reply. Because the platform at the Halt was a short one of just over 30 feet in length passengers joining or alighting at it had to travel in the rear carriage of the train.

The area served by the Maldon line became an important centre of green pea growing. The summer 1938 working timetable shows a Wednesday only return passenger working commencing on 1 June which, during the green pea season, ran from Maldon to Woodham Ferrers as a mixed train and arrived at the latter station four minutes later than when running as a passenger train. Dairy farming was also important in the area served by the line and this is reflected, not only in a photograph (not reproduced here) of Barons Lane Halt showing milk churns, but also in the poster for the opening of Stow St Mary's Halt which

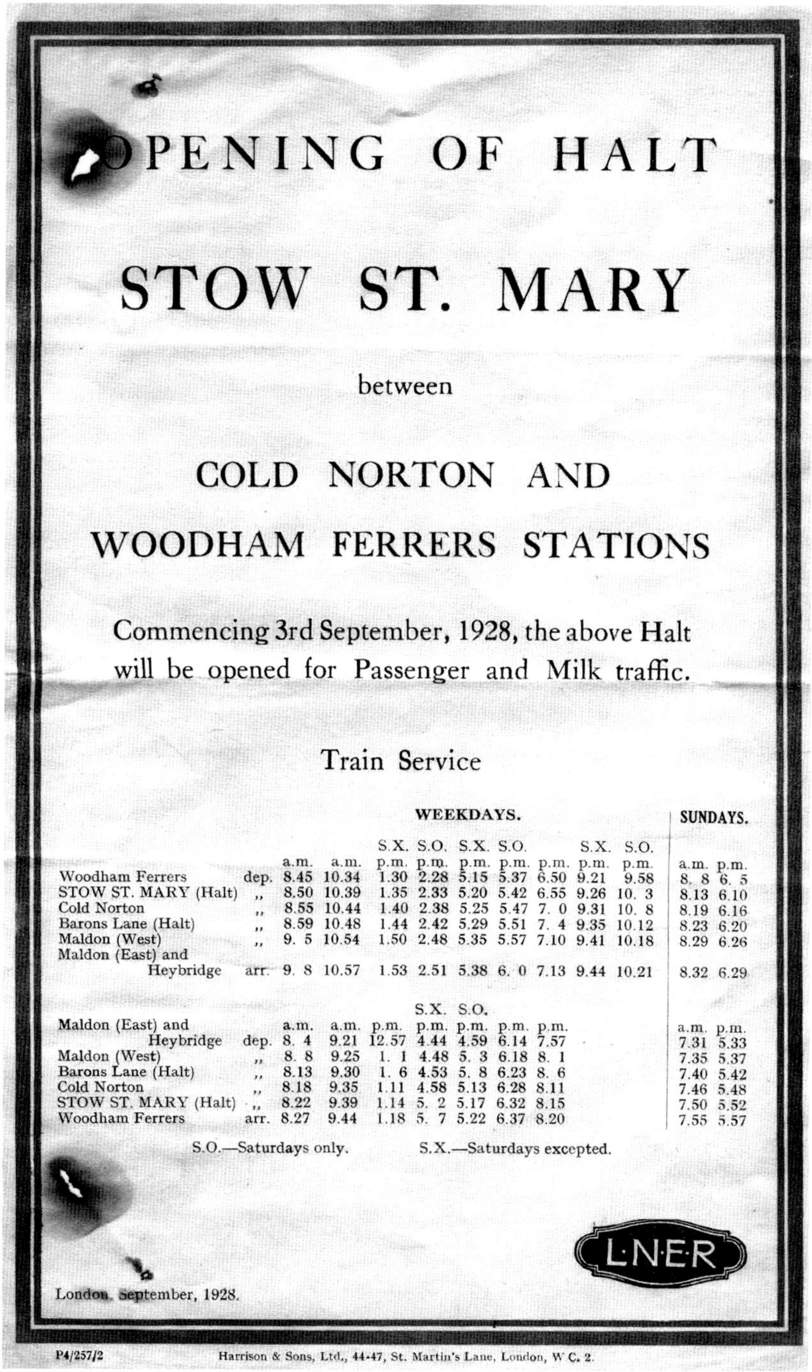

OPENING OF HALT

STOW ST. MARY

between

COLD NORTON AND

WOODHAM FERRERS STATIONS

Commencing 3rd September, 1928, the above Halt will be opened for Passenger and Milk traffic.

Train Service

| | | WEEKDAYS. | | | | | | | | | SUNDAYS. | |
|---|---|---|---|---|---|---|---|---|---|---|---|---|
| | | | | S.X. | S.O. | S.X. | S.O. | | S.X. | S.O. | | |
| | | a.m. | a.m. | p.m. | p.m. | p.m. | p.m. | p.m. | p.m. | p.m. | a.m. | p.m. |
| Woodham Ferrers | dep. | 8.45 | 10.34 | 1.30 | 2.28 | 5.15 | 5.37 | 6.50 | 9.21 | 9.58 | 8. 8 | 6. 5 |
| STOW ST. MARY (Halt) | ,, | 8.50 | 10.39 | 1.35 | 2.33 | 5.20 | 5.42 | 6.55 | 9.26 | 10. 3 | 8.13 | 6.10 |
| Cold Norton | ,, | 8.55 | 10.44 | 1.40 | 2.38 | 5.25 | 5.47 | 7. 0 | 9.31 | 10. 8 | 8.19 | 6.16 |
| Barons Lane (Halt) | ,, | 8.59 | 10.48 | 1.44 | 2.42 | 5.29 | 5.51 | 7. 4 | 9.35 | 10.12 | 8.23 | 6.20 |
| Maldon (West) | ,, | 9. 5 | 10.54 | 1.50 | 2.48 | 5.35 | 5.57 | 7.10 | 9.41 | 10.18 | 8.29 | 6.26 |
| Maldon (East) and Heybridge | arr. | 9. 8 | 10.57 | 1.53 | 2.51 | 5.38 | 6. 0 | 7.13 | 9.44 | 10.21 | 8.32 | 6.29 |

| | | | | | S.X. | S.O. | | | | |
|---|---|---|---|---|---|---|---|---|---|---|
| | | a.m. | a.m. | p.m. | p.m. | p.m. | p.m. | p.m. | a.m. | p.m. |
| Maldon (East) and Heybridge | dep. | 8. 4 | 9.21 | 12.57 | 4.44 | 4.59 | 6.14 | 7.57 | 7.31 | 5.33 |
| Maldon (West) | ,, | 8. 8 | 9.25 | 1. 1 | 4.48 | 5. 3 | 6.18 | 8. 1 | 7.35 | 5.37 |
| Barons Lane (Halt) | ,, | 8.13 | 9.30 | 1. 6 | 4.53 | 5. 8 | 6.23 | 8. 6 | 7.40 | 5.42 |
| Cold Norton | ,, | 8.18 | 9.35 | 1.11 | 4.58 | 5.13 | 6.28 | 8.11 | 7.46 | 5.48 |
| STOW ST. MARY (Halt) | ,, | 8.22 | 9.39 | 1.14 | 5. 2 | 5.17 | 6.32 | 8.15 | 7.50 | 5.52 |
| Woodham Ferrers | arr. | 8.27 | 9.44 | 1.18 | 5. 7 | 5.22 | 6.37 | 8.20 | 7.55 | 5.57 |

S.O.—Saturdays only. S.X.—Saturdays excepted.

L·N·E·R

London, September, 1928.

P4/257/2 Harrison & Sons, Ltd., 44-47, St. Martin's Lane, London, W.C. 2.

**Poster for** the opening of Stow St Mary's Halt in 1928. (*David Holden Collection*)

**Stow St Mary's**
Halt about 1938.
(*Author's Collection*)

states that the Halt will be opened for passenger and milk traffic on 3 September 1928.

There was more bus competition. In 1926, the National Omnibus Company started a route from Brentwood to Billericay. In about the same year, Edwards Hall Motors company started a daily service from Southend to Wickford via Rayleigh. Whilst most ran via Leigh, some ran via Prittlewell. In 1927 Edwards Hall Motors became a subsidiary of Westcliff-on-Sea Motor Services Limited.

More serious competition emerged in 1927. On 27 May 1927, A.H. Young started a bus service running from Wood Green in North London to Southend from a base at Palmers Green. On 28 February 1928 a company known as Service Saloons Ltd was registered to compete with Mr Young's service and started running between Southend and Brentwood with occasional journeys extended to King's Cross in Central London. On 3 July 1928, New Empress Saloons was registered to take over the business of Mr Young. On 25 October 1928, the City Motor Omnibus Company, an independent bus operator in London (as opposed to the 'official' London General Omnibus Company), purchased a controlling interest in the company although it was not until 31 March 1932 that the City Company completely purchased New Empress Saloons. Under the control of the City Company, the route was first extended to Camden Town and then on 8 December 1929 to Kentish Town. Westcliff-on-Sea Motor Services Ltd decided that it would have to compete with the new coach services, as their operations threatened its route from

Southend to Wickford, which it had acquired from Edwards Hall Motors in 1927. On 18 June 1928 a new service of Royal Red Pullman Saloons started between Southend and Wood Green. Obviously, in late 1928, Westcliff-on-Sea Motor Services Ltd and New Empress Saloons must have decided that the competition between the two companies was rather wasteful, because on 1 January 1929, Westcliff-on-Sea Motor Services Ltd and New Empress Saloons started a co-ordinated service between Southend and Wood Green. In the middle of 1929, Service Saloons got into financial difficulties and their vehicles were repossessed by the finance company. Westcliff-on-Sea Motor Services Ltd stepped in and picked up their licence and extended the former Service Saloons route to Seven Kings. The occasional journeys to King's Cross were no longer operated. At the beginning of 1935 Westcliff-on-Sea Motor Services Ltd sold its share in the Southend to Wood Green route to the City Motor Omnibus Company. Following the formation of the London Passenger Transport Board in 1933 all road and railway passenger services within its area with the exception of those operated by the four main line railway companies had to be operated by the Board, which saw the end of the City Motor Omnibus Company's operations wholly within London. In 1936, the City Motor Omnibus Company was dissolved and on 16 March that year the name of the New Empress Saloons changed to the City Coach Company.

With a service between Wood Green and Southend every 15 minutes, and every other bus starting from or running to Kentish Town, plus convenient connections to the London Underground at both London termini, the City Coach Company was a very formidable competitor to the LNER's Southend service. By comparison, the best the LNER could offer between Liverpool Street and Southend was a service of one or two trains an hour. The steam trains of the LNER were quicker than the bus between London and Southend, taking about on average one and a half hours (twenty nine minutes Billericay to Southend) as compared to two and three quarter hours by bus from Kentish Town to Southend. However, with running times of two hours and twenty-five minutes from Wood Green to Southend or fifty minutes between Billericay and Southend, the buses held several advantages over the train. They were smart, they were frequent and they were modern. The brown and cream six wheeled metal-bodied saloon buses represented the bright new world after the First World War, whilst the black or

**Southend interior** circa 1930 with D15 No 8857 on a train. (*Author's collection*)

**D15 No** 8889 leaving Rochford for Southend in 1928. (*J.E. Kite*)

green steam locomotives with teak wood carriages represented the pre-war world.

There was also bus competition on other lines. In 1929, Rayleigh Motor Services started a service from Southend to Colchester via Danbury or Latchingdon and Maldon. This prompted Eastern National to make it put on a similar service. In 1931, Borough Motor Services acquired control of Rayleigh Motor Services. In 1933, Eastern National acquired Borough Motor Services. In the area between Witham and Wickford via Maldon other operators sprang up. One company which arose was Quest Motor Services. This was acquired by Eastern National in 1935. Between them, the LNE and the LMS railways owned half the share capital in Eastern National. Eastern National (ENOC) had been formed in 1929 from the fragmentation of the National Omnibus Company's operating area, into operating areas identifiable with the four main line railway companies.

One line on which the railway did not suffer any competition from road transport, was the Wickford to Southminster line. Neither ENOC nor any other bus operator chose to run a service in competition with it. Equally, whilst ENOC ran daily in competition with the railway from Woodham Ferrers to Maldon, the buses served only Stow Maries and Cold Norton. Purleigh was served by buses only on Thursdays and Sundays. These ran to and from Maldon with some starting and finishing their journeys at Purleigh and some running from and beyond Purleigh to Cold Norton.

At the end of April 1931, the Sunday service on the Woodham Ferrers to Maldon line was withdrawn presumably due to poor custom. There is nothing about it in the minutes of the LNER or the minutes that have survived of the parishes served by the line.

It wasn't that the LNER didn't want to make any improvements. Serving a lot of the industrial areas of the north, unfortunately it was hit by the depression and so didn't have the money.

During 1932, in connection with quadrupling of the main line to Shenfield, a single line connection was made off the local lines to Mountnessing siding. This was signalled for down trains only.

With the aid of a Government loan, the LNER installed colour light automatic and semi-automatic signalling between Liverpool Street and Chelmsford and Southend. On the Southend line, the new signalling was brought into operation at Southend station on 27 February 1938, between Shenfield and Billericay on 8 May, between Billericay and Wickford on 22 May and between Wickford and Southend on 26 June. Except for Wickford junction signal box, all intermediate signal boxes between Shenfield and Southend were abolished. Ground frames were provided for shunting purposes at the intermediate stations and sidings. Whilst not directly affecting the New Essex Lines under the Government's 1935 New Works Plan, the main line from Liverpool Street and Fenchurch Street to Shenfield was to be electrified at 1,500 volts direct current. The completion date was to be 1941. Local services between Liverpool Street and Shenfield and Fenchurch Street and Stratford would then be operated by multiple unit electric trains.

At Southend, improvements were made to the station from 1936 to 1938. The improvements included enlarging the circulating area. Also two new train indicators were provided, ten additional sidings were laid down and a one hundred ton mechanical coaling plant built.

In 1939, the LNER was looking at ways of making economies on a number of lines by the introduction of push-pull trains. A group of lines that was discussed by the Traffic Committee at its meeting on 29 June 1939 was Ipswich to Felixstowe, Wickford to Southminster, Parkeston Quay to Harwich and a group of lines in the Sheffield area. It was estimated that in this scheme, the introduction of push-pull trains would enable five guards and two porters to be dispensed with and effect a saving of £1,262. The cost of the scheme was £2,465 of which £630 was dedicated to the Wickford to Southminster line. The trains would consist of an engine and three carriages. However, owing to the outbreak of the Second World War in September, push-pull working was not implemented.

On 20 and 21 May 1933, the LNER held an exhibition of rolling stock at Southend. Amongst the exhibits were A1 class 4-6-2 No 4472 *Flying Scotsman,* W1 class 4-6-4 No 10000, B12/3 No 8516, D16/3 No 8900 *Claud Hamilton,* B17 No 2800 *Sandringham,* Y5 class 0-4-0ST (SaddleTank) No 7230 and a steam crane giving aerial rides in an open wagon body. The Health and Safety people of later years would have had a fit! Other attractions were pulling the signal, riding on the permanent way inspector's velocipede and rides in a Lister truck. Yet more things to give the Health and Safety people of later years severe angst! According to the *LNER Magazine* for July 1933, 21,350 visitors passed through the exhibition and £550 was raised for distribution to charities, of which £362 10s went to Southend New General Hospital, £50 to Southend Mayor's Distress Fund and £137 10s to railway charities. The *Magazine* said that the exhibition was opened on 20 May by the Mayor of Southend, Alderman R. Tweedy-Smith LLD JP.

**D16 No** 8785 on an up Southend to Liverpool Street train near Billericay in May 1936. (*H.C. Casserley*)

**B12 No** 8505 near Billericay on a down Liverpool Street to Southend train in May 1936. (*H.C. Casserley*)

The interwar period saw substantial housing development around stations on the Southend line. According to Peter Erwood writing in *Railways South East* Summer 1990 edition, one member of staff at Rayleigh took advantage of the housing boom and ran an estate agency business on the side.

On the Woodham Ferrers to Maldon line there were attempts to increase traffic by running Hunt Specials.

By the mid-1930s, it would seem that the operation of the passenger service on the Woodham Ferrers to Maldon line was becoming a liability to the LNER and the company wanted the Eastern National Omnibus Company (ENOC) to provide a bus service as a substitute. According to Peter Paye in *Branch Lines to Maldon*, the first attempt to do this was made by the LNER in 1935. In my researches I was not able to find anything in the LNER's records concerning this and the earliest mention that I found was in 1937 in the records of ENOC in the Essex Record Office. At the meeting of the Local Working Committee between the ENOC and the LNER and LMSR on 2 April 1937, the Chairman of the Committee (Mr F. Bryan – Traffic Manager of the ENOC) asked whether any progress on the matter had been made. The answer was that no progress had been made. From the papers that have survived it has been established that in 1937, ENOC wrote to the Hants and Dorset Omnibus Company (HDOC) in connection with a similar service they operated for the Southern Railway (SR). HDOC informed ENOC that it was only necessary for them to replace the SR service by two return journeys, one in the morning and one in the afternoon. The SR had agreed to pay them the difference between the costs as shown in the monthly returns and the receipts from the two journeys in question. After that the HDOC board had agreed to charge the SR only what they considered to be the actual cost of operation and reduce the sum charged to 6d per mile. From a study of the history of the SR it is clear that the line in question was that from Ringwood to Christchurch via Hurn which closed on 30 September 1935.

Rumours of the proposal to withdraw the passenger service reached the ears of Stow Maries Parish Council and other parish councils. According to the *Essex Chronicle* of 30 April 1937, at the meeting of Woodham Ferrers Parish Council on the 27th of the month, it was recorded that 'Stow Maries Parish Council wrote concerning rumours about the closing down of the railway line to Maldon to passenger traffic'. According to the report, it was stated that other councils were taking up the question and that a 'petition containing fifty-five names protested against any closing'. Woodham Ferrers Parish Council endorsed the petition and it was decided to send a protest to the LNER. The *Essex Newsman* of 1 May also carried a report about the proposal to withdraw the passenger service. According to the report, the LNER:

> 'had under contemplation for several years the closing of the line for passenger traffic, but it has been stated that the line will not be closed at any rate until next winter. It will not be closed for goods traffic.'

The *Essex Chronicle* of 21 May in its report of the Maldon Town Council meeting of 18 May included an item on the proposed closure of the line. According to the item, the Town Clerk had said that he had received a petition from 150 people of the town and the adjoining parishes who would be affected by the line's closure. Alderman Baker said that he did not think that enough people used the line. Alderman J.G. Sadd said that if the railway company improved the service, they could get more people travelling. If they put on a one carriage train operated by one man it could be run at a minimum cost. He said that he would like 'to see some economic effort made to maintain the line in the interests of tradesmen and all concerned'. The Council decided to support the petition. Clearly what Alderman Sadd had in mind was a double-ended diesel powered railbus or railcar operated by one man who was both the driver and conductor-guard. The *Chronicle* of 16 May in its report of Woodham Ferrers Parish Council's recent meeting, recorded that the LNER had written to the Council that:

> 'It will be appreciated that the retention of the present facilities must depend on the support forthcoming from the local residents and traders and perhaps you would kindly advise me whether the Council can do anything to encourage the use of the railway service.'

Maldon Town Council at its meeting of 15 June had included in its business a letter from the LNER in which the Company stated that it:

> 'had under examination the economic position of this part of their railway with a view to ascertaining whether revenue obtained there from was sufficient to justify the retention of

the existing facilities. No decision had yet been reached but the representations received would receive consideration.'

The LNER had then said the same thing to Maldon Council as it had said to Woodham Ferrers Parish Council. I can find nothing further in the local press prior to the closure of the line in September 1939.

Had the LNER withdrawn the passenger service between Woodham Ferrers and Maldon at this time, as the Company said they would, then the goods service would not have been withdrawn either. In the late 1920s and early 1930s, the company had withdrawn the passenger service on a number of lines in the Eastern Counties, including those from Bentley to Hadleigh and Mellis to Eye in Suffolk. They did not withdraw the goods service on these lines and the lines survived as goods only until their closure in the mid-1960s.

On 3 September 1939, following the invasion of Poland by Germany on 1 September, Britain and her allies declared war. On 1 September, the government took over the railways and started an evacuation of children and pregnant women from London and the large cities. National treasures were removed from art galleries and museums. Following the outbreak of the war, in order to make

**G4 No** 8105 on a train approaching Maldon West station in 1931. (*Author's Collection*)

economies, the railways closed a number of branch lines. One was the Woodham Ferrers to Maldon line, which was closed to passenger traffic from 10 September. On the Southend and Southminster lines, services were reduced and slowed down. The fastest trains in both directions between Southend and Liverpool Street took between an hour and fifteen minutes and an hour and twenty minutes according to the working timetable for May 1943. The Southminster line service on Sundays was only two trains in each direction. For some years, Bradshaw's Railway Guide showed the services on the Woodham Ferrers to Maldon line as a blank. Other forms of transport were reduced as well. For example ENOC's routes from Chelmsford to Southend via Billericay and Billericay to Brentwood were withdrawn in 1939, and later the City's route from London to Southend was divided into sections.

Initially, the goods service on the Maldon branch ran through from Maldon to Woodham Ferrers. The working timetable for October 1939 shows a train leaving Maldon East at 11.15am for Maldon West, arriving at the latter station at 11.20am. The return journey commenced at 12.15pm with arrival at Maldon East at 12.20pm. At 2.30pm, a train left Maldon East for Woodham Ferrers and called intermediately as required. Woodham Ferrers was reached at 3.05pm. The return train left Woodham Ferrers at 3.25pm and again called intermediately as required. Maldon East was reached at 4.20pm. The working timetable for January 1940 shows a train leaving Maldon East at 8.30am, calling at Maldon West, Barons Lane and Cold Norton as required and reaching Woodham Ferrers at 10.15am. The train returned from Woodham Ferrers at 10.40am calling at Cold Norton, Barons Lane and Maldon West, reaching Maldon East at 11.40am. According to Peter Paye, during the summer of 1940, the LNER decided to abandon the section of line between Woodham Ferrers and Cold Norton. He says that this officially took place in April 1941 but in practice this happened by October 1940. However, from a study of the working timetables for the line for 1940, the last day of operation between Woodham Ferrers and Cold Norton is thought to have been Saturday 26 October 1940, as the timetable commencing Monday 28 October 1940 does not show any working over this section of line. Under the new timetable, the train for Cold Norton was to be worked by the engine of the 9.32am passenger train from Witham to Maldon. The Maldon East stationmaster was to arrange the running of it. In other words, it was to run as required. Paye says that the abandoned section was then used for the storing of wagons and coaching stock and exercises by military and railway staff in the relaying of track and the re-railing of rolling stock. However, according to him, from evidence given to him by relatives of his wife who farmed adjacent to the line, trains worked between Woodham Ferrers and Cold Norton until at least the spring of 1942. Such workings would have been by special traffic notice. This would seem to be borne out by the Southminster line goods working timetable commencing Monday 28 October 1940, which has a note concerning the daily goods from Wickford to Southminster that it was 'to call at stations to detach only, except at Woodham Ferrers where Maldon traffic will be attached'. Any track that had been removed for an exercise would have been reinstated for such a working.

According to the late Dennis Swindale in his book *Branch Lines to Maldon* (East Anglian Railway Museum 1978) one of the buildings at Maldon West station was used by Marconi of Chelmsford as a warehouse. However, the book does not state whether it was the booking office or the platform buildings. If it was the latter, it would have been before the demolition of the buildings in 1954. Sadly, the Marconi Records for that period are not known to have survived. The withdrawal of the passenger service on the Maldon line gave rise to hardship and inconvenience. The minutes of the meeting of Woodham Ferrers Parish Council on 25 October 1939 record that a letter had been received from a Mr Smith regarding the withdrawal of the passenger service. It was decided by the Parish Council to forward the letter to the LNER together with a covering letter from the council giving full details of the hardships and inconvenience caused by the closure of the passenger service on the Maldon line and to ask for a modified service on the line, i.e. a reinstatement of a passenger service. There is no mention in the minutes of the Council of a reply having been received from the LNER.

Purleigh was the place worst affected by the withdrawal of the passenger train service. From six trains a day on Mondays to Saturdays plus a rather limited bus service it was now reduced to one bus a day in each direction on Mondays to Fridays routed via the village on ENOC service 62 which ran from Maldon to Bradwell plus three buses on Thursdays, two of which ran to and from Cold Norton and four buses on Saturdays, of which two ran to and from Cold Norton on service 66. The routing via Purleigh on service 62 took place earlier in 1939 before the outbreak of the war. Cold Norton and Stow Maries both had several buses daily on ENOC service 19A which ran from Southend via Woodham Ferrers, Maldon and Colchester to Clacton. The situation did not improve until 14 January 1941, when ENOC started an enhanced service on service 66 between Maldon and Cold Norton on behalf of the LNER. The timetable dated 16 January 1941 shows two buses a day on Mondays to Fridays plus an additional bus on Thursdays: all of these ran to and from Cold Norton. Under the arrangement ENOC agreed that the LNER would pay them one shilling per mile for the journeys in question less revenue earned on the journeys. Although not all the minutes of the Local Working Committee between ENOC and the LNER and the LMSR from the period of the Second World War appear to have survived, from what has, it appears that for most of the time the bus service was making a loss. Indeed, at the meeting of the Committee in February 1942, the LNER expressed concern at the continued increase in subsidy payments and suggested that they should be withdrawn. ENOC replied that if the subsidy was withdrawn they would feel bound to ask for the withdrawal of the service. After considerable discussion, it was agreed by the LNER that ENOC should participate in the loss occasioned by the operation of the bus service. It was agreed by the bus company's representative to put the matter forward to the company for consideration. ENOC's surviving records do not state the outcome. Anyway, the enhanced service continued. There was a suggestion in May 1942 of extending it to North Fambridge, but it was decided that the extension was not justified. From the beginning of August 1943, service 66 was extended to Stow Maries: the timetable dated 1 August 1943 shows the service running from Maldon to Cold Norton via Purleigh on Mondays to Saturdays with two buses running on to and from Stow Maries on Thursdays and Saturdays. The minutes of the Local Working Committee throughout this period and after the end of the war refer to the service only running as far as Cold Norton.

During the early part of the war, the Woodham Ferrers to Maldon line remained available for use as a diversionary route. In 1940 the Southern Area Civil Engineer's Department of the LNER introduced a system of route availability for locomotives. This was extended in late 1947 to the whole of the LNER. One was the lowest and nine the highest. This meant that in general a locomotive was not permitted to work over a route of a lower route availability than that which had been allocated to its class. An exception applied where a plus sign was allocated to a line's route availability which indicated that certain classes of locomotive in a higher route availability group were permitted over that route. Shenfield to Southend was seven plus, Wickford to Southminster was six plus and Woodham Ferrers to Maldon was three plus. Witham to Maldon was three because it had wooden viaducts which precluded the use of anything larger than a J15 or an E4 using that line, but as there was a war on, that would not invalidate the case for keeping the line open. Peter Paye is of the opinion that using the line for diversions was a red herring as the Route Availability was too restrictive.

At Rochford, the former First World War aerodrome, which during the inter-war period had initially been used for agriculture, but in 1935 was acquired by Southend Corporation and turned into its municipal airport, was taken over by the government. Troops were billeted in the area.

Leading up to the Second World War, surveyors from the Air Ministry inspected the former Stow Maries First World War airfield to see if it could be re-opened, but apparently because of the clay soil, it was considered unsuitable and it was decided to upgrade Rochford instead. However, no attempt was made to demolish any of the buildings or to obstruct or camouflage the former aerodrome. with the result that it still resembled an operational airfield. As a result, it received a fair number of German bombs as well as an RAF Hurricane of 242 Squadron with combat damage which made a forced landing on 7 September 1940 at the height of the Battle of Britain. In September 1942, the airfield was again surveyed as the possible location for a bomber station to serve the American VIII Bomber Command (later Eight Airforce) of the United States Army Airforce (USAAF). It was allocated USAAF Station Number 163 and would have had the name of RAF Cold Norton. The new airfield would have taken most of the existing airfield. The land was requisitioned but because of the need to finish other airfields that already being built, the project was shelved in December 1942 and the requisitioned land returned to the owners. It is not known whether the Woodham Ferrers to Maldon line would not have closed to passenger traffic if the airfield been reopened by the RAF at or just after the beginning of the Second World War. Possibly not. Nor is it known that had RAF Cold Norton been built on the site whether the passenger service might have been restarted. Because the RAF and the USAAF had their own road transport, it does not necessarily follow that this would have happened.

In Suffolk at Raydon (near Raydon Wood on the then goods only Bentley to Hadleigh branch line) and at Eye on the then goods only branch line from Mellis, the USAAF had airfields during the war. Neither of these had a passenger service restored. There were also proposals for USAAF Stations in the vicinity of Southminster and Maldon. Burnham-on-Crouch is also mentioned by one source. At Mountnessing public siding an oil fuel depot was established, to which a large amount of aviation fuel was conveyed.

Initially, the area served by the New Essex Lines was part of the evacuation zone of London. The railways were not however used for the transport of evacuees to the area from London in 1939. In the spring of 1940, with the fall of France, everything changed. Children and expectant mothers were evacuated from areas near the coast, and anyone else who had no good reason to stay there was encouraged to leave. On Sunday 2 June 1940, 9,300 children were evacuated from the town by train (both LNER and LMS) to locations in Derbyshire. Entry to an area extending a depth of twenty miles from the coast was prohibited 'for the purpose of a holiday, recreation, pleasure or as a casual wayfarer'. Whilst most people obeyed the ruling, there were some who did not and were turned back at their destination station barrier. The prohibited area was reduced in December 1940 and withdrawn completely during the winters of 1941/2 and 1942/3 and completely withdrawn north of the Thames from 1 April 1943. New powers were then announced for the imposition of 'regulated area'. Under these, any coastal area between Hull and Penzance could be prohibited to outsiders whenever the government saw fit to do so. Prior to the D Day invasion in 1944, a ban was again introduced on 1 April and remained in force until 25 August. A number of defence lines were put up round the outskirts of London. The GHQ or General Headquarters Line ran through the Southend, Southminster and Maldon West lines. Various fortifications and other anti-invasion measures were erected not only on the defence line, but also at other places. The Battle of Britain followed the fall of France. Rochford airfield, which was a satellite station of Hornchurch airfield, was used by various squadrons during the battle. In October 1940, Rochford became an RAF station in its own right and was known as RAF Southend. It remained operational until 1944 and was given back to the civilian authorities at the end of 1946. At Bradwell Bay, the pre-war grass landing ground used for the nearby air to ground firing range was developed as a fighter satellite landing ground.

At the airfield, surfaced runways and hangers were added in 1941. These were used by fighters and in an emergency, by bombers. In 1946 the airfield was closed down.

Early in the afternoon of 28 August 1940, during the Battle of Britain, Rochford airfield was heavily bombed, with buildings damaged. About thirty craters were left behind on the airfield and the railway line was blocked. The LNER terminated services on the line at Rayleigh and a replacement bus service was provided between Rayleigh and Southend until the line was repaired. During that time, passengers from Liverpool Street for Southend were told to go to Fenchurch Street to use the LMS to Southend.

The winter of 1939-40 was a severe one. The *Essex Chronicle* of 9 February reported that six foot snow drifts had developed on the Southminster line and that for the first time in the line's history a snow plough had been sent to clear the line. On the evening of the day in question, the weather had deteriorated and a train leaving Woodham Ferrers had become snow-bound a mile outside the station and the engine had its fire extinguished. In an attempt to assist the train, another engine was sent, but this also became snow-bound, blocking the line. It took over twenty-four hours to clear the line. Because it was wartime, the exact date was not mentioned.

In 1940, all locomotives were moved away at night from engine sheds near the coast including Southend and Maldon so, that in the event of the Germans landing, they could not make use of them. I don't know, but I suspect that the locomotives at Southminster may also have been moved to a different location at night. The locomotives returned to their sheds in the morning. The timetable for evacuation routes by rail from the areas covered by the New Essex Lines should the Germans have landed are not known to have survived.

There were a number of attacks on the lines by the Luftwaffe. At Southend on an unknown date, the engine shed was damaged by machine gun fire. Also unknown is the date an enemy aeroplane machined-gunned a train travelling from Shenfield to Billericay and thereafter bombed Harts Corner (Billericay) killing several people. On 26 October 1942, a high explosive bomb brought down telephone wires at Rochford. On 12 March 1943, a marauding German aircraft machine-gunned a passenger train at Woodham Ferrers station without causing any casulties or damage to property. On 10 February 1945, a V2 rocket fell about 20 yards from the line at Wickford at 11.40am, severing all telephone and control communications, blocking both lines with debris. Everything was cleared up by 4.30pm. On 18 February 1945, a rocket fell and exploded at Billericay in the vicinity of the railway at 8.15 am. causing damage to the telephone lines. Repairs were effected by 9.45am. Several V1 flying bombs came to earth in the vicinity of Southminster and in 1944, one destroyed the railway cottages at Battlesbridge. Luckily, in the latter incident, there were no casualties. At about a 1.45am on the morning of 20 September 1944, a V1 fell in the vicinity of Maldon West station. This caused superficial damage to the stationmaster's house and three railway cottages in the Spital Road. A V2 rocket fell at Fambridge, exploding in the air above the railway line. On 10 January 1945, a V2 fell near Maldon East station at 11am, shattering several windows and causing damage to the station's buildings. At a 10.45pm in the evening of 21 March 1945, a V2 fell in the vicinity of Woodham Ferrers station causing blast damage to it and railway cottages.

One thing that has been quoted in several sources as happening but actually did not, was that for two weeks in 1942, when a huge bomb crater blocked the main line at Ingatestone, trains on the main line were diverted via Billericay, Woodham Ferrers, Maldon and Witham. Firstly, a bomb was dropped at 9.45pm. on the main line between Shenfield and Ingatestone, late on the evening of Wednesday 4 March 1943, blowing out part of the embankment half a mile north of the bridge over the single track loop of the Southend line. The signalman at Shenfield heard the explosion and lost block communication with Ingatestone signal box. A ganger was sent to investigate what had happened, but before he could report back, the 8.45pm Liverpool St to Harwich, hauled by B12/3 class locomotive No 8580 (which had been held at Shenfield) was ordered by the District Control Office to proceed at caution thus avoiding any further delay. In the pitch black darkness, hampered by the blackout, the engine and tender fell into the crater killing the driver and the fireman. The only other casualties were injuries to a passenger and the guard. This was the only instance of an LNER locomotive hauling a train falling into a bomb crater. According to a history of the Eastern National Omnibus Company, the bus company ran a shuttle service between Shenfield and Ingatestone for nearly three days whilst the line was being repaired. Another source also mentions the City Coach Company providing some buses for the shuttle. As the City Coach

Company had a garage at Brentwood, this was logical. The event was not reported immediately in the press, as it was wartime. The *Manchester Guardian* of 2 June 1943, giving information on the incident, reported that a notice was posted at Liverpool Street station one morning telling passengers that because of a 'failure' at Ingatestone the main line service to Colchester and beyond was subject to delay. The paper then described what had happened. No mention is given of the date of the incident. Both the *Essex Chronicle* and the *Essex Weekly News* reported the incident in a similar vein. As far as is known, no goods trains were diverted via Maldon and local residents assuredly have no knowledge of this happening. As mentioned earlier Peter Paye is of the opinion that using the line for diversions was a red herring (as the Route Availability was too restrictive), he does say in *Branch Lines to Maldon* that the idea of diverting trains via the two Maldon lines was briefly considered but equally speedily rejected. The limited route availability of the locomotives that could use the lines, combined with the restrictive single line Train Staff and Ticket working would have hampered the number of trains that could have used the lines. Besides the section of line from Woodham Ferrers to Cold Norton was regarded as non-operational and was used only for wagon storage and military and civil defence exercises furthermore making diversions impractical.

A Liverpool Street to Southend train was involved in an accident at 10.46am on 10 February 1941. The 10am Liverpool Street to Norwich express train hauled by B17 class locomotive No 2828 *Harewood House,* which had come to a stand at an automatic colour light signal on the 1 in 100 bank between Harold Wood and Brentwood for want of steam, was run into at about 30 m.p.h by the 10.04am Liverpool Street to Southend stopping train hauled by B12/3 class locomotive No 8556. In the collision, seven people lost their lives and nineteen were injured. The cause of the collision was due to the driver of the Southend train failing to maintain a proper lookout ahead on a straight stretch of line when the weather was fine and sunny and visibilty was unusually clear. According to the evidence given by the driver, he had apparently become drowsy and may even have fallen asleep. No blame was attached to the fireman who was fully occupied with attending to the fire.

On 13 June 1944, a V1 flying bomb fell on the main line near Coborn Road station in east London. Whilst the damage was being repaired, trains for Southend (and probably Southminster and other destinations) ran from Fenchurch Street via Bow Road.

During the latter part of the war, proposals were put forward for the post-war years. The most important proposal was the Greater London Plan of 1944. The key to the plan was the movement of people away from central London to newly built towns in the surrounding Home Counties. The plan not only included proposals for new towns, but motorways and railway electrification. The plan proposed the electrification of all lines into London from a point in the suburbs. The Shenfield to Southend line, as well as the LTS line, were proposed for electrification.

With the end of the threat of invasion and the war turning in the way of the allies from about the end of 1943 or early 1944, the need for the possible use of the Woodham Ferrers to Maldon line as a diversionary route ceased and the section of line between Woodham Ferrers to Cold Norton was used for the storage of damaged goods wagons. The exact date however has not yet been established. At Cold Norton Station those sidings not needed for the existing goods traffic were used for the storage of unwanted carriages and wagons. As to when they were first used is not known. Newspaper reports state that they became a great source of scrap metal for thieves. After the end of the war in 1945, things did start to get back to normal, albeit slowly.

There were even a few new services put on. The winter timetable for 1946-47 shows a weekdays through train from Chelmsford to Southend. Whilst the summer timetable for 1947 shows a weekdays only through train to Chelmsford from Southend and a Sundays only through train from Southend to Colchester via Chelmsford. The summer timetable for 1946 had a Sundays only train between Enfield and Southend and return, but this service was not revived in the 1947 summer timetable.

On the roads, the City Coach Company re-started running from London through to Southend. Eastern National's services from Chelmsford to Southend via Billericay and Billericay to Brentwood did not resume.

Following the end of the war in Europe, the *Essex Chronicle* of Friday 11 May 1945 reported that Woodham Ferrers Parish Council was asking for the Woodham Ferrers–Maldon line to be re-opened. No (passenger) train had run on the line for several years. The *Essex Newsman* of Tuesday 19 June 1945, in its report of the meeting of Woodham Ferrers Parish Council meeting of

Saturday 16 June, recorded that the LNER had replied that the line from Woodham Ferrers to Maldon could not yet be re-opened. The *Essex Chronicle* of Friday 3 August 1945 reported that at the meeting of Woodham Ferrers Parish Council the previous Tuesday, a letter signed by seventy residents asked the Council again to press for the re-opening of the Woodham Ferrers to Maldon branch line. It was resolved to approach the Ministry of Transport and the Ministry of Education concerning the service and also the bus service which was causing problems for the residents. The minutes of Woodham Ferrers Parish Council on 16 May 1945 record that a letter had been received from the LNER which stated that consideration would be given to a request for passenger trains to be resumed between Woodham Ferrers and Maldon as soon as circumstances made it practical to augment services as a whole and promising to communicate as soon as a decision was reached. It is clear from reading between the lines that the LNER had no intention of doing so and was stalling. It would have had to admit that it had no intention of restoring the passenger service. At the meeting of the Parish Council on 31 July 1945, the Clerk of the Council presented a petition signed by seventy-nine residents of Stow Maries asking for a restoration of the passenger service on the Maldon line. The Clerk was directed to write to the LNER about the matter. On 30 June 1945, the following article appeared in the *Burnham-on-Crouch and Dengie Advertiser*:

'Now that the war in Europe is over, the Woodham Ferrers Parish Council are trying to induce the LNER Company to re-open for passenger traffic the branch railway between Woodham Ferrers and Maldon. The closing of the line some years ago was a decided hardship to residents of Cold Norton and district, many of whom built their houses there because of the existence of railway facilities. Some whose businesses necessitated a daily visit to London had to seek residences elsewhere. Whilst not at present prepared to re-open the line, the railway company hold out hopes that this maybe done at a later date, for in their reply to the Woodham Council they say that while nothing can be done at present, they will "inform the Council when there is a possibility of such a service being restored". The closing of the branch also practically cut off Burnham and Southminster from railway connection with Maldon, and so increased the pressure on the bus service. A railway trip to Maldon from this district nowadays involves a journey via Wickford, Shenfield and Witham, a distance of about forty miles, this to a town which is only ten or twelve miles away by road'.

At the meeting of Cold Norton Parish Council on 30 August 1945, a letter was received from Purleigh Parish Council asking for support in a petition to the railway company to restart the passenger train service from Maldon to Woodham Ferrers. After discussion, the Council came to the unanimous decision that it was useless to petition the railway company, but if Purleigh Parish Council decided to take the matter to the Ministry of Transport Cold Norton Parish Council would support them in any way possible. At the meeting of Woodham Ferrers Parish Council on 8 September 1945 a letter was read from the LNER promising to provide better facilities on the Woodham Ferrers to Maldon line as soon as labour conditions permitted. At the meeting of the Local Working Committee between the ENOC and the LNER and LMSR on 9 January 1946, the Bus Company's representative confirmed that the existing arrangements for the subsidised Service 66 would be continued. The LNER's representative asked the ENOC to consider the extension of the service to Woodham Ferrers. Mr F. Bryan, the Chairman of the Committee, agreed to examine the suggestion. At the meeting of Woodham Ferrers Parish Council on 9 March 1946, a letter was read from a resident of South Woodham, calling for the attention of the council to the failure of the LNER to restart passenger services on the Maldon line and to the lateness of trains at Woodham Ferrers. The clerk was directed to write to the railway company pointing out the urgency of the matter. Failing a satisfactory reply, it was suggested that the Essex Association of Parish Councils take up the matter.

At the meeting of Woodham Ferrers Parish Council on 30 March 1946, a letter was read from the Traffic Superintendent of the LNER stating that the company would consider the possibility of re-starting passenger services on the Maldon line and promising to report to the council if it proved possible to do so. At the meeting of the Local Working Committee on 5 April 1946, it was decided that the suggestion of the extension of bus Service 66 to Woodham Ferrers and also an increase in its frequency should be left in abeyance. At the meeting of Cold Norton Parish Council on 18 April 1946, a letter was read from Mrs L. Morris, the secretary of the local Women's Institute, requesting improvements to the bus service. It was decided by the council to send a letter to her stating that it (the Council) had written to the LNER with little effect and adding that nothing short of the combined efforts of the interested parties would produce results.

At the meeting of Stow Maries Parish Council on 29 April 1946 a complaint made at the Parish Council meeting on 11 March 1946 about bus services to the parish was discussed. Mr Franks offered to interview the Traffic Manager of the ENOC at Chelmsford with a view to improvements being made to the service.

At the meeting of 21 May 1946 of Woodham Ferrers Parish Council, Councillor Mr Algar reported that the LNER were arranging for an improved service of buses from South Woodham to Maldon to start shortly. At the meeting of Stow Maries Parish Council of 27 May 1946, Mr Franks stated that he had had an interview with the Traffic Superintendent of the bus company who had stated the company intended to commence a new service on a trial period from Woodham Ferrers to Maldon East station to serve parishes previously served by rail and that the service would serve Stow Maries. The probable reason why the Traffic Superintendent of the bus company mentioned that the service would serve Stow Maries, even though it was already doing so, is that it is likely that Mr Franks was asked by the Parish Council to get a firm assurance on that point so that it could be minuted in the Parish Council minutes in case there was a comeback, such as the bus company diverting the route away from Stow Maries. At the meeting of the Local Working Committee on 10 July 1946, the Chairman of the Committee confirmed the extension of Service 66 to Woodham Ferrers station as from 3 June 1946 which the LNER had agreed to subsidise at 1/3d per mile less receipts for an experimental period of six months. This contradicts another source which says that the service was extended to Woodham Ferrers station from 28 July 1946. The LNER asked for the 8.10am bus from Woodham Ferrers to be delayed to connect with the up train from Southminster departing at 8.13am. The Chairman agreed to this. As the extended service must have been deemed to have been a success nothing further is heard of the proposal to restart a passenger service on the Maldon line in either of the minutes of the Parish Councils or the Local Working Committee.

From 1947 or 1948, the section of line from Cold Norton to Woodham Ferrers was used for the storage of unwanted carriages. These were visible from the road where it and the railway were in close proximity. Some of the sidings at Cold Norton were also used for this purpose. Local children played on the line.

Both Dennis Swindale in *Branch Line to Southminster* (East Anglian Railway Museum 1981) and Peter Paye in *Branch Lines to Maldon* mention an incident involving some wagons which were being stored on the Maldon branch. One winter Sunday at dusk during a heavy snow storm, a J15 locomotive arrived at Woodham Ferrers to undertake some shunting. A rake of wagons were left on the Southminster line just beyond the level crossing and the junction for the Maldon line. The J15 then went and propelled a rake of forty wagons a short distance on the Maldon line. The hand brakes on the wagons were pinned down at the place they were parked, which was on a 1 in 100 gradient, and the locomotive returned to the station coming to a halt beyond the points for the junction and near to the level crossing. Just after the points had been changed and the J15 was moving back to pick up the first rake of wagons, the wagons that had been left on the Maldon line rolled downwards out of the snow towards the junction at increasing speed. Obviously the brakes on the wagons had not been pinned down properly. On the footplate of the locomotive were the driver, the fireman, the guard and Woodham Ferrers stationmaster. With commendable presence of mind the four men decided to stay on the locomotive. The runaway wagons collided with the J15 with great force. Its tender took the full impact and was split open from the collision, in the process losing all its water, putting out the locomotive's fire. In the station the stationmaster's wife and teenage son heard the crash and feared the worst. They rushed out to see what had happened and were greeted by a vast cloud of steam from beyond the level crossing. After the steam and the dust had subsided the engine crew, the guard and the stationmaster emerged out from the wreckage a bit shaken but unscathed. Their decision to remain on the footplate without question saved their lives. Of the wagons involved, three were totally destroyed. At the resulting inquiry, the conclusion reached was that insufficient handbrakes had been applied on them to prevent their movement on the 1 in 100 gradient and that their combined weight had contributed to the runaway. Because there was still the Sunday evening passsenger train to come, a bus was procurred to bridge the gap from Woodham Ferrers to Fambridge. By now it was completely dark and the snow was falling even heavier. The bus driver had no knowledge of the route so the stationmaster's son volunteered to pilot him. At that time the road from Woodham Ferrers was rather narrow with many bends and a steep hill. The bus slipped and slid on its journey to Fambridge where the driver said in no uncertain terms that was going to be his only journey and set off on the return trip dropping off the stationmaster's son at the top of the road to Woodham Ferrers station before disappearing into the snowy night. The date that this incident happened is not recorded.

Creeksea and Hogwell sidings closed by the end of 1946. The 1946 working timetable shows them as being served by trains as required, whereas the 1947 working timetable, although showing them, it does not indicate that trains would stop at them.

The winter of 1946-47 was a particularly bad winter. *The Times* for 29 January 1947 and the *LNER Magazine* for March 1947 recorded snow drifts five feet deep between Burnham-on-Crouch and Southminster. *The Times* said that the drifts were cleared by snow ploughs.

Although it did not take place on the New Essex Lines but at Gidea Park on the main line, there was a serious collision in fog about 11.17pm on 2 January 1947 when the 10.28pm train from Liverpool Street to Southend hauled by B12/3 class locomotive No 1565 was run into by the 10.25pm. train from Liverpool Street to Peterborough hauled by B17 class locomotive No 1602 *Walsingham*. Unfortunately, seven passengers lost their lives in the accident. Forty-five people needed to be detained in hospital for injuries received in the crash. All four lines through Gidea Park station were blocked, but two were cleared for traffic within a couple of hours and the rest by about noon the following day. The cause of the accident was the mistake by the driver of the Peterborough train to continue running at a fairly high speed in the fog on the section of line from Romford to Gidea Park whilst uncertain of his location. This was not the only incident involving Southend line trains in 1947. Following the snow came the thaw. On Monday 17 March, after an engineer's occupation of the line, the engine of a Southend to London line train somersaulted down an embankment near Rayleigh and landed upside-down. The fireman sustained some slight injuries, but the driver and the passengers were unhurt. The cause of the accident was subsidence trouble with a section of the embankment between Rayleigh and Hockley. From the information available it is clear that until the derailment was cleared up, an emergency bus service was put on from Rayleigh to Hockley. Two days later, the 5.45pm train from Liverpool Street to Southend became derailed between Liverpool Street and Stratford.

The engine broke away from the train and the front carriage of the train crashed across two sets of lines and ended up less than fifteen feet from a thirty-foot drop into a canal. In an empty luggage van, three men were flung from one end to the other. Passengers were forced to walk from the train to Stratford station. Four lines of railway were blocked and passengers from other trains began to walk along the lines.

In 1947, a private siding on the alignment of the curve from the former Belchamps Junction on the Southminster line to Fanton Junction on the Southend line was opened for the engineering firm of Edward Farr Ltd. To gain access to the siding Belchamps Junction was re-opened. There was no access from the Southend line. It was announced as ready for traffic on 11 August 1947.

In 1945, some of the pre-war projects were resumed, notably the electrification of the railway from London to Shenfield. The LNER had also developed plans for the post-war years. The railway company intended to electrify the suburban services of the former Great Northern Railway first. Further electrification of the Great Eastern's lines would have been the lines from Liverpool Street to Chingford, Palace Gates, Enfield and Hertford East.

In 1945, a Labour government under Clement Attlee was returned to power following the General Election of that year with a pledge to nationalise a number of major industries such as the coal mines and the railways. The nationalisation of the railways took place on 1 January 1948.

# CHAPTER FIVE

# The British Railways Years

British Railways, as the new nationalised railway system was known, came into existence on 1 January 1948. The railways along with some road services and some waterways that were nationalised came under the umbrella of the British Transport Commission (BTC). The railways were controlled by the Railway Executive (RE).

The former GER lines together with the former Great Northern and Great Central lines became part of the Eastern Region of British Railways (BR). The former LTSR line became part of the London Midland Region. Not a great deal happened at first. British Railways started appearing on notices and on the sides of trains instead of LNER. On 1 January 1949, the LTSR line was transferred from the London Midland Region to the Eastern Region. The summer Sundays only service between Enfield and Southend was revived during the summer 1948 timetable and in the summer 1949 timetable, a service from Chingford was added. On 1 May 1949 Southend station was renamed Southend-on-Sea (Victoria).

The first electric trains for the Liverpool Street to Shenfield electrification were delivered to Ilford depot in March 1949 and the first trial runs took place between Ilford and Chadwell Heath at the end of the month. Later in the year, these trial runs were extended to Shenfield. There were also trial runs from Ilford to Liverpool Street. The public electric service started on 26 September 1949. The new service was inaugurated by the Minister of Transport, Alfred Barnes, who drove an electric train from Liverpool Street to Stratford. On the morning that the new electric service was started, a Southend line train broke down due to the steam engine developing some form of trouble which caused the train to be forty minutes late into Liverpool Street, with the result that many trains lost their paths and this caused more congestion. At the start of the electric services, some of the trains were still worked by steam locomotives and it was not until 7 November 1949 that the service went over to full electric operation.

On the LTS line, business travellers were wondering when they were going to get electric trains. The LMSR had done nothing about electrification. All the LTS received were some new carriages and some 3 cylinder and 2 cylinder 2-6-4 tank engines, which the LNER had allowed into Fenchurch Street station in London. On 4 January 1949, Southend Borough Council decided to ask the Railway Executive to receive a deputation concerning the railway services to Southend, which were described as appalling. It was said that the absence of a fast and reliable service was likely to affect the town's future posterity. Sir Eustace Missenden, the Chairman of the RE, informed Southend's Town Clerk, that provided that no restrictions were imposed on capital expenditure, it was intended that the electrification of the LTS line would be one of the first conversions to be taken in hand. Missenden met the deputation from Southend on 18 January 1949 and told them that a committee of experts were considering improvements to the Fenchurch Street to Southend line, which included electrification, an improved system of signalling and increased number of tracks. He added that any programme which might arise from the investigation, would be subject to the overriding considerations of the national economy, but the RE was treating the matter as one of urgency, and a report was expected in the near future.

Questions were asked in parliament and eventually BR gave a commitment to electrify the line. This would prove to be a long job as all the bridges except for one had to be rebuilt. In 1949, the new town of Basildon was created in the area of south Essex covering Pitsea, Vange and Laindon. According to *The Times* of 21 March 1950, Sir Cyril Hurcomb, the Chairman of the BTC, speaking in London the previous night, had said that the electrification of the LTS line should be regarded as of a higher priority than proposals that had also recently been put forward for new tube lines. He also foresaw the possible extension of the then recently electrified Liverpool Street to Shenfield section of line to places somewhat further afield.

On 2 June 1950 at the Transport Tribunal's inquiry into the BTC's fares equalisation scheme for the London area, Alec Valentine, the Commission's commercial expert, stated that electrification of the LTS railway had been given high priority by the RE. In the BTC report for 1950, one finds the first mention in post-nationalisation days of extending the Liverpool Street to Shenfield electrification to Southend-on-Sea (Victoria).

At the begining of 1951, there was a shortage of coal and for a time the Sunday service on the Southminster branch was withdrawn.

During the spring of 1951, the turntable at Liverpool Street station was taken out of use so that it could be lengthened to accommodate the new Britannia class 4-6-2 locomotives. During this period many Southend trains were hauled by tank locomotives. Three classes of tank locomotive were used – A5 (4-6-2T), L1(2-6-4T) and N7 (0-6-2T). The former were all borrowed from the North Eastern Region and managed to prove themselves to be unpopular not only with engine crews, but also with passengers. Engine crews especially regarded them as useless. They were not up to the job and held up other traffic at busy times. However, whilst they and the N7 class were permitted by their route availability to be able to work to Southminster, the L1 class were in theory prohibited from doing so. According to *Trains Illustrated* for June 1951, the L1 class were regarded with reasonable favour, whilst the N7 class performed surprisingly well. However, not every train was worked by tank locomotives, only those duties where there was insufficient time for the locomotive to go to Stratford for turning. I have not been able to establish whether the through trains to and from the Southminster line were worked by tank locomotives during this time.

In a memorandum dated 20 October 1951, the BTC informed the RE that they would be glad to receive a report on the economic effects of electrification from Shenfield to Colchester and Southend.

On the Woodham Ferrers to Maldon branch the service had now got to the point where it was left to the Maldon East stationmaster to decide if the train should be run.

Hogwell public siding was briefly re-opened, as it is shown in the working timetable for the summer of 1950. One of the two goods trains on the Southminster line, which ran on Mondays to Saturdays in the up direction, called at Hogswell public siding. From the evidence available it would seem that the siding closed for good after the end of the summer 1950 timetable.

At the meeting of the REC on 14 August 1952, Charles Bird, the Chief Regional Officer of the Eastern Region, undertook to examine the possible extension of the Liverpool Street to Shenfield electrification to Chelmsford and Southend-on-Sea (Victoria).

In the minutes of the meeting of the BTC dated 23 December 1952, under the section headed Motive Power, there is a reference to a memorandum from the Chief Secretary of the Commission dated 18 December 1952, with a letter from the REC containing recommendations with regard to electrification policy. Not all of the items concerned the GE and LTS sections of the Eastern Region. Of those that did it was (a) agreed to reaffirm the approval in principal of the LTS electrification scheme with full financial details of the scheme were to be estimated, (b) confirm that plans be developed for extending the Liverpool Street to Shenfield electrification to Ipswich with completion to Chelmsford as quickly as possible if financially justified and (c) propose that the merits of an extension of the electrification from Shenfield to Southend (Victoria) should be assessed. Note that the eastern end of the main line proposed for electrification was altered from Colchester in the memorandum of 20 October 1951 to Ipswich.

On 31 December 1952, the Chief Secretary of the BTC, S.B. Taylor, forwarded the Commission's recommendations to the Chairman of the RE, John Elliot. These recommendations were then forwarded to the Eastern Region of BR who set up a committee to report on the extension of the electrification from Shenfield to Chelmsford and Southend (Victoria). The committee was chaired by A.J. White. The terms of reference of the committee were (i) to prepare an outline scheme for the extension of the Liverpool Street to Shenfield electrification to Chelmsford and Southend (Victoria) including proposals for the working of freight services and excursion traffic and the Southminster branch passenger service and (ii) to furnish broad estimates of capital expenditure, changes in working costs and possible revenue from additional traffic. Note the further change in the eastern extremity of main line electrification which became Chelmsford rather than Ipswich.

Eastern National and Westcliff-on-Sea Motor Services as part of the Tilling Group had been nationalised in 1948. On 1 February 1952, the owners of the City Coach Company sold out to the state. The City Coach Company was absorbed into the Westcliff. As part of a reorganisation of bus services owned by the state, control of the Westcliff passed to Eastern National on 18 May 1952. On 1 January 1955, the assets of Westcliff-on-Sea Motor Services were transferred to Eastern National.

On the night of the 31 January to 1 February 1953, severe gales and high tides caused some of the worst flooding that the east coast of England had ever seen. Whilst the New Essex Lines were not greatly affected by the floods, the LTS line was. Three miles of the line between Benfleet and Leigh was flooded to a depth of ten feet. All rail traffic from Southend to London was diverted over the GE line. Whilst there were sufficient locomotives to run additional trains from Southend (Victoria) to Liverpool Street only four trains of high capacity suburban stock were available. The solution was to run a special service of steam trains from Southend to Shenfield and from there a special service of electric trains was put on to Fenchurch Street and vice versa. The line from Stratford to Fenchurch was included in the 1935 Liverpool Street to Shenfield electrification scheme with the intention of running a shuttle service from Stratford to Fenchurch Street. Although the section of line was wired up following a change of heart the shuttle service was never implemented and services between Fenchurch Street and Stratford and stations beyond were withdrawn with effect from 7 November 1949. This special service was on top of the normal service on the Southend-on-Sea (Victoria) line. The steam trains from Southend to Shenfield called at Prittlewell, and Rayleigh. The electric service ran non-stop to Fenchurch Street every fifteen minutes and reverse in evening and was formed of nine carriage sets. Later in the week, these trains also called at Stepney East. Emergency bus services were put on between Shoeburyness and Benfleet, Leigh and Benfleet and Leigh and Rayleigh using double deck buses.

There was also a shuttle service of trains between Shoeburyness and Leigh. On the LTS line, trains were able to run from Benfleet to Fenchurch Street via Upminster, but not via Tilbury as the sections of line from Tilbury to Low Street and Purfleet to West Thurrock were also closed by flooding. Things at first did not go to plan. It is recorded that on Monday 2 February, the first working day after the floods, whilst the special trains between Southend-on-Sea (Victoria) and between Shenfield and Shenfield and Fenchurch Street ran on time, they were carrying less than their full capacity. A mere 1,100 passengers travelled on them. By comparison, the trains from Benfleet to Fenchurch Street were packed solid. That evening a concerted effort was made to stop a repeat of this happening in reverse and almost brutal efforts were made to separate the Benfleet passengers from the Shenfield passengers. This effort bore fruit and within two days, 8,000 extra passengers were using the Shenfield route each peak period. The emergency services lasted until the end of the week when through running was resumed between Benfleet and Leigh on the LTS line. Until 19 February when everything got back to normal on the LTS line, four relief steam trains a day worked by GER line engines were run in each direction from Southend GE to Fenchurch Street calling at Prittlewell, Rayleigh and Stepney East and Vice Versa. Apart from having to convey LTSR line passengers from Southend, goods traffic for LTSR stations in the Southend area also had to be diverted to the GER line. Although I have not found any information as to the precise goods yards on the GER line, that the additional goods traffic was diverted to it implies that it was Southend (Victoria). A mention in *Trains Illustrated* for April 1953 records the first appearance of ex-WD 2-8-0s at that station since 1945. The magazine records members of the class on goods trains at Southend on 5 and 12 February. A problem directly affecting not only Southend (Victoria) locomotive depot, but also Maldon locomotive depot was that in both cases, the locomotive feed water was badly contaminated by the flooding. At Southend, water supplies for the locomotives were taken from the town's water supplies from 4 to 12 February. What happened before that is not clear. At Maldon, arrangements were made for the branch engines to take water at Witham until 16 February. As a postscript to this, the *Eastern Region Magazine* of April 1953 carried some letters from LTSR line passengers thanking the GER line staff for all that they'd done to help them during the period that their line was affected by the flooding.

By mid-1952, BR neglected to publicise facilities on the Woodham Ferrers to Maldon line and failed to encourage its use. According to Peter Paye, traffic consisted of occasional farm traffic and a weekly coal wagon to Cold Norton plus two or three coal wagons to Maldon West. In the autumn of that year BR made the decision to close the line between Woodham Ferrers and Maldon West which took place from 1 April 1953 although this was opposed by Maldon Borough Council and Cold Norton Parish Council. It was initially decided to keep the section between the two Maldon stations open, but because of dwindling traffic at the West station it was decided to close this section as well and this duly took place on 1 September 1954.

As to what effect the closure of the Woodham Ferrers to Maldon line had on the population of the villages that it served is difficult to judge. A comparison could be made by comparing the populations of Cold Norton with that of Althorne of the Southminster line for the years 1931, 1951 and 1961. Because of the Second World War there was not a census in 1941.

|  | 1931 | 1951 | 1961 |
|---|---|---|---|
| Cold Norton | 384 | 401 | 416 |
| Althorne | 394 | 451 | 483 |

On 3 January 1957 the section of line from Maldon East to Maldon West was reopened for goods traffic. The rest of the Maldon West branch was taken over by local farmers (often to serve as farm tracks) or else just left in situ. At Cold Norton, houses were built on the station site. The working timetable for 1957 to 1958 shows the goods service from Maldon East to Maldon West consisting of just one return working in the morning on weekdays. However no times are given for the train and the service is shown as 'Suspended'. It is claimed by Dennis Swindale in *Branch Lines to Maldon* that before closure of the line through to Woodham Ferrers, a railway enthusiasts' special visited the line. Dennis' recollection is perhaps questionable. On 6 April 1957 the Railway Enthusiasts Club ran an excursion which included a trip in brake vans over the surviving part of the Tollesbury branch which had closed to passengers in 1951. The excursion also included passenger carriages which visited the Witham to Maldon line and the line from Maldon East to Maldon West. Whether any railway enthusiasts had unofficial rides over the Woodham Ferrers to Maldon line following closure to passenger traffic but before the line was lifted remains unknown.

The canopy of Cold Norton station was removed soon after the closure of the line south of Maldon West. It is thought from looking at a photograph of the train that was used to carry away the dismantled canopy that this was in the autumn of 1953. It is not known when the points at Woodham Ferrers were disconnected. The lifting of the track south of Maldon West commenced from the Woodham Ferrers end of the line in late 1953 or early 1954 and was completed by June 1954. Brian Pask photographed track lifting taking place north of Barons Lane in mid-March 1954. Wagons for the track to be lifted each day were propelled by the Maldon goods engine to just north of the site to where lifting was to take place. A platelayer's trolley was pushed to where the lifting was required. The workmen engaged in lifting the track removed the rails from the chairs and placed them on the trolley. A crowbar was then used to prise the chairs off the sleepers, which were subsequently placed on the trolley. Presumably the sleepers were then lifted and placed on the trolley as well. The trolley with its material was then pushed to the waiting wagons which were then loaded with the contents and taken away at the end of the day by the Maldon goods engine. Cold Norton station had been demolished by June 1954, although there is some evidence that this might have occurred in April. A photograph taken of the signal box dated 17 April 1954 would suggest that that was the time that the station building and signal box were demolished. The demolition of the station buildings at Cold Norton must have been carried out using road vehicles, as track lifting had reached north of Cold Norton by 13 February 1954. The station platform had been demolished by the middle of September 1956. It is not known when the platform at Barons Lane Halt was demolished. The railings at the Halt are known to have gone by April 1953. The goods office/waiting room at Barons Lane Halt is believed to have been demolished earlier. A photo taken about 1950 of stock stored at Barons Lane shows the building with what looks like fire damage to the roof which may have led to its demolition. A photograph taken of the Halt after closure of the line but before the lifting of the track shows the platform in a very overgrown state with no sign of the railings and the waiting room/goods office. The waiting room at Stow St Mary's Halt was possibly demolished soon after the closure of the Halt in September 1939 or some time during the Second World War. The platform of Stow St Mary's Halt remained in existence.

According to one source, a resident of Stow Maries who dug out a swimming pool in his garden in the 1960s deposited the soil dug out on the remains of the Halt including the track bed. All I can say from personally visiting the site of the Halt, is that the height of the platform from the track bed is not as great as one might expect. The stored carriages had been removed earlier, certainly no later than the autumn of 1953 and most likely either just before or just after the closure of the line. It is not known precisely when the last working over the line occurred. I was also told that some of the stored carriages were removed by road using a crane to lift the bodies off.

As mentioned earlier, the Maldon West branch's remains were put to other uses. At Cold Norton, houses were built on the station site. At Stow Maries, the site of the halt and part of the trackbed has been turned into a nature reserve which is accessible to the public. Mountnessing and Ramsden Bellhouse sidings ceased to appear in the working timetable after that from 21 September 1953 to 13 June 1954.

In June 1953 the committee set up to prepare an outline scheme for the extension of the Liverpool Street to Shenfield electrification to Chelmsford and Southend-on-Sea (Victoria) produced its report.

The report began by stating the then current position concerning passenger trains. The section of the main line from Shenfield to

Chelmsford was served by a roughly hourly shuttle service between the two places connecting with the Shenfield electric trains and the Southend-on-Sea (Victoria) service and there were also trains from London to East Anglia. On the Southend-on-Sea (Victoria) line, the basic weekday service was an hourly Liverpool Street to Southend (Victoria) service in both directions stopping at all stations between Shenfield and Southend (Victoria) and between one and three stations in the electrified area. In the peak hours there were four trains per hour from Liverpool Street to Southend (Victoria) and vice versa with additional trains from Shenfield to Southend (Victoria) and vice versa. To cater for the growing workmen's traffic there was one early morning train from Southend (Victoria) to Chelmsford with a corresponding return service in the late afternoon. In the summer, the Southend (Victoria) service increased considerably, especially at weekends to cater for holiday and excursion traffic. At the height of the holiday season, the number of excursion specials rose to fourteen in a 24 hour period including five from outside the electrified area.

The Southminster line was covered by a shuttle service to and from Wickford. Within the area examined by the committee, the report stated that the annual value of originating and inward passenger traffic, which would be directly affected by electrification, was estimated at £300,000. Planned population increases in the area were expected to ultimately produce an additional £150,000 in passenger revenue apart from electrification. The report said that the shuttle service for local traffic between Chelmsford and Shenfield should be increased to give more connections at Shenfield with the Southend line itself and with the electric suburban service.

On the Southend line there was a need for faster services between Southend, Brentwood, Romford, Ilford and Liverpool Street. It would not be possible to fulfil all the requirements with steam operation. In the main body of the report there is mention of the B1 class steam locomotives that were starting to be used on the Southend line services. Even with the use of these locomotives, the service could not be improved to the desired level. The committee recommended that the sections of line from Shenfield to Chelmsford and from Shenfield to Southend (Victoria) should be electrified at 1,500 volts direct current on the overhead system. Excursion traffic from outside the electrified area and freight traffic should continue to be steam hauled pending the introduction of electric haulage for freight traffic in the Stratford District.

There was no immediate change recommended for the operation of the Southminster branch as the capital costs of conventional electrification could not be justified, but other possibilities had not yet been studied in detail. The report stated that a faster and more frequent service on the Shenfield to Chelmsford section could be provided at little cost by the extension of existing Liverpool Street to Shenfield trains. On financial grounds, the Shenfield to Southend section service could be provided by an hourly service covering the forty-one and a half miles from Liverpool Street to Southend in sixty minutes with six intermediate stops and an hourly all stations service from Shenfield to Southend. To carry the additional peak hour traffic resulting from the developments of population the report recommended that new electric multiple unit stock should be constructed for the service. It said that the stock should be composed of four car units identical with those proposed for the LTS electrification. twenty-three units would cover all the requirements at the outset and the existing repair and cleaning facilities at Ilford depot could be used.

The use of electric locomotives for the Southend (Victoria) line service is mentioned in the main body of the report but nothing would be gained in from their use, as platform limitations at Liverpool Street would not increase seating capacity of the trains. According to the report, the power required for the trains would be purchased from the British Electricity Authority and delivered to the railway at Chelmsford and Rochford. The electricity distribution system would be controlled from the existing electrical control station at Chadwell Heath. The design of the overhead equipment would be of the simplest and the most economical type based on the experience gained on other electrification schemes.

Few civil engineering works would be needed apart from safety measures and those necessary to provide clearance for the overhead equipment. Estimates provided for signal and telecommunications circuits to be cabled and track circuits with associated apparatus altered from DC operation to AC operation. The report estimated the capital outlay for the scheme to be £2,593,000 of which £1,486,000 represented financial betterment. The provision of the proposed electric services would be achieved with a decrease in annual operating costs for operation and maintenance of £104,000, excluding interest, below the cost of the existing steam service. Apart from the additional revenue expected rising from the growth of population, it was estimated that the electrification would

**Billericay station** in about 1953 with a B1 arriving on a down train. Observe the rare three way point. (*David Collins*)

itself produce a twenty per cent increase on the revenue that was considered susceptible to electrification.

The report said that the decrease in annual costs and the increase in revenue from electrification, at its then existing population levels, would produce a return of over eleven per cent on the net financial betterment or over seven per cent after meeting revenues. It would secure a greater revenue from the rising population at less cost than would be possible by steam operation.

The report recommended that the scheme be approved in principle and that the work be started in successive portions as detailed estimates could be prepared and approved for each portion. By those means, it was estimated that it was possible to complete the whole of the work within approximately three and a half years if it was approved.

On 26 June 1953 Charles Bird forwarded to the Chairman of the Railway Executive and last General Manager of the Southern Railway, John Elliott, a report on the extension of the electrification. In it, he recommended authorising the possible extension of the Liverpool Street to Shenfield electrification to Chelmsford and Southend-on-Sea (Victoria) and referred to the undertaking given at the meeting of the REC on 14 August 1952. He said that he had pleasure in forwarding the report on the subject to Mr Elliot. Bird said that he did not doubt that, but for the war, the electrification would by then have reached Southend-on-Sea (Victoria) and at least as far as Chelmsford on the mainline, as with such extensions in mind, spare capacity was provided at Ilford car sheds and Chadwell Heath electrical control station (when the Liverpool Street to Shenfield electrification was being planned and built in the late 1930s and 1940s). The part of the sentence in brackets is implied but not stated in Bird's letter. According to Bird, because of the spare capacity at Ilford and Chadwell Heath the capital costs of the proposals for the extension of the electrification were thereby reduced. On the other hand, although the electrification to Chelmsford was desirable, on traffic grounds it would only cater for local traffic for the time being, and that some of the expenditure on the section of line should be considered as a preliminary contribution to the further extension of the electrification to Clacton and Ipswich and beyond. He recommended the authorisation of the electrification. Earlier in his letter, he had said that the LTS line was working to capacity in the peak hours and that the interim steam improvements only enabled the Eastern Region to keep pace with traffic demands. When work on building the flyover at Barking and the reconstruction of Barking station (which was a very necessary part of the work of electrifying the LTS) started, the capacity of LTS services through that station would be reduced. If the capacity of the Southend (Victoria) line was increased by electrification electric trains could temporarily be run over the route (from Stratford) to Fenchurch Street thus avoiding the Barking work. He was sure that the measure of relief afforded to the LTS line would be welcomed by the Eastern Region people and by the travelling public. The more that he thought about it, the more he was convinced, that the Southend–on-Sea(Victoria) electrification should be considered part of the LTS electrification scheme and this may have been in the mind of headquarters committee (his words) when they mentioned the extension of the electrification to Southend-on-Sea (Victoria) in their [BTC] report for 1950.

On 29 June 1953 Bird again wrote to John Elliot submitting the report on the extension to the electrification with a covering letter that in his view that the work should be undertaken at the earliest possible opportunity.

He said that the most cogent reason for carrying out the extension lay in the increased capacity of the Southend-on-Sea (Victoria) line (attainable only by electrification) that it would be able to give when work on remodelling Barking station started. In the peak

hours, thirty London Transport and twelve BR trains used Barking
in one direction and he expected to add four more trains before the
alterations began. However skilfully the engineers staged the work,
the complete remodelling would upset normal working and impose
serious delays unless pressure could be eased. He mentioned the
merciless criticism that occurred when anything went wrong on
the LTS line and he was really apprehensive of public reaction to
worsening services over a considerable period as electrification was
not entirely accepted (by so-called railway experts) in Southend
as an alternative to the widening of the LTS line. He said that the
BTC had mentioned the extension of the Shenfield electrification
in its report for 1952 and since there was a good economic case, he
did not imagine there would be much opposition to the scheme
on its merits. It was really important that the BR Eastern Region
should electrify to Southend (Victoria) as quickly as they could to
help the flow of traffic on the LTS line while preliminary work on
electrification was going on there. In his report of 26 June which he
mentioned in his letter to John Elliot, Bird had asked permission
to proceed with the electrification extensions without waiting for
detailed estimates of the whole cost so that there was no risk of
delaying the progress of events on the LTS line. He said that he
knew that what he asked for was unusual. However Elliot with his
experience on the Southern Railway would support his view that
there were occasions in which considerations of policy demanded
that the accuracy of the estimate be taken on trust for the ultimate
good of the undertaking.

On 4 July, Michael Bonavia, Principal Works and Development
Officer, British Transport Commission, wrote to the Railway
Executive supporting the proposed electrification. In summary, he
mentioned the planned population increase in the areas served by
the electrification from 252,000 to 320,000 (an increase of twenty
eight per cent), the estimated gross outlay of £2.6 million, the
net financial gain of £1.5 million, the operating and maintenance
savings of £104,000 which was equal to seven per cent on net
financial gain and a figure of £60,000 or a further four per cent on net
financial gain for additional traffic arising from the electrification.
The sum of the two net financial betterments gave a net financial
betterment of eleven per cent in total. Full estimates on a stage by
stage basis were to be submitted as the work proceeded. Approval
in principle with a view to immediate inauguration of detailed
technical planning was requested by the Chief Regional Officer.

The proposed service on the Southend-on-Sea (Victoria) line was a regular interval semi-fast service with hourly departures continuing on from how they were at that time between Liverpool Street and Southend augmented by a connecting stopping service between Shenfield and Southend (Victoria). The additional fast trains during the peak hours would continue as before. The proposed standard journey time from Liverpool Street to Southend (Victoria) was sixty minutes as compared to eighty-four minutes at that time. For the fast peak hour services the proposed journey times were fifty-five minutes down and fifty-nine minutes up compared with sixty-seven minutes down and sixty-eight minutes up at that time.

The electric stock for the Liverpool Street to Southend-on-Sea (Victoria) service was to be four-car sets of the pattern proposed for the LTS electrification. For the Chelmsford service, the existing Shenfield stock was to be used. The advantages of the electrification scheme were that no expensive equipment would be required at the London terminus and it would make the past heavy expenditure for the Shenfield service more fruitful. The existing carriage sheds at Ilford and the maintenance facilities had spare capacity and would not require extension. No costly signalling improvements were involved nor would there be any diversion of technical staff from major tasks. So much of the work merely represented a repeat order of existing work. As the money would practically all go into the electrical equipment and rolling stock, the mileage electrified per £m spent, would compare favourably with other schemes where big engineering works were required. The scheme was not an alternative to the LTS electrification nor would it conflict with it, but it would help mollify public complaints from the Southend area and would ease the otherwise inevitable deterioration of LTS services, pending major engineering works at Barking. It should appeal to the BTC who had a tendency to suggest much planning of electrification and other motive power development but produced little in the way of physical results. Mr Bonavia said that the economic staff at the Treasury were concerned about a trade recession starting and were beginning to consider a course of public work schemes which could be accelerated if necessary. These schemes took a long time to develop and the recession might have finished before work on them was underway, unlike the scheme proposed. The scheme should, he said, find favour from the point of view of capital investment control and the cost of it, for over thirty route miles, was less than the cost of one mile of a new London Transport tube line.

On 14 July, Bonavia forwarded to the Railway Executive, a copy of a submission which he had prepared following discussions which had taken place the previous Thursday 9 July. On hearing that they were in accord therewith, he would arrange for it to be despatched to the BTC. The submission followed the lines of his paper of 4 July. In a memorandum dated as July 1953, John Elliot wrote to the BTC recommending approval of the electrification scheme. In a memorandum dated 31 July 1953 from the Chief Secretary of the BTC to the Eastern Region Commission, he recommended approval of the extension of the electrification from Shenfield to Chelmsford and from Shenfield to Southend. He said that the Eastern Regional Committee of the Commission might feel that the RE should give consideration to the use of light diesel units for the Southminster line. He also mentioned that the original electrification scheme to Shenfield (as constructed) provided for later extensions, and that extensions to Southend, Clacton and Ipswich were envisaged by the LNER. At this point it is worth mentioning that I have not found anything in the LNER minute books suggesting that the company was, before the war, thinking of extending the electrification beyond Shenfield. As I mentioned in the previous chapter in the period between the end of the War and Nationalisation, the LNER's thoughts concerning electrification of the former GER lines were to electrify to Chingford, Enfield Town, Palace Gates and Hertford (East). This does not mean that before the war, the LNER did not have plans to electrify to Southend, Clacton and Ipswich and dare one say Chingford, Enfield Town, Palace Gates, Hertford (East) and Cambridge.

When the Shenfield electrification was completed in 1949, the overhead wires were extended for some way along the main line towards Ingatestone. This indicates that post-war at least, further extensions of the Shenfield electrification were contemplated.

At the BTC's meeting of 6 August 1953, it approved the scheme for the electrification from Shenfield to Chelmsford and Southend-on-Sea (Victoria) and for diesel units on the Southminster line. On 12 August, the Chief Secretary of the BTC wrote to the Minister of Transport asking for approval for the electrification scheme.

On 21 August 1953, John Elliott replied, saying that much goodwill would come from the announcement that BR had obtained approval from the British Transport Commission for the electrification scheme and that it was anticipated that work would start the next year. It was to be emphasised in any announcement that the electrification would not affect the programme for the electrification of the LTS line, that had been agreed, and would be a preliminary to it. He would be pleased to know if the BTC agreed. He also said in his letter that consideration was being given to working the Southminster line by the ACV three-car diesel multiple unit, which was then doing a series of test runs throughout BR and on the un-electrified sections of London Transport's railways.

On 12 September 1953, the Ministry of Transport wrote to the BTC giving approval for the electrification scheme. The ACV or rather ACV/BUT three car diesel multiple, to give it its correct designation, went into service on Mondays to Fridays on the Southminster line on 21 September 1953 and remained there until 9 October. The train ran empty between Shenfield and Wickford. The date or dates that the train undertook test runs on the line before going into passenger service on the branch are not known. Although the train only carried passengers on the branch, it is known to have reached Southend before the commencement of its trial on the branch, as, according to David Butcher in a post to the Great Eastern Railway Society e-group, he photographed it passing Warners Bridge alongside Southend Airport on 18 September 1953. The train was (according to David) returning to Wickford from Southend. The train merited a mention in the *Essex Weekly News* of 2 October. In an article titled 'The Railways Launch A Diesel Dipper', the columnist Joseph Billio said that one would have thought that poor old Southend had had enough to put up with. If it wasn't enough that the Coronation decorations took all the village outings to London rather than Southend and that just when the trippers began to flock back to Southend, the place began to smell, British Railways had to go and start a scenic railway. By scenic railway he meant just that. The new grey and red diesel train took you from somewhere to somewhere else, dazzling you all the while with a new view of a familiar slice of the Essex scene. The train made six round trips a day on the Southminster line between 7.4 am and 10.30pm. It took thirty-six minutes to cover the sixteen and a quarter mile single journey and the fare was five shillings return. Its maximum speed was forty-eight miles per hour. The glass fronted leading coach gave a novel view of rail travel. The distant convergence of parallel tracks hypnotised the traveller. Even the gentle gradients made the line dip out of sight. The running cost of the train was 5d a mile compared with 1/8d a mile for a steam train.

The *Southend Standard* of 1 October also had an article on the train. Understandably, it chose not to describe it as a scenic railway. According to the *Standard*, the train weighed thirty-nine tons and fourteen hundredweight, the total length of its three carriages was 120 feet and the seating capacity was 117 passengers. The *Standard* said that if the experiment was successful, it was possible that this type of train would be put into operation on the branch line and also some other branch lines in Essex, some of which had recently closed down because they were uneconomical. One suspects that the *Standard* was referring in particular to the Braintree, Dunmow and Bishop's Stortford line which had lost its scheduled passenger service on 1 March 1952. *British Railways Magazine (Eastern Region)* for December 1953 said that during the diesel train's trials on the Southminster line, it had run 2,790 train miles and had maintained the steam train timings for the line without experiencing any difficulty. On most occasions it had had to wait at stations. On three occasions, the train had been worked using one instead of both of its engines and had still kept to the steam train timings. The magazine reported that passengers had generally expressed their appreciation of it.

On Sunday 27 September 1953, British Railways announced the extension of the Shenfield electrification to Chelmsford and Southend. According to *The Times* of Monday 28 September, the

**The ACV** 3 car diesel multiple unit at Southminster in September 1953. (*Frank Church/Essex Bus Enthusiasts Group*)

cost of the electrification would be about £2.5m and that work would start as soon as possible. In its report, the newspaper said that the BR scheme formed an essential and preliminary step to form part of the plan to electrify the LTS line and unlike the latter, this would be fairly straightforward. When complete, the reserved capacity on the Liverpool Street line would be of benefit to Southend travellers. It was hoped that the work would be finished by January 1957. The electrification was the same as the Liverpool Street to Shenfield electrification at 1,500 volts direct current using overhead pickup, whilst the new electric service to Chelmsford would be provided by extending twenty-two of the existing Liverpool Street to Shenfield services. The Southend service would have new all-steel trains. The new trains for the Southend line would be specially designed to suit both daily travellers and holidaymakers. They would be made up of four coach units providing 373 seats of which 354 would be third class. Of the 354 third class seats, 145 would be in open-type vehicles with centre gangways and the remainder in compartment type coaches. The standard journey time of the regular-interval services to Southend would be one hour with six intermediate stops. There would be faster trains in the morning and evening peak periods. The new service which would be working by January 1957 in time on the Southend line to relieve travelling delays arising from the more complicated electrification of the line from Fenchurch Street to Southend-on-Sea (Central) of which the Shenfield to Southend-on-Sea (Victoria) section was an essential and preliminary step. BR said that technical planning for the electrification of the line from Fenchurch Street was then well in hand, but exceptionally important engineering works would first have to be completed including the reconstruction of Barking station. This involved the re-arrangement of tracks with a flyover and the construction of a new large marshalling yard at Ripple Lane. These works would take some years to complete. On the other hand, the extension of the electrification from Shenfield to Chelmsford and Southend was a straightforward scheme with no major engineering works, which it was hoped would be finished by January 1957. Fast electric trains should already be running on the Southend–Liverpool Street route by the time the big engineering works on the Fenchurch Street line began to cause some delays on the latter; the reserve capacity of the electrified Liverpool Street line would then be of considerable benefit to Southend travellers. The news of the electrification also made the *Essex Weekly News,* the *Essex Chronicle* and the *Southend Standard.* All three newspapers carried articles on the impending electrification.

The *Essex Weekly News* in its editorial for 2 October 1953 observed that the occasional traveller on the line would almost certainly prefer the greater speed and comfort of a steam train. It said that there was something about an electric train which did not lend itself to deep reading, comfortable feeding or quiet conversation. The *Weekly News* said that all these pleasures were possible on a steam train and indeed seemed sometimes heightened by the circumstances of locomotion. Electric trains might have been cleaner, but they rattled. They may have been lighter and airer, but they were less intimate. You can't please some people!

The *Southend Standard* of 1 October in its comments column expressed the opinion that the Southenders whose lifeline with London was the former LTSR line, long viewed with suspicion, the possibility of the extension of the electrification from Shenfield and feared that it might be used as an excuse for delaying the electrification of the LTSR line. The *Standard* went so far as to suggest that it might be a further twelve years before the LTSR line was electrified.

The *Essex Chronicle* of 2 October, whilst including details of the electrification to Southend as well as to Chelmsford slanted its article on it, rather more towards the benefits to be enjoyed, by the latter town. Both *Trains Illustrated* and the *Railway Magazine* in their issues for November 1953 carried similar information. In describing the new electric trains, they said that two carriages would have toilet accommodation and that doors would be provided for each compartment and for each bay of the open stock.

*The Times* of 13 October 1953 carried a report that the previous day, BR had announced some details of the £250,000 programme of preliminary engineering works for the proposed electrification of the LTS line.

Work on the electrification began in the summer of 1955. Before that though, there had been a strike by the footplatemen's union ASLEF between 29 May and 14 June 1955. Understandably, the strike caused disruption to travellers, but ASLEF had good reason to call the strike! Just to confuse things, not all footplatemen belonged to ASLEF. Some belonged to the NUR and chose not to strike. Some trains did run on the Southend line, but as far as can be ascertained, no services ran on the Southminster line. I was told that there was a better service of trains on the LTS line. The strike is remembered for the use of Britannia class locomotives on some Southend trains. This was not the class's first appearance on the line for at least two had worked to Southend before then. Nor was it their last.

During the electrification of the Shenfield to Southend line, a certain amount of single line working was in force at various times. Some trains were cancelled. During the morning rush hour, London trains had priority and during the evening rush hour, Southend trains were given precedence. Buses replaced trains in the opposite direction. To compensate for unbalanced locomotive workings, a couple of trains in the middle of the day were double headed. On the Southminster branch, push-pull trains were operated to reduce locomotive movements at Wickford. This brought a rather interesting selection of locomotives to the Southminster line of not only Great Eastern, but also Great Northern and Great Central origin.

**Electrifying the** railway at Billericay on a hot sunny day in 1955. (*David Collins*)

**Electrifying the** railway near Billericay in 1955. (*David Collins*)

**B12 No** 61573 double heads another member of the class over the single train line from Shenfield to Mountnessing Junction and Siding during the period of electrification of the Southend line. (*Kidderminster Railway Museum*)

**B17 No** 61611
*Raynham Hall*
double heads
another member
of the class on a
train at Wickford
during the period of
single line working
through the
station whilst the
Southend line was
being electrified.
(*Kidderminster
Railway Museum*)

According to a leaflet produced by BR on the electrification, sub-stations were built at Ramsden Bellhouse, Rayleigh and Prittlewell. Electricity was supplied to these at 33,000v DC (three phase-fifty cycles) by the Eastern Electricity Board where it was rectified and supplied to the overhead contact wires at 1,500 volts direct current. Track sectioning cabins were built at Billericay, Fanton and St Mary's. The substations and track sectioning cabins were supervisory controlled from the then existing Liverpool Street to Shenfield electric control centre at Chadwell Heath. During the electrification, nine bridges were rebuilt and two were also widened. Station platforms were lengthened. Extensive track maintenance was also carried out to bring the permanent way up to the modern standards for electric traction. The colour light signalling operated by direct current was converted to alternating current to avoid interference. Telephone lines were transferred either to cables laid in concrete troughing on the line side or where this was impractical the telephone lines were carried on concrete stakes. In open country, the structures for the overhead line equipment were erected with the aid of on-train earth boring, steel erection and concrete mixing units, which enabled the work to be performed in one visit to the site. Much time was saved in comparison to the earlier method of manual excavation and concreting. In the vicinity of Southend Airport, between Rochford and Prittlewell, the overhead structures were kept much closer together than was usual, to keep the equipment as low as possible and they were painted white in order to be spotted by low-flying aircraft. All the stations from Shenfield to Southend were cleaned. The new trains for the service were comprised of thirty-two four carriage non-corridor stock. Each unit had a mixture of compartment and open carriages. Each unit provided nineteen first class and 344 second class seats. Of the latter, 140 were in open type vehicles and 204 in compartment type vehicles. The combination of open and compartment type stock was adopted to cater for both regular business travellers and holiday visitors. Note the increase in the number of trains from twenty-three to thirty-two and the decrease in seating from 354 third to 344 second class seats. Also the decrease from 145 in third class open to 140 in second class open. There was a corresponding decrease in third class accommodation in compartment type carriages from 209 third class to 204 second class. The seating accommodation for first class passengers remained at nineteen. Third class accommodation on Britain's railways was abolished on 3 June 1956. Since by that date only a few boat trains had second class accommodation, the latter was abolished and third class renamed second. At the beginning of March 1956, the inhabitants of Southend had their first chance to see one of the new electric trains when an exhibition was held at the former LTS station at Southend Central to celebrate one hundred years of the railway to Southend. Besides having the last surviving former LTSR 4-4-2 tank locomotive *Thundersley* and a former LTSR carriage, amongst other things, on view, there were also electric multiple unit 02s for the Southend line, one of the new class EM2 Co-Co electric locomotives for the Manchester to Sheffield electrification No 27002, 0-6-0 diesel shunter No 12134, Metro-Cammell diesel multiple unit (dmu) No E79054/E79270, Standard class 4 2-6-4T No 80080, Britannia class 4-6-2 No 70038 *Robin Hood* and the A4 class 4-6-2 locomotive 60022 *Mallard* – the holder of the world speed record for a steam locomotive. On Saturday 3 March, *Thundersley* at the end of the exhibition hauled a special train from Southend Central to Liverpool Street, then a return working to Southend GE was made in a diesel multiple unit.

On 11 June 1956 the electrification from Shenfield was extended to Chelmsford and the start of it was duly mentioned in the *Essex*

*Chronicle* and the *Essex Weekly News*. During the period between then and the inauguration of end of December, some of the trains destined for the Southend service were run on the Chelmsford service to give the drivers training on them. At the same time, they would also have received training on the older electric trains built for the Shenfield electrification of 1949. As mentioned earlier, the new trains had a mixture of compartment and open accommodation for both first and second class passengers unlike the original Shenfield electrification units which only had open accommodation and no first class accommodation. The formation of the new trains was driving trailer second, trailer composite open lavatory (although the first class accommodation was in compartments with a side corridor providing access to the lavatory), non driving motor brake second and driving trailer second open lavatory.

According to the *Railway Observer* for September, 9 August 1956 saw the first visit of a diesel unit in regular passenger service to Southend (Victoria). As the normal services were unable to cope with the additional traffic because no Southend crews were available to work relief trains, Stratford despatched a two-car dmu to work non-stop between Shenfield and Southend. This working proved very popular and continued until 17 August.

Not only did the Southend line see modernisation, but also the Southminster line. On 17 September 1956 according to *The Times*, the *Manchester Guardian* and the *Essex Weekly News*, diesel trains took over the Wickford to Southminster line. According to the *Essex Weekly News* of 21 September 1956, on the previous Friday, representatives of local authorities, the press and railway officials were entertained to a lunch at Burnham after travelling on a diesel train from Wickford. G.F. Huskisson, the Eastern Region's District Passenger Manager for London, spoke of plans for the new service on the Wickford to Southminster line and praised its staff for the 'jolly good job' they were doing. Mr O.T. Bowton, the Chairman of Burnham Urban District Council, said that he hoped that the new service would be more beneficial to the residents of the area and that the diesel trains would reduce the time taken to travel to London. He asserted that the current poor service was one of the reasons why Burnham had not developed in the previous fifty years to the extent that many people hoped that it would. The *Southend Standard* of 20 September carried a similar article.

According to its report, at the lunch in Burnham, Mr Huskisson had also said that he supposed everyone felt a little sorry about steam trains going, but he could assure them that there would still be steam goods trains on the line. The driver of the special train, W. Mason, clearly preferred the diesel and wished that they had been brought in twenty years earlier. The start date for diesel services on the Southminster line has been wrongly quoted as 11 June 1956 by Dennis Swindale in *Branch Line to Southminster* (1981) and myself in *The Shenfield to Southend Line* (1984). The correct date, as mentioned earlier, is 17 September.

Diesel trains also made their first timetabled appearance on the Shenfield to Southend line, albeit only between Shenfield and Wickford. In the timetable commencing 17 September 1956, there was, on Saturday evenings, a through return working from Southminster to Shenfield. The train left Southminster at 5.22pm and called at all stations to Shenfield, which was reached at 6.20pm. In the opposite direction, the train left Shenfield at 6.36pm and called at all stations to Southminster, which was reached at 7.28pm. The working was withdrawn with the start of electric services to Southend on 31 December. According to the *Railway Observer* for

**A Derby**
Lightweight dmu at Fambridge just after the start of diesel working in September 1956. (*Frank Church/Essex Bus Enthusiasts Group*)

**Wickford station** December 1956 with B17 No 61602 *Walsingham* on a Southend train. In the Southminster branch platform are a pair of Derby Lightweight diesel multiple units. (*Brian Pask*)

October 1956, the last steam passenger train on the Southminster branch was hauled by B12 No 61569. The initial diesel service on the Southminster line was eleven trains a day between Wickford and Southminster and twelve trains in the reverse direction on Mondays to Fridays, with twelve trains between Wickford and Southminster and thirteen trains in the reverse direction on Saturdays, of which, as mentioned earlier, one in each direction ran to and from Shenfield. The Sunday service was two trains a day in each direction between Wickford and Southminster.

The first trial runs of an electric train on the Shenfield to Southend line took place on 30 November 1956 when a nine car train of three Shenfield units ran as far as Rayleigh. The first trial run of one of the Southend units took place on 3 December, but only as far as Rayleigh. The following two days trial saw runs to Wickford and then on the subsequent three days, to Rayleigh.

The first electric train reached Southend on 11 December 1956. It comprised three three-car Liverpool Street to Shenfield electric units – Nos 04, 29 and 69. The first train of Liverpool Street to Southend units reached Southend on trial on 12 December 1956. Further trial runs to Southend by the new trains occurred on 13 and 14 December.

The engine siding at Wickford and the engine shed at Southminster both closed in the early 1950s. The *Railway Observer* for November 1954 reported that Wickford engine siding had been closed. Southminster engine shed hung on a bit longer until the end of steam on the branch and perhaps a short while beyond, but by February 1958, the turntable had been abandoned and the shed was in a rather parlous state and only suitable for demolition.

According to the *Railway Observer* for February 1957, the final weeks of steam services proved to be of interest. From 20 December 1956, Southend locomotive shed ceased to have a permanent allocation of locomotives and replacements from various other sheds were drafted in. The only engines remaining at the shed were the engines used on the three daily goods turns.

On 28 December 1956, the formal opening of the electrification to Southend took place. According to *The Times*, the *Manchester Guardian* and the *Essex Weekly News*, the ceremonies started at Liverpool Street station just after 9am when a steam train from Southend (that had disgorged its passengers who were mainly workers in London), returned to Southend with special guests for the opening of the electrification. At various points along the journey, the train picked up railway officials, mayors, councillors and other people of relevant importance including the press. The journey to Southend took ninety minutes. In the late afternoon when the formalities at Southend had been completed the party, including the Mayor of Southend returned to London in one of the new electric trains comprised of units 15s and 16s. The *Manchester Guardian* of 29 December 1956 reported that under the new timetable the fastest train from Southend would take fifty-five minutes compared with sixty-eight minutes taken by the fastest steam train and that stopping trains would be considerably speeded up. The newspaper said that the Liverpool Street line had always been something of a Cinderella and that City workers (who lived in Southend, using the rival Fenchurch Street) had for many years gloated that their lot at least was not so grim. Henceforth, things were to be reversed. The Fenchurch Street line was getting into the throes of being electrified itself. In many compartments on the line, commuters could be seen furtively studying the new timetable for the rival line to see if it was worth them changing their allegiance. The *Manchester Guardian* concluded that unfortunately, the peculiar geography of Southend (not to mention the bus services) would thwart most of them and that the officers of the Southend Railway Travellers Association would be busier than ever. The account in the *Essex Weekly News* differs from that in *The Times* and the *Manchester Guardian*, in that it states that the electric train from Southend proceeded only to Shenfield where the train returned to Southend. Motorman John McEnanie of Newington Avenue, Southend, was the driver, but the Mayor of Southend Alderman H.H. Smith JP took over the controls at the end of the journey and drove the train into Southend (Victoria) station. The *Essex Weekly News* for 4 January 1957 said that the new service provided for 119 electric trains a day on Mondays to Fridays compared with the previous service of sixty-four steam trains. The figures for Saturdays were 106 electric trains compared with fifty-six steam trains. Figures for Sundays were not given. However, from a study of the last steam timetable and the first electric timetable, there were forty-three electric trains compared with thirty-one steam trains. Steps to be taken, in connection with bus services to meet the new electric train services were contained in a report issued by the Southend Transport Co-Ordination Committee. It was felt that the existing services were more than adequate to deal with any build-up of traffic at Southend (Victoria) station. It was not anticipated that the electrification would greatly increase the traffic from Prittlewell station and there would be no need to increase or modify the existing services. Some traffic build-up could be anticipated at Rayleigh station and it was understood that holders of season tickets from Leigh could use Rayleigh. The *Southend Standard* of 27 December 1956 had an article on the forthcoming electric service. The *Standard* for 3 January 1957 carried an article on the inauguration of the electric service on 28 December. Whilst the *Southend Standard* was full of praise, the new service did have its teething problems. On Tuesday 1 January, the 6.02am from Southend to Liverpool Street was terminated at Rochford due to brake trouble, the following train about twenty minutes later was packed and many passengers were left on the platforms. British Railways put on an additional train from Wickford to ease the situation, but the 6.48am train from Shenfield to Liverpool Street, the 7.36am train from Liverpool Street to Southend and the 7.38am train from Liverpool Street to Gidea Park had to be cancelled. Reading between the lines, one surmises that the train to form the 6.48am from Shenfield to Liverpool Street and the 7.38am from Liverpool Street to Gidea

Park was used to form the additional train from Wickford. One would deduce that it was formed of the original Shenfield stock of 1949. There were complaints in the *Southend Standard* about the new service being overcrowded and the off peak service being too slow. There were also complaints regarding places such as Rochford and Prittlewell not being served by the off-peak fast trains. *The Times* of 1 January 1957 reported that the introduction of electric services went well.

The *Southend Standard's* edition of 27 December, in addition to having an article on the forthcoming electric service, also had an article which said that there were hopes that a new station would be built to serve Southend Airport. According to the article, plans were being discussed for the construction of a new airport terminal which would include a railway station. The article said that the rapid development of the airport was such that the present terminal which had been opened in October 1955, was already inadequate to deal with the flood of passengers to and from the continent. There was insufficient waiting room for passengers, which had been particularly evident over the Christmas of 1956, when British European Airways had used Southend Airport as a diversionary airport. The report concluded by saying that no proposals had been placed before Southend Council, although discussions had been held with BR, concerning the possibility of a combined rail-air terminal building.

On the last full day of steam working, the last steam train into Southend was hauled by B12 class locomotive no 61553. On the final day of steam working, most of the up workings were operated by steam trains and on their arrival at Liverpool Street an electric train was despatched for the return working. The drivers of all the electric trains were accompanied by an instructor for back-up because although they had been trained on the trains earlier in the year (on the Chelmsford service) for some months, not all had received refresher courses. The first public train from Liverpool Street to Southend was worked by units 02s and 04s departing at 11.15am. According to the *Railway Observer*, the honour of making the final steam run fell to B1 class locomotive No 61335 with the 8.50pm service to Liverpool Street.

The sound recordist Peter Handford made a couple of recordings of steam trains on the Southend line near Billericay before electrification, one of a B12 and one of a B17. BR made a film of the electrification of the Southend line called *Service to Southend*.

**B1 No** 61335 at Southend on the last day of steam working. (*Brian Pask*)

However, two small parts of it were filmed on the former LTSR line! These were not the only misleading shots in the film. The film includes what is purported to be the last steam train from Liverpool Street to Southend. Whilst the engine of the train is B12 No 61553, the whole thing is shot in daylight whereas in fact the last steam run was completed in darkness – to be precise 12.15am on the morning of 30 December 1956. For railway purposes this was regarded as Saturday. The film also shows the official inaugural electric train from Southend, mostly taken of (or from) its interior, including passing, on arrival at Shenfield what the narrator claims is the last steam train from Liverpool Street to Southend, which is not necessarily the train shown earlier in the film. As mentioned, the official inaugural electric train ran on 28 December over a day before the last scheduled steam train ran from Liverpool to Southend. The film commentary even implies that the electrification is for the whole route and not merely an extension from Shenfield. This was a bit of a case of not how it was, but how BR wanted to show it.

*Trains Illustrated* for February 1957, *Railway World* for February 1957 and the *Railway Magazine* for March 1957 all had articles on the Shenfield to Southend electrification. In addition, *Railway World* had an article by R.C. Riley on 'Steam to Southend (Victoria)', the

*Railway Magazine* also had an article on the history of the New Essex Lines by B.D.J. Walsh, who was an expert on the history of the Great Eastern Railway. *Trains Illustrated* for March 1957 included in the section 'Motive Power Miscellany', a brief summary of the journey of the last regular steam hauled train from Southend (Victoria) to Liverpool Street. In 1982, in the February issue of *Railway World,* an article was published on the latter days of the steam services to Southend (Victoria) by I.R. Stewart.

The first timetable of the electric service had a Mondays to Saturdays off-peak service of three trains per hour between Liverpool Street and Southend (Victoria) and vice versa. Two of these called at Stratford, Ilford, Romford and all stations to Southend whilst the other called at Shenfield then all stations to Hockley, then Southend. The Sunday service comprised just one train an hour calling at Stratford, Ilford, Romford and all stations to Southend and vice versa. Note the change from the original proposed service of one through train per hour in each direction between Liverpool Street and Southend with an hourly shuttle service in each direction between Shenfield and Southend. The timetable also included a through train from Stratford to Southminster on Sundays. There was however no return working. The summer timetable commencing 17 June 1957 had, on Sundays, one through train from Stratford to Southminster, one through train from Liverpool Street to Southminster and two through trains from Southminster to Liverpool Street.

The significance of the electrification to Southend and the cause of all the fuss, was that, with all due respect to Chelmsford, Southend was the first major town north of the Thames to receive electric trains. Further, unlike the extension of the electrification to Chelmsford which used existing electric trains, the Southend service had new trains built for it. A major effect of the electrification was an increase in the number of season tickets. The only station for which I have seen information on is Billericay. According to Ken Butcher, writing in *Great Eastern Journal* No 127 (July 2006), at Billericay these increased from 6,400 in 1955 to 14,000 in 1957 and 34,000 in 1962.

The contracts for equipment for the electrification of the LTS line were let on 16 January 1957 according to *The Times* of 17 January 1957.

The new electric trains took traffic away from the former City Coach Company route from North London to Southend. The new electric

**A class** 307 electric multiple unit leaving Billericay for London in 1957. (*David Collins*)

**Wickford in** June 1958 with a pair of class 307 emus on a Southend train and a Wickham dmu on a Southminster train. The very model of a modern railway in 1958. (*Ken Nunn*)

trains were an improvement not only on the existing steam trains but even on the new buses that had been put on the route by Eastern National. The electrification of the railway also benefited from petrol rationing which had been introduced in December 1956 as a result of the Suez Crisis and which meant that not only was private motoring restricted, but also some bus services had to be reduced.

Here are some figures which relate to both the Chelmsford and the Southend lines. In the last year of steam working 2.6 million ordinary passengers were carried between Shenfield and Southend and Chelmsford. In the first year of electrification, these rose to 5.4 million and in the second year to 5.9 million. Because of even greater increases in the number of season ticket holders, receipts rose by 117 per cent in the first year of electric working whilst operating costs fell. An unfortunate effect was an increase in house prices in the area served by the lines, which started to put houses out of the reach of the indigenous population. In the rush hour, the fastest down trains accomplished the run from Liverpool Street to Southend in fifty-six minutes and the fastest up trains in fifty-five minutes, while the hourly fast off-peak trains accomplished the journey in each direction in one hour. According to the summer timetable for 1957, not all of the trains were worked by the new electric stock specially built for the service. Some of the trains were worked by the old trains built for the Shenfield electrification of 1949. Apart from the earlier mentioned Sunday through workings from Liverpool Street and Stratford and Southminster and return workings there was in addition a Sundays only through train from Southend to Chelmsford. This latter service however did not last very long though and ceased in 1958.

At this time, there was a possibility, but no more, of long-distance passenger trains from Manchester and the North running through to Southend (Victoria). The same edition of the *Southend Standard* which mentioned the problems with the service on 2 January 1957 also mentioned that the idea of a car rail-air link to the continent was being discussed in railway and civil airline circles. The idea was that through trains conveying motorists and their cars would run from, say, Manchester or Newcastle to Southend (Victoria). At Southend, the motorists would then drive their cars to Southend Airport where they would put their vehicles on to passenger/vehicle carrying aircraft and fly to the Continent. The air service had been started in 1954 by Freddie Laker under the name of Channel Air Bridge. The newspaper said that the introduction of petrol rationing had given an impetus to the idea. However, nothing came of it.

The impact of both the new electric trains on the Southend line and the new diesel trains on the Southminster line on the travelling public was positive. The new trains on both lines were clean, unlike the steam trains that they replaced. One would have had to be extremely sentimental to not appreciate the new trains.

One very noticeable effect of the electrification to Southend was an upsurge in the urbanisation of towns served, some of which still retained some of their country character. It also turned neighbouring villages of these towns into suburbs of them and as mentioned caused an increase in property prices in the former villages. This came about because those at the higher end of the income scale moved into the former villages, often buying up property and redeveloping it, thereby putting any subsequent purchase beyond the reach of local people. Regrettably, they were often put in the position of having to move into the larger towns. Whilst some of the newcomers did have an interest in the community into which they moved, many did not, merely regarding these places as dormitories. However, even some who may have wanted to contribute to the life of their communities, were prevented from doing so because the time that they spent in travel plus the time that they spent in work meant that they were away from their community for a very large portion of time and had no incentive to take part in community life. Most of the day their 'community life' revolved around work, and it was only when these people retired (deciding to stay in the community) that they were able to take any part in it.

The increase in the population of towns on the Southend line following electrification may be judged from the following table showing populations of five towns from 1951 through 1961 to 1971. Apart from Hockley, which suffered a slight decline between 1951 and 1961, the natural trend was upwards, even if the increase at Rochford in 20 years was more modest.

|            | 1951 | 1961  | 1971  |
|------------|------|-------|-------|
| Billericay | 6949 | 10940 | 17246 |
| Wickford   | 7250 | 11270 | 15787 |
| Rayleigh   | 8500 | 19032 | 26740 |
| Hockley    | 3553 | 3462  | 7790  |
| Rochford   | 5188 | 6049  | 7509  |

Whilst some part of the increase can be put down to London overspill development, in Billericay for example, most of the increase can be directly attributed to electrification.

The effects on the population of the three major centres on the Southminster line following the introduction of diesel traction were:

|                     | 1951 | 1961 | 1971 |
|---------------------|------|------|------|
| Woodham Ferrers     | 2303 | 2015 | 2215 |
| Burnham-on-Crouch   | 3416 | 4167 | 4920 |
| Southminster        | 1403 | 1444 | 3241 |

The effects on the population of the three major centres on the Southminster line following the introduction of diesel traction were quite pronounced except at Woodham Ferrers which showed a slight unexplained decrease.

As mentioned earlier, the introduction of electric traction on passenger services did not mean the complete end of steam services. For a while, goods and parcels services as well as summer Sunday through trains from Enfield and Chingford and excursions beyond the line were for a time worked by steam locomotives.

A train double headed by an L1 and a B1 leaving Southend on a return excursion in 1957. (*Brian Pask*)

Nor did it bring the end of scheduled locomotive haulage of passenger trains. Some of the through Sunday Southminster trains are known to have been steam-hauled even up to 1957. BR Standard class 4 2-6-0s are known to have been one class used, according to Brian Pask. Later BR Brush Type 2 (later class 31) diesel locomotives were used. According to *Trains Illustrated* for August 1958, Brush Type 2 diesels worked the Sunday through service to Southminster as well as summer Sundays through trains from Enfield and Chingford. For many years, when engineering work was being undertaken on all or part of the Southend line which necessitated switching the electric current off over the section on which the work was being undertaken but without closing the line to rail traffic, diesel trains were used over the affected section, substituting for the electric trains. So far as the author is aware, this practice continued at least into the 1970s. However, such flexibility ceased in the mid-1980s, when Stratford depot ceased to have an allocation of diesel multiple units. They were superfluous following the electrification of the Stratford to North Woolwich line in May 1985 and the Romford to Upminster and Wickford to Southminster lines in May 1986.

Following the electrification the fastest off-peak trains were taking an hour in each direction, whilst the fastest trains in the peak hours were taking fifty-seven minutes from Liverpool Street to Southend and fifty-five minutes from Southend to Liverpool Street. At last, the times of 1914 were being equalled and even bettered, although one has to say that non-corridor electric trains, some of whose carriages had individual compartments, were not the same as the best trains of the period before and after the First World War, which boasted corridors and refreshment facilities.

As mentioned previously, on 3 January 1957, the section of line from Maldon East to Maldon West was reopened for goods traffic only to close again on 31 January 1959. On 6 April 1957, the excursion organised by the Railway Enthusiasts Club visited Maldon. There is some conflict as to when the track (other than a short section at Maldon East) was lifted. According to the late Bernard Walsh, it was later in 1959, whilst the late Dennis Swindale in *Branch Lines to Maldon* says that it was mid-1960. As Dennis lived in Maldon, the mid 1960 date is plausible. The lattice span of the bridge over the River Blackwater was removed in 1965 according to the British Railways Bridge Register. However according to Geoff Baker writing in the *Great Eastern Journal* in 1978, it was removed in 1964.

On the evening of Friday 5 September 1958, violent thunderstorms accompanied by torrential rain, swept over southern England. The former LTS line received quite a bit of damage on the direct line from Barking to Pitsea via Upminster, the old line from Barking to Pitsea via Tilbury and the line from Upminster to Grays. Communication was lost between Southend Central and Fenchurch Street. The GE line was less affected, but there were times when trains to and from Liverpool Street could not get through owing to flooding in the cutting on Brentwood Bank. For a time, a replacement bus service was put on between Gidea Park and Shenfield. The up electric line was cleared by 12.30am and the down main by 12.45am. The down electric and the up main were cleared by 6.30am. Those trying to get home that evening had a very long journey and it must be remembered at this time most people in London had to work on Saturday mornings.

Additional traffic was generated for the Southminster line following the decision of the government to build an atomic power station at Bradwell-on-Sea. Work started in 1957 and was completed in early 1961. The first reactor became critical in August 1961 and was put on load in July 1962. The second reactor became critical in April 1962 and was put on load in November 1962. Fuel for the power station was conveyed to and from Southminster by rail in a sealed flask and thence by road to the power station.

**Maldon West** with J67 No 68628 on the occasion of the enthusiasts special to the station in 1957. (*R.C. Riley/ Transport Treasury*)

When the power station opened, there was a special train for the guests at the ceremony, which was hauled by two Brush Type 2 diesel locomotives from Liverpool Street.

Following a decision by BR that all future overhead electrification would be 25,000 volts alternating current, the lines out of Liverpool Street using 1,500 volts direct current were converted to the new system. However, because of concerns regarding clearance with bridges, it was decided that whilst the main line beyond Shenfield would be converted to the 25,000 volts, the lines from Southend to Shenfield and thence to Liverpool Street would be converted to 6,250 volts alternating current This meant that all electric trains had to be dual voltage. The existing electric trains were also converted to alternating current. Work first commenced on converting the original Shenfield three-car stock. This involved retaining the original motors and direct current control gear in the motor coach and moving the guard's compartment and pantograph to the intermediate trailer which was fitted with a transformer and rectifier fed by 1,500 volts direct current. On the Southend four-car stock the pantograph and luggage compartment was moved to the driving trailer second as the trailer composite open lavatory or the driving trailer second open lavatory were unsuitable vehicles. Some re-marshalling of each set was involved so, that the formation was driving trailer-brake second-non driving motor-second-trailer composite (open in second and side gangway in first)-driving trailer open second. Only one unit No 03s was converted before the changeover was made. Meanwhile 112 four car units built to a similar design to the four-car direct current units but built for alternating current were delivered from 1958 to 1960. These were ultimately intended for the LTS line electrification, but in the meantime some of these were used on the section of line from Colchester to Thorpe-le-Soken, Clacton and Walton-on-the-Naze, which was electrified at alternating current, whilst some of the others were used to cover for the original Southend direct current electric units whilst they were being converted to alternating current. There was, however, a suggestion, that rather than convert the Southend four car direct current units to alternating current they should be sent north and used to provide a limited stop service on the former Great Central line between Manchester and Sheffield which had been electrified at 1,500 volts direct current in 1954. However nothing came of this.

For the start of the alternating current services on both the Shenfield local and Southend lines ten trains of Shenfield units plus forty-two trains of four-car LTS line stock were needed. The change-over took place over from 4 to 6 November 1960. Before the change from direct current to alternating current, electric multiple units built for alternating current were taken to Southend. The trains were hauled by steam locomotives of class L1 (which were fitted with air brakes) following a runaway and collision with a direct current electric train at Wickford by a train of the new stock hauled by a vacuum braked diesel locomotive on 1 November. The direct current electric train was standing in Wickford station for ten minutes because of a derailment at Hockley earlier in the day, when it was decided to cancel the service. A porter stated that he could see the train coming and shouted at people on the platform to get back. The diesel engine was braking hard with smoke coming from the wheels. Passengers were told over the loudspeaker to get out of the train, but only those at the back did and were not injured in the collision. The rear carriage of the stationary train was telescoped into the next carriage and lifted three feet above the platform. The injured were in the front of the train. According to *The Times*, ten people were taken to St Andrew's Hospital in Billericay and two were detained with shock and abrasions. The *Guardian* says that eight people were injured. The *Southend Standard* of 3 November 1960 said that eight people were slightly injured.

The same edition of the newspaper contained information about the change from direct current to alternating current. Before the change of current on both Shenfield and the Southend lines the disposition of alternating current electric trains was supposed to be: ten nine-car sets of converted Shenfield three-car units at Ilford of which nine sets were for service and one set was spare; nineteen eight-car sets made up of LTS line four-car units at Ilford of which fourteen sets were for service and five sets were spare; nineteen eight-car sets of LTS line four-car units at Southend which were all for service; one eight-car set of LTS line four-car units at Wickford which was spare; one eight-car set of LTS line four-car units at Rayleigh which was spare; one eight-car set of LTS line four- car units at Shenfield for trial running; and one eight-car set of LTS line four-car units at Liverpool Street for trial running.

On the evening of 4 November, electric current was switched off between Shenfield and Southend at 8pm. Between 8pm and approximately 11pm a service of diesel trains was in operation between Shenfield and Southend after which time a replacement service of buses was operated. For a few hours on 5 November, it was possible to see direct current and alternating current electric trains at Shenfield and to travel in both directions between Liverpool Street and Southend and vice versa (with a change at Shenfield) in trains of two types of electric current. During the night, the power supply for the Shenfield to Southend line was changed from direct current to alternating current and a service of alternating current electric trains was run from Platform 1. Direct current between Shenfield and Liverpool Street was finally switched off at 4pm on 5 November and between then and approximately 9am on 6 November a service of diesel trains were operated in lieu of the electric trains, whence electric trains took their place. With a few exceptions, cheap facilities tickets were withdrawn in the affected area on 5 and 6 November. On the days in question, a restricted freight service was operated and on 5 November some use of road traffic (and the former LTS line) was made for the conveyance of newspapers, parcels and fish. Road traffic was also used for the conveyance of parcels between Liverpool Street and Stratford on 6 November. Whilst passengers were allowed to use the former LTS line on 4 and 5 November as an alternative route, because of engineering works on the line on 6 November, this was rarely permitted and then only after prior consultation between Liverpool Street and Fenchurch Street control. As mentioned earlier, whilst some direct current electric trains had been converted for alternating current not all were so equipped. The conversion of all the direct current electric stock to alternating current took some years. In the meantime (beside some of the four- car alternating current stock built for the former LTS line mentioned earlier) some four -car electric multiple units were borrowed from the London Midland Region and used on the line. Most of the direct current electric stock used on the Southend line was taken to Ilford except for three trains of eight carriages which were taken to Goodmayes. The trusty L1 locomotives were used to haul the trains from Southend.

The Times of 7 November 1960 reported that the conversion was progressing according to plan and that it was expected that morning's peak service would operate satisfactorily. The Southend Standard of 10 November 1960 reported that the operation had been carried out without a hitch. A writer to the newspaper complained that cheap day fares had been withdrawn for the period of the change-over operation. Whilst the withdrawal of cheap day fares during the period of the change-over is mentioned in a staff notice dated 18 October 1960, it was not mentioned in the information on the change-over in the *Southend Standard* of 3 November.

November 1960 also saw the inauguration of the North East London suburban electrification. On 6 November 1961, the LTS line electrification was completed and the first electric trains started running. The full electric service came into operation on 18 June 1962.

On the section of main line between Shenfield and Chelmsford, the conversion from direct current to alternating current at 25,000 volts took place between 12 September 1960 and 20 March 1961. During that time, a shuttle service of diesel trains replaced the electric trains between the two towns.

Steam traction was being replaced by diesel traction on goods, parcels and non-electric excursion trains. Southend shed lingered on until the end of steam working. Latterly it was used to store withdrawn engines, including the last B17, Sandringham Class No 61668 *Bradford City*. The facilities were used until the end. The turntable at Southend was relocated to Doncaster in 1960.

What is believed to have been the final steam working on the New Essex Lines took place on 29 August 1961 when class B1 engine No. 61156 worked a ballast train from Burnham on the Southminster branch. It is thought that the last steam working out of Southend (Victoria) took place on 18 May 1961 when class L1 engine No 67729 worked a parcels train into and out of Southend. The last steam working from Southminster was on 26 August 1960 when class J20 engine No 64699 worked a goods train over the line. Apart from a few workings out of March depot in Cambridgeshire, steam on the former GE lines ceased on Sunday 9 September 1962.

Going back to the accident at Wickford in November 1960, it was not the only accident to befall the line that month. On 17 November a twin-engined Swedish freight aircraft overshot the runway at Southend airport and came to a halt near the railway after ploughing through the grass. No-one was hurt fortunately. This was not the only accident at the airport involving the railway. On 9 October that year, a four-engined British passenger aircraft carrying seventy-six people, failed to stop at the end of the runway after landing and after crashing through a barrier, finished with its tail high in the air and its nose lying across the railway. Five passengers and two of the crew were taken to hospital. A similar accident occurred on 13 August 1957, when a British car carrying aircraft, with ten passengers and crew of three, crashed through the safety barrier onto the railway. But no one was hurt other than a woman receiving bruising to one of her legs. On 4 May 1968, a British aircraft carrying eighty-three people crashed through the safety barrier onto the railway injuring ten. Just to complete the saga, on 24 September 1969, the blast of a jet aircraft taking off from Southend airport set off the trip mechanism which cut off power to the railway. Three trains to London had to be cancelled.

In the early 1960s, Althorne appeared in a cinema feature on Dorothy Palmer, who was one of two staff at the station. The film described Dorothy as Althorne's station mistress, although in fact she was also the porter, the signalwoman and everything else at the station.

According to I.R. Stewart writing in the *Railway Magazine* in October 1974, until 1960, Billericay station was a place full of character and characters. Whilst the passenger services may have been electrified, the station had not been modernised and still retained gas lighting and a very old-fashioned ticket office. According to him, it was the 'only fairly original station left on the Southend line'. In 1960, everything altered and the station was modernised – to Mr Stewart's disgust.

In the latter part of 1961, the single line connection from Shenfield to Mountnessing Junction, which had been signalled only for down trains, was re-signalled for working in both directions.

The Wickford to Southminster line was the subject of an article by Roma Branton in the *British Railways Magazine (Eastern Region)* for October 1961. The same edition of the magazine also included an article by her on Dorothy Palmer. According to Roma's article, Dorothy, who had been at Althorne for 20 years, was 'Porter, Signalwoman, The Lot'. The Southend line had to wait until the edition of March 1963 before an article by Roma Branton on it appeared in the magazine.

Until the 1962 summer timetable, there were still summer Sunday services from Enfield and Chingford to Southend, but these ceased after that. 1963 saw the end of Southend services not stopping at certain stations on the line.

The winter of 1962-63 was one of the worst on record. I am not aware of any incidents involving the New Essex Lines.

On 5 December 1964 there was a fire at Bishopsgate goods depot in London, which for a time meant that trains could not run into Liverpool Street. Until it was safe for trains to run into Liverpool Street some trains from Southend ran into Fenchurch Street station.

In 1963 the Beeching Report was published. Dr Richard Beeching was the Chairman of BR and produced two reports. One was on the reshaping of British Railways and the other was on the development of major trunk routes. It was the first which was the most notorious and the most damaging for this country. This recommended the closure of a lot of lines and goods yards. Whilst the Southend and Southminster lines were not included in the list of lines to be closed the Witham to Maldon line was. Even without the benefit of hindsight, the inhabitants of Maldon protested, but to no avail and the line was closed to passengers on 6 September 1964 and to goods on 15 April 1966. The track however remained in situ until 1969, except for a short bit at Witham which was used by a private company and lasted into 1982. Some of the sidings at Witham lasted into the early 1990s. The removal of track at Maldon, also saw the remains of the branch to Woodham Ferrers removed, which by then had been reduced to a long siding.

Ramsden Bellhouse siding had closed to public traffic on 22 August 1960, but remained in use for engineering traffic until 1983. Althorne, on the Southminster line, had closed to goods traffic on 19 December 1960. Shenfield had closed to goods traffic on 4 May 1964. On 9 August 1964 Mountnessing Siding had closed to all traffic except for oil traffic which continued to be handled until the mid-1970s. On the Southminster line, Battlesbridge, Woodham Ferrers, Fambridge and Burnham all closed to goods on 4 October 1965 except for some private sidings at Battlesbridge, which were closed a little later. Southminster also closed to general traffic on that date, but remained open for sand trains and traffic to the atomic power station at Bradwell. Also closed were the goods only passing loops at Battlesbridge on 7 December 1966 and Althorne on 21 January 1967. The passenger and goods passing loops together with the signal boxes at Woodham Ferrers and Burnham-on-Crouch closed on 21 January 1967. The private siding on the alignment of the curve from the former Belchamps Junction on the Southminster line to Fanton Junction on the Southend line closed to traffic on 26 February 1969.

All the remaining goods yards were closed on 5 June 1967, except for Southend. This stayed open for coal traffic which lasted until the 1980s and last appeared in the 1983 working timetable The fact that the closure of the goods yards along with the closure of the Maldon line would, and undoubtedly did, put extra traffic on the roads, obviously hadn't occurred to those behind the Beeching Report. Whilst the report reflected Beeching's thinking, there were also officials who had input into the report.

**Notice announcing** the proposal to close Ramsden Bellhouse public siding. (*Frank Church/ Essex Bus Enthusiasts Group*)

BRITISH RAILWAYS

# PROPOSED WITHDRAWAL OF FREIGHT TRAIN SERVICE

# RAMSDEN BELLHOUSE SIDING (PUBLIC)

The Eastern Region of British Railways announce that, because of the loss being incurred, they are shortly submitting proposals to the East Anglian Area Transport Users' Consultative Committee to withdraw the freight train service from Ramsden Bellhouse Siding (Public). Freight traffic in full wagon loads will still be dealt with at Billericay and Wickford stations

Persons who wish to make representations to the Consultative Committee should inform the Secretary, Mr. F. E. Tyler, 33 Station Road, Cambridge, in writing as soon as possible, setting out particulars of the grounds of such representations

Further information may be obtained from Mr. H. W. Few, Traffic Manager (Liverpool St.), British Railways, Eastern Region, Hamilton House, 155 Bishopsgate, London E.C.2

The fact that the Southminster line was not included in the Beeching Report did not mean that it was not felt that the line was not under threat of closure. At the time of the goods yards closures on the

Southminster line, the last passenger train of the day (10.10pm from Wickford ) was also withdrawn, which meant that the last connecting train from Liverpool Street left at 8.24pm. That was assuming that no problems arose between Liverpool Street and Wickford, which could happen. This was not exactly a way to encourage use of the line. Passengers felt that this was the beginning of the end. BR did nothing to discourage this feeling. This wasn't helped by a piece of bad publicity when it described Burnham as Burnham-on-Sea (!) rather than Burnham-on-Crouch. In the early 1960s, BR was looking at automatic train operation as a way of considerably reducing the cost of railway operation and an investigation into the automatic operation of the Wickford to Southminster branch was conducted by the British Railways Research Division (Electrical Research Division). The report of the investigation was produced by H.I. Andrews and H.H. Ogilvy and was dated 14 April 1964.

The authors of the report said that automatic train operation had reached the stage where a full scale trial was possible. The trial was to be confined to a self-contained branch line within easy reach of London, so that the experiment could be observed from BR's headquarters. The Wickford to Southminster branch met the criteria, mainly because it had a heavy commuting traffic in the mornings and evenings, particularly at weekends in summer owing to the yachting fraternity. At Burnham there was seaside and yachting traffic. The line was also used for staff training. It had a good deal of residential traffic, particularly at Burnham, whilst there was also the flask traffic for Bradwell nuclear power station.

The report said that the line was worked by one double motor coach and trailer (three-car dmu) and one motor coach and trailer (two-car dmu) as well as three daily goods trains on the line. There were six signal boxes, two attended level crossings and forty-one unattended level crossings. It was proposed to operate the line using two two-car battery electric units. The electrical system proposed, would be a semi-conductor system on the lines that were being introduced in West Germany, and would give a power saving of twenty per cent over the existing battery electric system that was being used by battery electric railcars on the Scottish Region. It would eliminate major items of maintenance cost, for instance brake block changing and contact cleaning. The units' batteries would be charged from short lengths of live rail at Wickford and Southminster to which contact would be made when the train was stationary. The live rails would be supplied by hundred kilowatt electricity from the national system through a transformer energising at 500 volts alternating current. This would give the railcars a wider range of operation with a smaller battery, though the bulk of the power would be drawn at night when cheap rate electricity was available.

All trains would be operated by automatic control through a continuous induction system actuated by two insulated wires along the centre of the track. Trains would be started by a push button actuated by the guard at the head of the train who would also stop the train in an emergency. The trains would be staffed by a guard, who besides starting the train and stopping it in an emergency would also be required to keep a look out at all times, and a travelling ticket clerk. It was intended to close all ticket offices and make all stations on the branch unstaffed halts except for Southminster, where there would be a small number of staff to maintain both trains. Headlights of the American pattern would be provided on both trains. The three daily goods trains would continue to be operated by diesel locomotives and the appropriate eight locomotives would be fitted with an indicating device actuated from the track system advising the driver to proceed. On entering the branch, a small indicating device would be attached to the last vehicle of the train together with the tail lamp.

All signal boxes would be eliminated and the passing loops at Woodham Ferrers and Burnham would be closed with only the passing loop at North Fambridge retained. The existing signal boxes would be reduced to ground frame status, used by pick up goods trains only and operated by the guard. Althorne and Woodham Ferrers level crossings were to be converted to the boom type and be automatically operated.

All stations on the branch were to be reduced to unstaffed halts exept the afore-mentioned Southminster. Here a skeleton staff was to be retained to deal with train maintenance, train cleaning, parcels, goods and general enquiries. Assistance to passengers on trains would be dealt with directly by the train crew.

According to the report the savings would be as follows:

| | |
|---|---|
| Savings in train crew | £0 |
| Savings in station and terminal signalling staff expense | £19,255 |
| Savings in train operating costs | £2,419 |
| Savings in signalling costs including maintenance, renewal and interest | £6,000 |
| Total savings | £27,674 |

As far as I know nothing, came of the report. Obviously it was considered but in the end I suspect that the savings made were not justifiable.

On the Southend line in the early 1960s, most of the platforms were lengthened to take twelve carriage trains. However there was deterioration in service from the end of 1965 when Southend lost its fast off-peak service which it would not regain until the early 1990s.

Around this time there were a number of derailments on the Southminster line. On 9 August 1967, seven sand wagons left the track at Althorne station, partly demolishing the platform and covering it ankle-deep in sand. Repairs to the line took four days and during that time a special bus service was put on for Althorne, Burnham and Southminster passengers. On 30 September 1968 three sand wagons and a guards van left the track at Battlesbridge ripping up eighty yards of line. The mishap caused the guard to break his collarbone. Until the line was repaired, a replacement road service of six buses and a taxi was laid on.

This was not the only derailment on the Southminster line. On 25 February 1965, the 10.18am from Liverpool Street to Southend formed of eight carriages (units No 158 and 221) became derailed at Wickford owing to the facing points for the Southminster

**Southend (Victoria)** station in 1970 with a Liverpool Street train awaiting departure headed by rebuilt class 307 emu No 107. *(R.F. Roberts/SLS Collection)*

line being moved under the seventh coach. Two people, both passengers, suffered minor injuries. The cause of the accident was the signalman needlessly manipulating the lever as the train passed over the points while demonstrating a fault in the electric locking system to a visiting technician. The Southminster branch was closed until 12.05pm the next day. The main line was available for non-electric trains from 6.30am the next day and electric trains from 4.45pm the next day.

In late 1967, British Railways announced that they were going to carry out demolition at stations on the Southminster line to cut costs. This happened in the spring of 1968 when many of the perfectly adequate Victorian buildings were taken down and replaced with something wholly inappropriate. Battlesbridge suffered more than the others. Dennis Swindale in *Branch Line to Southminster* described the transformation from a charming country station to a dismally basic halt. He says that with the destruction of most of the buildings, the old GER image of the line vanished.

The rationalisation was also accompanied in late 1967, by the full closure of some station ticket offices and the partial closure of other stations' ticket offices. Accompanying this was the introduction of conductor-guard working on the line.

At Burnham-on-Crouch the women's waiting room on the down platform was taken over by the British Transport Yacht Club to the disadvantage of women travellers.

On 20 February 1969, Southend-on-Sea (Victoria) was renamed Southend (Victoria).

At Maldon West, the booking office building was demolished in 1969; apparently because of complaints about its condition.

In early January 1969, a storm of protest on the Southminster line was unleashed when BR announced that there would be no more Sunday trains. According to the *Railway Magazine* for February 1969 this took place on 12 January. Understandably, the inhabitants of the area served by the line were not very happy with the Sunday closure. This seemed another subtle step towards the closure of the Southminster line. To give an example from elsewhere in the east of England, the line from Cambridge to Oxford via Bedford and Bletchley was not included in the Beeching Report, but BR had withdrawn all services from the Cambridge to Bedford section and passenger services from the Bletchley to Oxford section. Had the Southminster line closed to passenger traffic at this time it would have had to remain open for sand traffic and nuclear flask traffic.

It would have become something like the lines to Dungeness in Kent and Leiston in Suffolk which served Dungeness and Sizewell power stations respectively. Everyone took part in the battle to restore the Sunday trains: members of Parliament; local residents; local councils; residents' associations; season ticket holders; rail users' associations; hoteliers and licensees, but to no avail. BR's response was that the income from the Sunday trains did not cover the cost of running them.

From 17 May 1970, Eastern National started a Sunday bus service (Route 91) from Burnham to Wickford via Southminster, Althorne, North Fambridge, Cold Norton, Stow Maries, Woodham Ferrers, Rettendon and Runwell. There were two buses per day in each direction. One in the morning at 8.30am from Burnham returning from Wickford at 10am and one in the evening from Burnham at 6.30pm returning from Wickford at 8pm. In January 1971, an application was made to run the service throughout the year, but in June 1971 an application was made to withdraw the service. An application was then made by City Coach Lines of London W1 to continue the service. The application was made on behalf of Southend Corporation Transport as the service was operated outside of the Southend Corporation Transport/Eastern National co-ordination area. The service was run by Southend Transport on hire to City Coach Lines, but it proved un-remunerative. Several reasons could be put forward for this. The bus service provided only two buses a day in each direction as opposed to a Sunday service of eight trains in each direction between Wickford and Southminster plus two additional trains in each direction between Wickford and Burnham. There were no through fares to the railway network. The journey took sixty-nine minutes in each direction between Burnham and Wickford and fifty-eight minutes in each direction between Southminster and Wickford, as opposed to twenty-four minutes from Burnham to Wickford, twenty-three minutes from Wickford to Burnham, twenty-eight minutes from Southminster to Wickford and twenty-seven minutes from Wickford to Southminster by train.

The inhabitants of places served by the Southminster line would not have been happy in the spring of 1971 had they known of a letter dated 30 April and headed 'LONDON VIABILTY: CLOSURES' from the British Railways Board Executive Director, Passenger, to the General Managers of the four English Regions of British Railways. In the letter, the Director said that there were a number of services in London and the South-East, the continued existence of which made it harder to achieve and maintain viability on any interpretation of the term. He said that they should aim at getting the services withdrawn by the end of 1973 and that meant that they should not lose any time in approaching the Department of the Environment for their agreement to the publication that summer of advance notices of closure as required by Section 54 of the Transport Act 1962. Attached to the Director's letter was a list of services which appeared, prima facie, to represent the drain on the railway's resources which would hinder the achievement of any kind of financial viability. In the list in the Eastern Region section was the Wickford to Southminster line. The line along with all the others in the Region's list except one was suffixed with an asterisk. The asterisk indicated that those services failed to cover specific costs, 'i.e. movements, specific terminals, specific track, specific signalling and specific E.T.E [entertainment and travel expenses] costs'. The response of the Eastern Region General Manager did not mention any intention of wanting to close any of the lines within Essex and nothing more was done. Nevertheless, the letter showed that there were ideas for closing the Southminster line.

Early on the morning of 31 January 1971, there was a collision at Wickford between the 3.20am Liverpool Street to Southend Newspaper train hauled by class 31 locomotive No 5502 and the 4.04am Southend to Liverpool Street train formed of class 306 units Nos 084, 023 and 001. The up line was closed between Billericay and Wickford and single line working was in operation on the down line. The newspaper train was due to stop at Wickford to unload, but because it was running about fifteen minutes late arrangements were made for it to pass through Wickford and go on to the Southminster Branch, beyond the station. This meant that the passenger train, which was running to time, could be crossed over to the down line without delay before proceeding on that line to Billericay. Had all gone to plan, the newspaper train would have set back on to the down bay line at Wickford as soon as the passenger train had departed. The driver of the newspaper train did not set his locomotive's brakes properly when the train came to a halt on the Southminster line and as he was not properly familiar with the signals that controlled his setting back movement he left his controls to check the signals on the opposite side of the line and so allowed his train to run back down the gradient where it collided with the passenger train which had just crossed to the down line. The rear vehicle of the newspaper train was derailed and slightly damaged and two carriages of the passenger train were extensively damaged. Fortunately, no one was injured.

In 1972, Essex County Council announced plans for a new town at South Woodham Ferrers with an ultimate population of 15,000. From 12 August 1973 for eight weeks, an experimental Sunday service was run on the Southminster line. This was repeated in 1974 from June to August. It was not repeated in 1975.

In April 1971, the Government announced that Maplin Sands (Foulness) had been selected as the site for London's third airport. The project would have included a major airport, a deep water harbour and a high speed rail link from King's Cross which would have crossed over the GE Norwich line between Shenfield and Ingatestone and running north of the Southend line would have crossed over the Southminster branch. There would not have been any connections to the New Essex Lines. In 1973, because of the oil crisis precipitated by the Yom Kippur War, the project was abandoned.

The period 1970 to 1974 saw a number of industrial disputes including those involving the railways. Some of the disputes were official and some unofficial. Not all the industrial action took the form of a strike. Some involved a work to rule and a ban on overtime. One such dispute took place in the spring of 1972. However, it did produce an interesting working on the Southend line. The *Railway Magazine* of June that year recorded that on 12 April a Southend (Victoria) to Liverpool Street train was worked by class 309 Clacton emus. This is as far as I am aware, and I stand to be corrected, the only time a service train on the Southend line was worked by Clacton units. One must assume though that the units worked a corresponding down train. During another industrial dispute in early 1974, a class 31 diesel locomotive and a rake of nine coaches worked a Liverpool Street to Southend train on 4 February. In this case one must assume again that there was a corresponding up working by the locomotive and coaches.

During a ban on overtime and Sunday working by maintenance supervisors in the spring of 1975, some Southend line trains were worked by diesel locomotives hauling main line corridor stock. Those classes of locomotives noted were classes 31 and 37.

In the late 1970s, I remember there was talk of electrifying the Southminster branch. I was told by staff at Billericay in 1978, that the plan was to operate the service with four of the electric units which had been built for the Shenfield electrification of 1949, but converted to conductor guard working. I have never heard anything else of this and if any files ever existed on such a plan, they have not survived. Perhaps it was just a rumour.

In autumn 1977, the Southminster branch had featured on television in an episode of the *Dick Emery Show*. Dick Emery was a popular comedian of the time. In the episode, Fambridge and Southminster under disguised names, had appeared as two stations competing for the award for the most efficient station on the line. Fambridge was portrayed as rather down at heel and Southminster as highly efficient. By a degree of skulduggery, Fambridge went and won the award.

November 1978 saw the cessation of sand traffic on the Southminster branch, following the exhaustion of the pit at Southminster. In early 1979, a meeting was held at Latchingdon with the aim of getting sand from a new pit at Asheldham, which was only one and half miles from Southminster, on to the railway and thereby taking heavy lorries off the roads of Dengie. Part of the battle was won, when in the spring of 1979 sand trains resumed; however these did not last long, and the last one ran in early November of that year.

1978 saw publication of the first history of any of the New Essex Lines when Dennis Swindale's very successful *Branch Lines to Maldon* came out. He followed this up in 1981 with *Branch Line to Southminster*. In 1984 I went into print with *The Shenfield to Southend Line*.

BR had revised the clearance for 25,000 volts alternating current under bridges and during the weekend of 20 and 21 January 1979 the Shenfield to Southend line had its voltage raised to the higher voltage from 6,250 volts. Two London Midland Region Class 86/0 class locomotives Nos 86 001 and 86 008 were used to test the voltage. They were hauled dead from Willesden by class 47 No 47 431 to Shenfield on Saturday 20 January and were used in multiple – one for loading and one for braking to test voltage conversion of the line. On the Sunday morning, they were hauled back to Willesden by the same locomotive that hauled them to Shenfield. According to the April 1979 *Railway Magazine,* a correspondent understood that they ran at least twice to Southend Victoria during the night and he observed them at Wickford during the morning of 21 January. I am not sure what the arrangements were concerning passenger services during that weekend.

In 1980, an experimental Sunday service in the summer was run on the Southminster branch. This was repeated in 1981 and became permanent. The 1982 ASLEF strike saw dmus work some Southend trains.

In 1976, class 312 four-car electric multiple units were put into service on the GE lines. These were gangwayed within the sets and did not have compartments. Although mainly used on the Colchester, Clacton and Walton services, some of these appeared on off-peak services to Southend. From the mid-1980s, they also started appearing on peak hour services to Southend. They were later joined by class 310 four car units built for the London Midland Region in the mid-1960s. In 1980 new class 315 four-car electric multiple units were put into service to replace the original 1949 three- car units. These units were gangwayed within the sets. Beginning in 1981, BR started refurbishing all of its original GE and LTS sections four-car electric multiple units beginning with those built for the 1956 electrification to Southend. Non-gangwayed trains with compartments were no longer regarded as acceptable. No such trains had been built since the beginning of the 1960s. Refurbishment, in most instances, involved converting all carriages to open carriages and fitting gangway connections between the carriages within each unit. Not all units built for the LTS electrification were refurbished by the time replacement stock arrived on that line. Some of the units built for the LTS electrification were semi refurbished by having the partitions in compartment carriages removed. The insides of the carriages concerned were not the most elegant. You could see round the walls and under the roof remains of the partitions.

In 1979, at the general election, the Conservatives under Margaret Thatcher were returned to power. Whilst the Conservatives decided to privatise many things, one thing that Margaret Thatcher would not have privatised was the railways. There was however talk in the early 1980s of some experiments with some self-contained lines, one being the LTS line, the case being that it would have been in competition with the still nationalised Southend GE line. Nothing developed at the time.

Under the sectorisation of BR, 4 January 1982 saw the creation of the London and South East Sector of which the Southend (Victoria) and Southminster lines were a part. On 10 June 1986, the sector was relaunched as Network SouthEast, along with a new red, white and blue livery. It was presided over by Chris Green. The relaunch was not a mere superficial rebranding and was underpinned by considerable investment in the presentation of stations and trains, as well as efforts to improve service standards.

In 1988, the Eastern Region, which in 1967 had been enlarged by absorbing the North Eastern Region, was divided into the Eastern

Region and the new Anglia Region. The former GER and LTSR lines becoming part of the new combination.

On 13 November 1983, owing to a signalman's error, an electric train was wrongly signalled at Wickford on to the Southminster branch. The train did not get very far as it soon ran out of overhead wires.

On 23 January 1984, one finds the first mention of the proposal that resulted in the electrification of the Southminster branch, when the Principal Investment Manager of BR wrote a draft paper regarding the electrification of the Wickford to Southminster branch. In it he said that in May 1985, 3rd rail electrification would be introduced from Dalston to North Woolwich by the extension of the Richmond and Broad Street electric multiple units. This would leave Stratford [motive power depot]with diesel multiple unit maintenance of just the Romford to Upminster and Southminster units. The case for electrification of the Romford to Upminster branch was being developed, but electrification of the Southminster branch, involving a greater number of units, would enable diesel multiple unit maintenance to be discontinued at Stratford and the residual work transferred to Cricklewood. The only freight traffic on the Southminster branch was the Central Electricity Generating Board nuclear flask trains. There was no potential for further development of freight traffic on the line. Romford to Upminster was later approved for electrification in June 1984.

According to the paper if nothing was done and the present level of service continued, it would not be able to cater for the traffic on offer and would not provide the improvements discussed with Essex County Council. From this, it is clear that discussions had taken place between Essex County Council and BR about the line and its service. If the level of service provided continued, it would undoubtedly lead to difficulties during the peak period, public complaints and loss of revenue. This was not an acceptable option because it failed to maximise revenue and reduce costs, but it was the base option against which the non-electrified option and the proposal for electrification was compared.

The report gave details of the non-electrified option. This was an improved service to be operated using high density diesel multiple units with some two three car sets running to and from the down running platform at Wickford as the bay platforms could not take more than five cars and the cost of extending them was prohibitive. The augmented service would require the reinstatement of the crossing loop at Woodham Ferrers by reinstating and refurbishing of the former up platform. Both platforms would have to be of six car length. At Wickford, a new footbridge would be needed as the current footbridge was inadequate for future levels of passengers crossing between the up and down platforms in the morning peaks. The platforms were not to be extended under this option though they were inadequate. The report said that this appraisal showed it to give a worse financial result than maintaining the present position or electrifying it and it was therefore rejected.

The report gave details of the electric option. The proposed electrification was using standard 25,000 volt equipment and replacing the diesel multiple units with electric multiple units from the existing fleet of units. The Southminster track layout was to be simplified to accommodate the flask trains. Signal boxes were to be abolished and track circuit block signalling was to be introduced between Wickford and Fambridge and one train working, to be introduced between Fambridge and Southminster. Woodham Ferrers and Althorne manned level crossings were to be automated and converted to automatic open crossings locally monitored, which would provide staff savings. In the peak hours, the electrified service would provide through trains to and from Liverpool Street. Approval and dispensation from the Department of Transport would be needed for the extension of some of the platforms. The estimated cost of the electrification would be £2,966,000 at what the report says in Q4/1983 base level. The report approved delegated authority to E.K. Foulkes of £2,966 for individual items with a total of £29,660 as project manager. The estimated effect on revenue accounts at full electrification (1989) would be £643,000 better without population growth and £1,036,000 better with population growth. The draft report did mention closure of the branch and immediately dismissed it as being totally unacceptable. A case should have been made for the reinstatement of the crossing loop at Woodham Ferrers and reinstating and refurbishment of the former up platform under the electrification.

Following discussions on the draft paper on 23 March 1984 the Principal Investment Manager authorised the electrification at an estimated planning +/- cost of £2,966 million at Q4/1983 price levels. The justification being, that it would eliminate a pocket of diesel operation in an extensive 25,000 volt electrified area under Anglia electrification. After all financial improvements were excluded, the proposal remained financially attractive.

At the meeting of the Investment Committee of the BRB on 2 April 1984, the Board authorised the electrification. The only reference that I can find to an announcement of the electrification in the press is an article in *The Times* for 4 August 1984 in relation to the on-going miners' dispute. The article headed 'Work on, BR asks railmen' says that the previous day, British Rail rushed out a special 'good news' edition of its newspaper *Rail News*, in a clear effort to sway railwaymen against taking action in support of the miners. The article mentions that (amongst the electrification schemes approved) was that from Wickford to Southminster.

Work on the electrification started at the end of November 1984. On 17 March 1986, electric current had been switched on and the first test run of an electric train took place on 23 March, formed of units Nos 305510 and 307104. Later that day, unit No 307104 did test runs on its own on the branch. The first use of electric trains in passenger service took place on 14 April with an early morning train in both directions. Services on the branch were disrupted for three days in April by a dispute over the running of the new service. Finally, on 12 May, the full electric service started. To be sentimental, something was lost with the electrification of the line. There was always a feeling of a journey in the wilds. I have found nothing in the national press on the start of the electric services. With the electrification of the Southminster line came the introduction of winter, as well as summer services, on Sundays.

**Class 08** 08 520 at Southminster on an electrification train in 1985. *(James Jolly)*

**Rebuilt and** refurbished class 307 emu No 112 at Southminster shortly after arrival in July 1986. (*R.F. Roberts/SLS Collection*)

From 3 June 1985, there were changes to the bus services serving Stow Maries, Cold Norton and Purleigh. An effect of the changes was that, for practical purposes there was no useful bus service to these places. This put those inhabitants not possessing a car or motorcycle in a worse position than those during the Second World War. The situation was clearly unacceptable and subsequently improvements were made to the bus services serving those places starting in late October 1999 and since June 2004 they have enjoyed a reasonable level of service.

On the night of Thursday 15-Friday 16 October 1987, there was a hurricane. Mature trees were uprooted as if they were mere saplings, telegraph poles were torn up, roads were blocked with fallen trees and power cables were brought down. For a time, both the Shenfield to Southend and Wickford to Southminster lines were put out of action. Whilst the Shenfield to Southend line was cleared in time for Monday's rush hour, the Southminster line was, according to *The Times* of 19 October, not likely to open that day. The *Guardian* said that the Southminster line remained closed. On 25 January 1990, there was another hurricane, this time during the day. Trees were uprooted, roofs were ripped off and bus shelters were toppled. It is recorded that trains couldn't run through Billericay due to fallen trees on the overhead lines and BR organised a fleet of buses from Shenfield to Billericay and Wickford.

In the late 1980s, the Maldon western bypass was built over the course of the line from Maldon West to Maldon East. The remains of the Chelmer viaduct were demolished and replaced by a new viaduct. The road opened on 9 October 1990.

The former City bus route from North London was curtailed to and from Walthamstow, instead of Wood Green to Southend in 1981. For a time, following the deregulation of bus services, the route was extended to Oxford Circus in central London (initially as an express variant of the route from October 1986, but by October 1987 as part of the main route), before being curtailed back to Walthamstow by July 1990 and completely abandoned in 2000, by which time it been altered to run from Walthamstow to Basildon. Bits of the route were parcelled off with a different service pattern on Sundays and public holidays from Mondays to Saturdays.

1989 saw the centenary of the New Essex Lines. In that same year, John Jolly of Mangapps Farm at Burnham-on-Crouch opened a railway museum, which includes a running line on which rides are given. The museum includes a lot of items of interest, both from the immediate area, and also further afield. It is most certainly worth a visit. Steam and diesel traction are used. A number of celebrations took place to celebrate the centenary of the New Essex Lines. On 1 July a party of Maldon District Council dignitaries, and others including BR officials and the author Dennis Swindale boarded the 9.56am train from Wickford to Southminster, the front coach of which was commandeered as a mobile hospitality unit. At various stations on the line, representatives of the parishes through which the line passed joined the train. At Southminster, the platform was full of a large crowd of school children and Southminster Parish Council. Following a visit to a tent dispensing refreshment in the station forecourt the guests boarded a bus for a trip to Mangapps Farm Railway Museum. At the public library in Southend, the South East Essex Railway Society organised an exhibition on the centenary of the lines. On August Bank Holiday Monday 28 August, there was an exhibition at Southend (Victoria) station which included diesel and electric locomotives, electric multiple units and restored N7 class 0-6-2 tank locomotive No 69621, which worked a shuttle service up and down the yard. On the Southminster branch, services were worked by preserved 1949 Shenfield electric multiple unit No 306 017 and green liveried LTS line electric multiple unit No 302 200.

**Preserved N7** No 69621 at Southend on centenary day in 1989. (*Dave Brennand*)

**Preserved class** 306 emu No 017 at Southminster on centenary day in 1989. (*Author*)

From the end of 1988, new class 321 four-car electric multiple units began to appear on Southend services. These units boasted sliding doors and were equipped for driver only operation.

In April 1990, the Chairman of BR, Sir Robert Reid, announced that sectorisation would be made complete, with regions disbanded by 1991/2 and the individual sectors becoming directly responsible for all operations other than a few core long-term planning and standards functions.

On 1 April 1994, Network SouthEast was officially disbanded as train services passed to various train operating units ready for privatisation through a franchising process.

With effect from 4 October 1993, the mail terminal at Southend (Victoria) ceased to be used. The final mail working was on the night of Friday 1/Saturday 2 October, but rail access to the terminal was left intact.

# CHAPTER SIX

# From Privatisation to the Present Day

Margaret Thatcher was against the privatisation of the railways. She saw the logic of keeping the system as a unified entity. John Major replaced Margaret Thatcher in 1990. John Major was not against the privatisation of the railways. His idea for privatising the railways was something akin to the big four companies that existed prior to nationalisation. The European Union would not allow this. What happened was the biggest mess going. The infrastructure was owned by one company (Railtrack) and the trains were operated by around twenty-six train operating companies. In the east of England, on the former GE lines, privatisation took place on 1 January 1997. There were three companies operating passenger services out of Liverpool Street. West Anglia Great Northern operated the North East London suburban and main line services to Cambridge. Anglia operated the main line services to Norwich together with rural services in East Anglia. First Great Eastern operated the remaining services out of the station to Essex including the New Essex Lines.

This was a complex arrangement with little real benefit. The Labour government that came to power in the General Election of 1997 had promised to renationalise the railways, but vacillated, procrastinated (despite John Prescott's fine words) and in the end maintained the status quo.

The former LTS line had been privatised on 26 May 1996 and was initially operated by Prism. In July 2002, it was renamed c2c extinguishing the historical name. Bradwell power station was coming to the end of its active life and on 1 December 1999 British Nuclear Fuels announced that it would close in March 2002 with decommissioning taking up to three years to complete. This took a bit longer than expected with the last recorded nuclear flask train running on Thursday 31 August 2006. Since then there have been a number of workings over the line in connection with decommissioning the power station.

Steam made a brief reappearance on the lines on 6 May 2002 when preserved (former LMSR) class 5 4-6-0 No 45407 and

BR class 4 2-6-0 No 76079 worked a special train from Liverpool Street to Southend. The special train then ran to Wickford before making one return trip to Southminster. After that, it returned once more to Southend before embarking on a final run from Southend to Liverpool Street. Since then there have been a number of other steam-hauled excursions from the Southend line.

Obviously someone in the offices of the government decreed that it was perhaps not a good idea to have three different train companies operating out of the same station in London. When the franchises for East Anglia came up for renewal, it was decided to have one franchise for the whole lot. This was won by National Express, with a new franchise taking effect from 1 April 2004. National Express originally marketed itself under the name 'One'. Personally I liked the name 'One'. It was logical, but others thought it was ridiculous. In early 2008, following the acquisition of the East Coast Main Line franchise, the East Anglia franchise was re-branded National Express East Anglia. At the end of May 2015, some of the North East London services and the Romford to Upminster line were transferred to the London Overground, whilst in preparation for CrossRail, the Liverpool Street to Shenfield local service was transferred to TfL Rail. Crossrail will be renamed the Elizabeth line when it opens through central London. After the commencement of services to all destinations, it will become part of London Underground. With c2c operating some services into Liverpool Street, mainly at weekends, things have now gone backwards.

On 20 May 2007, Fambridge station was renamed North Fambridge and Woodham Ferrers station was renamed South Woodham Ferrers.

From the December 2007 timetable, the Southminster branch, which had a gap in the service on Thursday afternoons for the nuclear flask train, had that gap filled as the nuclear flask train no longer operated.

In November 2009, the government announced that Bradwell was earmarked to be the site of one of the new nuclear power stations. An opposition group (Blackwater Against New Nuclear Group) was formed in opposition. On 23 June 2011, it was announced that Bradwell had been chosen as one of eight sites deemed suitable for new power stations by 2025. This will, if it is built, bring back freight traffic in some form to the South Essex Lines; albeit very limited. What effect the running of nuclear flask trains will have on passenger services on the Southminster line will not be known until the power station is ready for operation.

On 12 December 2010, with the start of the new timetable, all off-peak Southminster line trains terminated at Wickford. As compensation for passengers having to change there once again, the service on the line does at least enjoy an enhanced off-peak frequency of a train every forty minutes. Over the years there have been proposals to reconnect Maldon to the railway network. In 1979 Gordon Harvey, the Secretary of the Southminster Line Standing Committee, advocated that the line from Woodham Ferrers to Maldon be reopened. Like so many ideas, nothing came of this A lot of the former branch line from Woodham Ferrers to Maldon has been built over. At Woodham Ferrers, for example, part of the line is now occupied in part by a housing development. At Maldon, part of the line was used as the site for the construction of the western bypass, whilst the West Station, like that at Cold Norton, has been demolished and the site built over the goods shed remains together with the East station which is stranded in an industrial estate. The East goods shed was demolished in late 2008. At Barons Lane, some of the land has been reclaimed for farming, but both there and at Stow Maries some of the track bed remains. The site of Stow St Mary's halt is now a nature reserve.

In 1999, Regional Airports Ltd, who had acquired Southend Airport from Southend Borough Council in 1993, obtained planning permission from Rochford District Council to build a railway station at Southend Airport. The airport was to be named London Southend Airport. However nothing was done to advance the proposal. In 2008, the airport was sold to the Stobart group and work was then put in hand to push forward the scheme. Construction started towards the end of 2009 and the station was practically completed by the beginning of 2010. It had been the initial intention to open the station in December 2009, but this was put back to the summer of 2010, then December 2010 and finally the summer of 2011. The station was shown in the timetable commencing 22 May 2011 and the electronic station display in the trains showed Southend Airport as a stopping place even though the station was not open. The first train from Southend to Liverpool Street called at the station at 4.05am on 18 July 2011. The station and the new control tower were officially opened by the Minister for the Thames Gateway, Bob Neill MP. The station cost £12 million to build and is staffed by Stobart and not the train operating company.

**Southend Airport** station with a class 321 emu No 321 354 heading an 8 car train. (*Dr Ian Scotchman*)

During the week of 1 to 7 August 2011 services on the Southminster branch were suspended while the passing loop at North Fambridge was extended to take twelve carriage trains. During this time rail replacement bus services were provided for all stations except Battlesbridge, for which a rail replacement taxi service was provided.

On 25 March 2011, it was announced by the government that National Express was to lose the Greater Anglia franchise from 5 February 2012. On 20 October 2011 the Transport Minister, Theresa Villiers, said Abellio Greater Anglia Limited, which is part of the Nederlandse Spoorwegen,(Netherlands Railways)would operate the Greater Anglia franchise from 5 February 2012 until July 2014. Abellio Greater Anglia Limited have adopted the name Greater Anglia following their take over of the franchise on 5 February 2012. In March 2013, the Department of Transport announced that the franchise had been extended until October 2016. On 10 August 2016, the Company won the franchise to run services until 2025. Under the new franchise, the Company will replace its entire fleet between the beginning of 2019 and the end of 2020 with a mixture of electric multiple units for suburban, Intercity and Stansted Express services and electro-diesel multiple units for regional services. For the Southend (Victoria) line there is promised an off-peak service of four trains per hour between Liverpool Street and Southend (Victoria) instead of the current service of three per hour, two new fast peak hour trains in each direction between Liverpool Street and Southend (Victoria), an earlier first and later late train service between Liverpool Street and Southend Airport and later connections from Liverpool Street to Southminster.

Beginning at the end of June 2014, celebrations began to commemorate the 125th anniversary of the opening of the Wickford to Southminster line, which in Abellio Greater Anglia publicity material is known as the Crouch Valley line. Designs by fifteen young artists aged five to eighteen were unveiled in the windows of Burnham railway station and the artists were presented with prizes at the ceremony by ticket office employee and local resident Linda Campion. At the ceremony, there were music, stalls, workshops, and exhibits whilst an historic bus provided free transport to various locations on the Burnham Art Trail and to Mangapps Railway Museum. On Friday 4 July, railway archive photography and memorabilia was displayed at South Woodham Ferrers station. On Friday 11 July at Wickford station, John Whittingdale OBE, MP for Maldon, named class 321 unit No 321442 *Crouch Valley 1889-2014.* After a celebratory trip on the train to Burnham, John Jolly, managing partner and curator of Mangapps Railway Museum, was presented by Abellio Greater Anglia with a mounted replica name plate for permanent display at Mangapps. Over August Bank Holiday weekend of 23 to 25 August, Mangapps hosted a steam and diesel gala event to celebrate the 25th anniversary of the museum and a Changing Tracks exhibition to mark the 125th anniversary of the opening of the Southminster branch line. The event featured two steam locomotives running for the first time in several years and Chelmsford Model Club exhibited a model railway. For £10, people were able to drive one of the Museum's class 03 diesel locomotives.

In late October 2014, a class 379 electric multiple unit, No. 379013, which had been converted to operate on battery power was tested on the Southminster line out of traffic hours. class 379 EMUs, introduced in service in 2011, are normally used on the Liverpool Street to Stansted Airport and Cambridge services. The purpose of the trial was to see if a battery powered electric train could be made to operate reliably. This would enable those lines in electrified areas which are not currently electrified to be converted to electric traction without the need for expensive electrification equipment and so dispense with the need for diesel trains on the lines. The train in question did keep its normal electrical equipment and was also able to operate using the overhead electric power supply.

During its test runs, the train was reported in the *Railway Magazine* for December 2014 as having reached 100 miles per hour on the Southminster line. This was an error on the part of the magazine as the maximum line speed on the Southminster line is sixty miles per hour. The speed reached was most likely 62.5 miles per hour or 100 kilometres per hour. In early 2015, the train went in to passenger service on the Harwich to Manningtree branch. After the trials on the latter branch it was converted back to its normal mode of power.

BR Standard Class 4 2-6-4T No 80078, which originally worked on the former LTSR line, was returned to service at Mangapps Railway Museum on Monday 29 May 2017 and on Sunday 11 June took part in a steam event celebrating its connection with the former LTSR.

Over the years, all of the stations on the Southend line have seen some work done to them.

One can't help but think that the opportunity to re-open the passing loop at South Woodham Ferrers plus the running of some trains through central London via the CrossRail Line has been missed.

It is unclear whether a second nuclear power station will be built at Bradwell but if it is, it would bring freight traffic back to the lines. A decision as to whether a new power station (which would be built by the Chinese) will get approval to be constructed will not be made known for at least four years.

One would hope that at some time in the not too distant future a new railway serving Maldon could be built. Maldon is an attractive town with a goodly population of commuters as well as a number of historic buildings and a quayside on the River Blackwater where will be found a number of interesting ships. The building of a new railway would have the benefit of relieving commuter and visitor traffic on the roads to and from the town. Sadly, it would be impractical to rebuild either of the two lines that were closed and indeed, had the Witham to Maldon line not been closed, something would have had to be done about the timber viaducts along the route. Replacement of them or diversion of the railway round them would have been necessary, regardless of whether or not the line was electrified, as happened to the Braintree branch. Whether the political will to build a new railway to Maldon exists is another matter. As mentioned earlier, irrespective of whether a new line is built to Maldon or not, the passing loop and up platform at South Woodham Ferrers needs to be reinstated. This will enable the line to increase its current capacity to cope with any increases in traffic by allowing an extra train to run on the Southminster line.

# CHAPTER SEVEN

# The Lines Described

## Shenfield to Southend Victoria

Shenfield station is situated at the eastern end of a cutting partially on level ground, and partially on a bridge that dovetails into an embankment. Before the widening of the line in 1932, it consisted of three through platforms. The junction for the Southend line is at the eastern end of the station with the former goods yard situated at the western end. In 1932, a new island platform was added. Between 1979 and 1981, the buildings on the old up platform were demolished and replaced by new ones. Under the CrossRail scheme, a new platform 6 has been added to the north side of the station to accommodate Crossrail trains that terminate at Shenfield. The new platform was brought into use in May 2017.

Leaving Shenfield from the eastern side, the Southend line runs beside the main line for some distance then gradually descends a gradient of about 1 in 100 before curving away to Mountnessing Junction. Here the line is joined by the bi-directional single line

**Shenfield station** from the eastern end in 1968. (*R.F. Roberts/SLS Collection*)

which left Shenfield from the northern (down) side. This too descends at a gradient of about 1 in 100 before burrowing under the main line. At Mountnessing there was a goods yard on the south side of the line. Leaving Mountnessing, the line continues downhill until about two miles from Shenfield where it becomes level for half a mile before rising at 1 in 100 to Billericay. From the middle of Billericay's platforms there is a change of gradient, then the line descends almost continuously to Wickford.

Billericay is a two platform station and the only remaining example of the two stations on the New Essex Lines that were originally built in a cutting. The goods yard was on the north side of the line. Before it was filled in, there was a short bay platform on the north side of the down platform. Leaving Billericay, the line continues in a deep cutting intersected by two bridges towards Wickford. It is said that on a clear day, if your eyesight is good, you can see the Thames at Southend from the southernmost one, the Norsey Road Bridge. On the way to Wickford the line continues through Norsey Woods and past Ramsden Bellhouse. The siding here was on the north side of the line.

**Billericay station** from the Stock Road bridge in about 1953. (*Author's collection*)

**Billericay interior** in the 1900s. (*Author's collection*)

**The cutting** at Billericay with an L1 on a Southend train in about 1953. Taken from the Norsey Road bridge. (*David Collins*)

Wickford was in steam days, and still is to some extent today, the most important intermediate station on the line boasting two bay platforms at the eastern end of the two through platforms and two refuge sidings at the north end of the station. There is a refuge siding on the down side, with a siding leading off it for on-track machines. The refuge siding on the up side has now been disconnected. The up platform buildings have been demolished and replaced by modern buildings. The goods yard was on the north side of the line at the western end of the station. There was an engine siding with a turntable on the south side of the line at the western end of the station. For the accommodation of the engine crews there was a hut.

Leaving Wickford, which is on the level, the line rises half a mile at 1 in 100 before descending a further half mile at 1 in 100. There is then a level stretch of several miles followed by a long rise at mostly 1 in 100 towards Rayleigh. The junction for the

**Wickford interior** in the 1900s. (*Author's collection*)

**Wickford facing** west in March 1955. (*H.C. Casserley*)

Southminster branch is about half a mile east of Wickford station. Fanton Junction was at the eastern end of the cutting beyond Wick Lane level crossing. For many years, the course of the curve to the Southminster branch was still visible. It has now been built on. Between Wickford and Rayleigh was Bridge 774 where from 1 May 1922 to 30 April 1925 there was a platform for workmen employed by Messrs W. and C. French on building the Southend Arterial Road.

Rayleigh, Hockley, Rochford and Prittlewell are all conventional two platform stations. The goods yard at Rayleigh was situated on the Up side at the Wickford end of the station. There was also a refuge siding in the same area. Leaving Rayleigh there is an uphill climb to Hockley. Here, at the summit, there used to be a siding called 'Down Hall'. This consisted of two roads. Traffic was propelled from Rayleigh on the wrong line under special arrangements.

After the site of Down Hall siding, the line descends for about two and a quarter miles to Hockley. At Hockley, the goods yard was on the south side of the line at the western end of the station. There was a refuge siding at the western end of the up platform.

**Rayleigh interior** in GER days. (*Author's collection*)

**Rayleigh exterior** in the 1920s. (*Author's collection*)

Railway Station, Rayleigh.

Leaving Hockley, the run to Rochford is all downhill. Hawkwell siding was situated about a mile from Rochford and seems to have been on the south side of the line. A pair of former railway cottages still exist nearby. The siding was closed from 1 March 1901. Rochford goods yard was on the north side of the line and the former goods shed has been preserved as a community centre. Leaving Rochford, the line rises mostly at 1 in 150 to Prittlewell. On the south side of the line is Southend airport. The gantries for the overhead wires at this point have been constructed to the minimum possible height and have been painted white. They are very much closer together than elsewhere. As mentioned elsewhere in this book, there have been a number of incidents involving aircraft. Southend Airport station which was built in 2009 but not opened until 18 July 2011 has direct access to the new terminal building of Southend Airport.

Prittlewell station is located in the northern outskirts of Southend and is the nearest station for Roots Hall, home of Southend United F.C. Prittlewell goods yard was on the south side of the line at the western end of the station. There was a refuge siding at the western end of the up platform.

Leaving Prittlewell, there is a very short uphill climb into Southend Victoria station past the carriage sidings and the site of the former locomotive shed. The station signal box still exists although the entrance is boarded up. Southend Victoria is a four platform terminus. The goods yard was at the eastern side of the station. The locomotive shed boasted accommodation for up to six locomotives, a turntable, coaling stage and accommodation for engine crews. There is no covered accommodation for electric trains. There was, until the end of 1992, a Royal Mail depot siding on the north side of the station.

**Hockley station** in 1956 with overhead wires up ready for the start of electric services. (*R.C. Riley/ Transport Treasury*)

**Rochford interior** about 1910. (*Dave Brennand collection*)

**Prittlewell in** the 1900s. (*Author's collection*)

**Southend shed** in March 1955 with a N7 No 69725 and J20 No 68681. (*H.C. Casserley*)

**Southend shed** in late 1956 with B12 No 61578, an unidentified J39 and an unidentified tank locomotive. (*R.C. Riley/Transport Treasury*)

**Southend
(Victoria)** station
in 1970 looking
towards the
buffer stops
and concourse.
(*R.F. Roberts/SLS
Collection*)

## Wickford to Southminster

The Southminster line left the Southend line about half a mile east of Wickford station and curved away north past the site of Belchamp Junction which was the northern end of the curve to the Southend line. Part of the curve was relaid in 1947 for a siding to an industrial estate. It was announced as ready for traffic on 11 August 1947 and was closed to traffic on 26 February 1969. It has since been lifted. The line climbs for three quarters of a mile at 1 in 100 before descending on a similar gradient to a level stretch which leads to Battlesbridge station. Battlesbridge has a solitary platform on the south side of the line but at one time there was a passing loop on the north side of the line which could be used to pass a train in the station by a train that was not stopping there. The goods yard was on the south side of the line at the eastern end of the station.

Leaving Battlesbridge, the line continues with gentle gradients to South Woodham Ferrers station. (The name of the station was officially changed from Woodham Ferrers to South Woodham Ferrers on 20 May 2007.) At one time, there was a passing loop here, but this has now been removed. Remains of the former up platform are still visible. Whether the passing loop will be reinstated should a new power staion be built at Bradwell only time will tell. The goods yard was at the western end of the station on the north side of the line. On the south side of the line was an engine yard which once included a turntable.

RAILWAY STATION, BATTLES BRIDGE . 70

**Battlesbridge exterior** in the 1900s. (*Author's collection*)

**Battlesbridge interior** in the 1900s. (*Author's collection*)

**Battlesbridge station** interior in early 1950s. (*W.A. Camwell/SLS Collection*)

**Woodham Ferrers** interior in 1958. (*HMRS*)

Leaving South Woodham Ferrers on a short curve, the line runs eastward on a straight stretch of line alongside the riverside marshes. This stretch entails splendid views overlooking the Crouch estuary all the way to Burnham-on-Crouch. This is a flat watery landscape - almost treeless, inhabited by waterfowl and cattle. Settlements are few and far between. After one and a half miles it rises at 1 in 130/1 in 100 for three quarters of a mile before falling towards North Fambridge station at 1 in 110/1 in 130. On the north side of the line between South Woodham Ferrers and North Fambridge was Hogwell siding.

North Fambridge is now the only passing loop on the line. (The name of the station was officially changed from Fambridge to North Fambridge on 20 May 2007.) There are two platforms straddling the passing loop. The goods yard used to be on the south side of the line at the eastern end of the station. The Down platform is signalled in both directions allowing trains from Wickford to be terminated here before returning to the junction. During the week of 1 to 7 August 2011 the passing loop was extended to take 12 carriage trains.

**Fambridge interior** in the 1900s. (*Stephenson Locomotive Society*)

FAMBRIDGE STATION. 1616.

Fred Spalding.
Photo.
Chelmsford.
Copyright.

**Fambridge station** interior facing west in June 1969.
(*H.C. Casserley*)

**Fambridge signal** box in June 1969.
(*H.C. Casserley*)

Leaving North Fambridge the line rises at 1 in 110/1 in 300 followed by a short level section and then a sharp rise of 1 in 100 for three quarters of a mile before gently descending into the lonely station of Althorne. There is a real sense of isolation at this wayside stopping place.

Althorne, which can justifiably lay claim to be one of the most remote stations in the Eastern Counties, possesses merely a single platform positioned on the north side of the line. It serves what is little more than a hamlet. Like Battlesbridge, a passing loop existed long ago on the south side of the line and this too could be used to pass a train in the station by another train that was not stopping there. The goods yard was on the north side of the line at the eastern end of the station.

Leaving Althorne the line curves south-east into a straight section and rises at 1 in 200/ 1 in 100 for nearly two miles in the direction of the former Creeksea Ferry siding which was on the north side of the line. The line then turns north-east on a gentle gradient and enters Burnham-on-Crouch station. Burnham is a major yachting centre and the nearest station for the Mangapps Farm Railway museum. This may be reached by leaving the station and turning left over the bridge over the railway and continuing straight on for around one and a half miles. Burnham-on-Crouch station once sported a passing loop with platforms on both lines, but the loop has now been taken up and only the up platform is in use. The goods yard was on the south side of the line at the western end of the station.

**Althorne interior** in the 1920s. (*Kidderminster Railway Museum*)

**Althorne station** interior facing west in June 1969. (*R.M. Casserley*)

**Burnham-on-Crouch station** interior in the early 1950s. (*Kidderminster Railway Museum*)

Leaving Burnham-on-Crouch, the line heads in a north-easterly direction on a fairly level gradient to Southminster. The remote station of Southminster at the edge of the Dengie Marshes possesses just one platform. The goods yard was at the southern end of the station on the western side of the line. The yard once used by the weekly nuclear flask train, survives in the form of a set of rusting sidings. The locomotive depot which had a turntable and a shed which could hold two tender locomotives or four tank locomotives was on the eastern side of the line.

**Southminster station** interior in the 1900s. (*Author's collection*)

**Southminster station** and shed in 1938. F5 No 7590 is in the station with a Wickford train. (*W.A. Camwell. SLS collection*)

**Southminster signal** box.
(*Kidderminster Railway Museum*)

**Southminster shed** in April 1955.
(*R.M. Casserley*)

**The Maldon Branch – visible remains**

The Maldon line left South Woodham Ferrers station on a gentle alignment curving north and headed in the direction of Stow St Mary's Halt. Near South Woodham Ferrers station, the site of the line has been built over but later on, up to the bridge before Cold Norton station, the course of the line still exists This part of the former line is now a nature reserve.

Stow St Mary's Halt consisted of a wooden platform on the eastern side of the line in a cutting spanned by an overbridge. The Halt was at the southern side of the bridge. There was a small hut some distance up the embankment against the bridge retaining wall. The platform still exists. Leaving Stow St Mary's Halt, the line continued north to Cold Norton.

Cold Norton was a single platform station with the platform on the west side of the line with a passing loop on the east side of the line which could be used to pass a train in the station by a train that was not stopping there. The goods yard was on the west side of the line at the northern end of the station. The station site is now a small private housing estate.

**The nuclear** flask gantry at Southminster. (*Myles Muncey*)

**Cold Norton** station interior in the 1900s. (*Author's collection*)

**Cold Norton** station in 1940 after the closure to passenger traffic. (*Author's Collection*)

Leaving Cold Norton, the line continued slightly north-west to Barons Lane. Here, the course of the line has now been assumed into fields as far as the former bridge over the line, which still exists. On the other side of the bridge, the course of the line can be traced as far as the site of Maldon West goods yard.

Nothing remains of Barons Lane siding and halt other than the entrance road. Goods accommodation was on the western side of the line and passenger facilities consisted of a platform and nothing else.

From Barons Lane, the line headed to Maldon West where there was a two platform station in a cutting at the start of the double track section to Maldon East. The goods yard was to the south of the passenger station and to the west of the line. The goods shed still exists.

Leaving Maldon West the line curved to the right and crossed the Chelmer and Blackwater Navigation on a viaduct. Beyond the viaduct a curve went north to the direction of Langford and Ulting, on the line from Witham to Maldon, whilst another curve went south-east to join the branch into Maldon East.

The course of the line to Maldon East including the site of Maldon West passenger station has been obliterated under the Maldon by-pass. Maldon East station was a single platform with a double bay terminus with a goods yard and a locomotive depot to the north of the station.

The goods shed was demolished in 2008. The station remains in an industrial estate.

**Maldon West** station in the late 1950s, looking through the tunnel after the removal of the platform buildings. (*Author's collection*)

**The viaduct** over the Chelmer between Maldon West and Maldon East stations in 1961. (*RCTS*)

**Maldon East** station interior in 1938 with F3 No 8046 on a train. (*W.A. Camwell/SLS Collection*)

**Maldon East** station exterior in 1948. (*W.A. Camwell/SLS Collection*)

# CHAPTER EIGHT

# Motive Power

It will never be possible to say precisely what classes of motive power ran over the New Essex Lines. Railway enthusiasts when the lines were opened were a rather rare breed. What follows are those that are known to have worked over them from the sources that are available.

## Steam locomotives

When the New Essex Lines were first opened, Southend depot had an allocation of some 2-4-0 locomotives of the No 1 Class. The class was originally built between 1867 and 1872 under the locomotive superintendentship of Samuel W. Johnson, who was the locomotive superintendent of the GER from 1866 to 1873. The class was built by Messrs Sharp, Stewart and by the GER. They were called the No 1 Class because that was the number of the first engine to be delivered to the GER from Messrs Sharp, Stewart in 1867. Another classification that could have been used was L7, as that was the order number under which the first GER built engine was built in 1869. There were forty engines in the class. From 1899 to 1893, the whole class was rebuilt under the locomotive superintendentship of James Holden, who was the locomotive superintendent of the GER from 1885 to 1907. The class lasted a long time; the last one in service was No 1 which was withdrawn from service in 1913. In a very early locomotive observation, No 28 was recorded as being on the Southminster branch on 12 October 1889. On the same day, No 5 was recorded as being on the Southend line. Before the LTSR obtained its own locomotives, some of the No 1 class worked on that railway, whilst two of those are known to have been stationed at Southend GER from about the opening of the line. In 1879, No 106 was photographed at Southend LTSR during the period that the GER provided the motive power for that railway. That photograph of a GER locomotive on the LTSR during the time that the GER provided the motive power for the railway is the only one known to exist. These locomotives were one of the most useful classes of GER locomotives and occupied the same place in the latter part of the nineteenth century, that the Y14 or J15 0-6-0s did in the twentieth century. It is a great pity that a replica cannot be built of one of these locomotives.

In October 1889, another class of locomotive noted working on the New Essex Lines was an example of the Y class. The Y class had been built as 2-4-0s between 1859 and 1866 under the Locomotive Superintendentship of Robert Sinclair. He was the locomotive superintendent of the ECR from 1856 until its amalgamation into the GER in 1862 then the GER from 1862 to 1865. There were 110 locomotives by Neilson, Robert Stephenson, R.W. Hawthorn, Kitson, Vulcan, and Schneider. During the locomotive superintendentship of William Adams, the locomotive superintendentship of the GER from 1873 to 1878, twenty of them were rebuilt as 4-4-0s, whilst between 1878 and 1883, under William Adams and his successors Massey Bromley (1878-81) and Thomas Worsdell (1882-85), the rest were rebuilt but still as 2-4-0s.The last member of the class was withdrawn in 1894. No 406, which was a 4-4-0, was observed working a Southend to Colchester train in October 1889.

There is a photograph taken at Maldon of a train crossing the viaduct over the Chelmer hauled by one of the 61 class 0-4-4 tank locomotives which were built between 1875 and 1878 under the locomotive superintendentship of William Adams. There were fifty locomotives in the class and they were built by Neilson, Robert Stephenson and Kitson. The identity of the locomotive crossing the viaduct is not known. The last member of the class lasted until 1913.

There is a photograph taken at Wickford of a train hauled by one of the E10 class 0-4-4 tank locomotives, No 244. A photograph also exists of the staff of Wickford station with another member of the class No 94. The E10 class consisted of sixty locomotives built by the GER between 1878 and 1883 under the locomotive superintendentship of Massey Bromley. The last member of the class survived until 1912. On 12 October 1889, No 239 is recorded as having worked a train on the Woodham Ferrers to Maldon line.

In April 1915, one of the 209 class or G40 class 0-4-0 saddle tank locomotives, No 0228 (originally 228), was photographed at Southend station being used to heat foot warmers. In the days before the heating of carriages from the locomotive, foot warmers were a means of warming carriages in cold weather. They were a sort of hot water bottle either made of stone or metal. At the Southend exhibition of 1933, another member of the class, No 7230, was on display. The class first appeared in 1874 and comprised eight locomotives. The first four were built by Neilson between 1874 and 1876, whilst the second four were built by the GER between 1897 and 1903. The LNER class number for the class was Y5. The last member of the class was withdrawn in 1948. No 229 was sold in 1918 to the government and has survived to the present day.

The two members of the C8 class of 4-4-0s are known to have operated on the Southend line. The C8 class was designed under the locomotive superintendentship of Samuel W. Johnson, but did not appear until 1874. They were built by the GER and were rebuilt in 1888, surviving until 1897 and 1898.

Another class known to have operated to Southend were the G16 4-4-0s. There were eleven members of the class, which were built by the GER between 1884 and 1885. These engines were originally compounds. Compound locomotives had both high and low pressure cylinders and were supposed to be more economical. The engines were converted to simple expansion in 1892. The class was withdrawn between 1902 and 1904.

The Y14 or LNER J15 class of 0-6-0s first appeared in 1883; between then and 1913 a total of 289 were built. All except nineteen were built by the GER. The nineteen exceptions were built by Sharp, Stewart. The locomotives were exceptionally well liked and could go anywhere. In 1922 three members of the class were shedded at Southend and one at Wickford. The engine at Wickford (No 911) was one of forty-two that were used by the British Army in France and Belgium during the First World War. The class survived until the end of steam on the former GE lines in 1962. No 564 (later LNER No 7564 and later 5462 and BR 65462) has been preserved.

The M15 class 2-4-2 tank locomotives comprised 160 locomotives built between 1884 and 1909. They were all built by the GER. The original thirty machines that were built between 1884 and 1886 had a boiler pressure of 140 pounds per square inch and were fitted with Joy's valve gear when built. The valve gear did not suit the locomotives and they were heavy on coal. They acquired the nickname 'Gobblers'. The remaining 130 locomotives built between 1886 and 1909 had a boiler pressure of 160 pounds per square inch and were fitted with Stephenson's valve gear; to which the original thirty were rebuilt. Between 1911 and 1923 under the locomotive superintendentships of Stephen Holden (1908-12) and Alfred Hill(1912-22), the GER rebuilt thirty of the locomotives with a boiler pressure of 180 pounds per square inch. Two further engines were also rebuilt with large cabs, which had side windows, in 1912.

The engines rebuilt with 180 pound per square inch boilers were classed M15R. In 1911 and 1912, the GER built twenty locomotives of class G69 which had 180 pounds per square inch boilers and large cabs with side windows plus the other two locomotives mentioned above. The LNER classified the M15 class as F4, the M15R class as F5 and the G69 class as F6. The last F4 was withdrawn in 1955, the last F5 in 1958 and the last F6 in 1958. A new F5 is now being built.

The T19 class of express passenger locomotives were frequent visitors to the Southend line and also visited the Southminster line. The class comprised 110 locomotives of the 2-4-0 wheel arrangement built by the GER between 1886 and 1897 under the locomotive superintendentship of James Holden. They remained as top link express locomotives until they were superseded from 1900 by the Claud Hamilton class, although from 1891 they shared the work with the D27 class of 2-2-2 locomotives and from 1898 with the P43 class 4-2-2 locomotives, neither of which are known to have visited the New Essex Lines. Many of the T19 class were fitted for burning oil fuel and one, No 760, was named *Petrolea*. Between 1902 and 1904, twenty-one of the locomotives were rebuilt with larger boilers and new cabs. This gave them the appearance of being 'front heavy' and they were nicknamed 'Humpty Dumpties'. A further sixty were rebuilt between 1905 and 1908 in similar fashion to the previous twenty-one but as 4-4-0 locomotives by replacing the two wheel radial truck at the front with a four-wheel bogie. Photographic evidence exists for all three variants of the class reaching Southend and for the rebuilt variants reaching Southminster. This does not mean that the original variant did not reach Southminster. Those locomotives that were not rebuilt were withdrawn between 1908 and 1913. Those that were rebuilt as 2-4-0 locomotives were withdrawn between 1913 and 1920. The five that survived after 1915 would probably have been withdrawn earlier but for the war. The locomotives that were rebuilt as 4-4-0s were withdrawn between 1922 and 1944. The LNER classified them D13.

The T26 class of mixed traffic locomotives were also frequent visitors to the Southend and Southminster lines. The class comprised one hundred locomotives of the 2-4-0 wheel arangement built by the GER between 1891 and 1902 and they were known as the 'Intermediates'. All survived into the LNER, which classified them E4 and eighteen survived into BR days. The last one of all was withdrawn in 1959 and is now preserved. No 62785 'formerly GER No 490' was the last 2-4-0 tender locomotive working on the British mainland.

The N31 class of 0-6-0s comprised of eighty-two locomotives built between 1888 and 1898. They tended to be used on goods workings, but they were known to have worked troop trains and photographic evidence exists of one on an excursion train to Southend at Rochford. They were somewhat sluggish locomotives and were withdrawn between 1908 and 1925. The LNER classified them J14.

The C32 class of 2-4-2 tank locomotives comprised fifty locomotives built between 1893 and 1902 and were a tank locomotive version of the 'Intermediates'. The LNER classified them as F3. The last member of the class was withdrawn in 1953.

The S44 and later LNER G4 0-4-4 tank locomotives were built by the GER between 1898 and 1901; the class consisted of forty locomotives. The class survived until 1939. Photographs exist of them working on the Woodham Ferrers to Maldon line.

The GER's 0-6-0 tank locomotives of classes R24, R24R and S56 appeared at various dates between 1890 and 1904. All were built by the GER. Class R24 consisted of 140 locomotives built between 1890 and 1901 and class S56 consisted of 20 locomotives built in 1904. There was some blurring between classes R24 and S56. The difference was that the R24s had a boiler pressure of 160 pounds per square inch, whereas the S56s had a boiler pressure of 180 pounds per square inch. Eighty of the R24s had their boiler pressure increased to 180 pounds per square inch between 1902 and 1919. The GER classified them R24R. The LNER classified the R24s J67, the R24Rs and S56s as J69. Just to confuse matters, some of the J69s had their boiler pressures reduced to 160 pounds per square inch and were reclassified J67. Fred Spalding photographed a member of the R24 class at Woodham Ferrers on a passenger train sometime during the 1900s. A J67 was noted at Southend in 1951 and a J69 a bit later. J69 No 68629 (old GER No 83) worked the very last passenger carrying train to run over any part of the Maldon West branch when it worked an enthusiasts' special from Maldon East to Maldon West and return on 6 April 1957. The last R24, R24R and S56 were withdrawn in 1962. S56 No 87, later 7087, later 8633 and later 68633, has been preserved.

Class C72 consisted of thirty 0-6-0 tank locomotives built between 1912 and 1923 by the GER and the LNER. They were the largest of the GER's 0-6-0 tank locomotives and the last ones were withdrawn in 1961. They were distinguished by having side windows to their cabs. The LNER classified them J68.

The Claud Hamilton classes consisted in total of 121 locomotives built between 1900 and 1923. They were of the 4-4-0 wheel arrangement and all were built by the GER, with the last few locomotives constructed by the LNER. There were three variants. The S46 class consisted of forty-one locomotives built between 1900 and 1903. The D56 class consisted of seventy locomotives built between 1903 and 1911, whilst the H88 class comprised ten locomotives built in 1923. The first member of the class was No 1900 and appeared in that year; named after the GER's chairman Lord Claud Hamilton. Class S56 had round-topped fireboxes, classes D56 and H88 had Belpaire fireboxes. There was rebuilding from S46 to D56 and from D56 to H88. The first H88 was a rebuild of a D56 in 1922. Some of the S46 class were originally fitted for running on oil fuel. The LNER classified them D14, D15 and D16. All of the D14s had been rebuilt to D15 by the end of 1931. The LNER under the Chief Mechanical Engineer Nigel Gresley(1923-41) rebuilt some of the D16 class with extended smokeboxes. Later still, some of the engines and some of the D15s were rebuilt with round-topped fireboxes and new cabs. The three variants of the class became D16/1, D16/2 and D16/3. The last D15 was withdrawn in 1952 and the last D16 in 1960. Sadly none have been preserved. The classes are known to have worked to Southend and Southminster from their very earliest days until about 1950 and even then they occasionally appeared on the New Essex Lines. In 1956, Brian Pask photographed one at Southend on a London train. John Plume told me that one worked a Southminster to London train in that year. There are plans to build a replica D16 to be named *Phoenix*.

The goods version of the S46 was the F48 class 0-6-0, whilst the goods version of the D56 was the G58 0-6-0. The F48 class consisted of sixty locomotives built between 1900 and 1903 and the G58 class of thirty locomotives built between 1905 and 1911. Class F48 had round-topped fireboxes except for one engine, No 1189, which had a Belpaire firebox. Class G58 had Belpaire fireboxes. The LNER classified the F48s J16 and the G58s J17. All the J16s were rebuilt to J17 by 1932. The last J17 was withdrawn from service in 1962. No 65567 'formerly GER No.1217' has been preserved. All were built by the GER.

Class Y56 consisted of twelve 2-4-2 tank locomotives built in 1909 and 1910. Apart from being used for the trial push and pull trains on the Southend line in April 1913, they were also used on the Woodham Ferrers to Maldon line. Of course, had the trials on the Southend line proved successful, they would have seen more use on the line. The LNER classified them F7. The last ones were withdrawn in 1948. All were built by the GER.

The ninety-one 4-6-0s of class S69 appeared between 1911 and 1928. Sixty-one of the locomotives were built by the GER, twenty by William Beardmore and ten by Beyer, Peacock. The last ten did not appear until 1928. The LNER classified them B12. When the ten locomotives built by Beyer, Peacock appeared in 1928, because they had Lentz valve gear, they were classified B12/2 and the original engines B12/1. From 1927, fifty-five B12s were fitted with ACFI (Societe l'Auxiliairc des Chemins de Fer et de l'Industrie) feedwater-heating apparatus. This apparatus was mounted above the boiler and consisted of two heater drums and a single steam cylinder, which operated two water pump cylinders. The drums gave the appearance of ruck sacks and earned the locomotives, so fitted, the nickname 'Hiker'. In their original form, they could even have worked to Maldon by both routes although as far as is known none ever did. From 1932 onwards, the B12s were rebuilt with round topped fireboxes, modified cabs and were classified B12/3. At the same time, the ACFI equipment was removed. According to Tony Gooding writing in the *Great Eastern Journal* for April 2008, No 61553 (formerly GER No 1553) hauled the last steam passenger train from Liverpool Street to Southend on 29 December 1956. The last member of the class in traffic No 61572, which survived until 1961, has been preserved.

**B12 61519**
at Hockley.
*(W.A. Camwell/SLS Collection)*

**B12 no** 61576 entering Hockley station in November 1956. (*R.C. Riley/Transport Treasury*)

Class E72 consisted of ten 0-6-0 locomotives built by the GER in 1912. Class T77 consisted of twenty-five 0-6-0s built by the GER between 1916 and 1920. The two classes were similar in appearance, but the E72 had tail rods added to their pistons which necessitated a rather large overhang at the front. The LNER classified class E72 as J18 and class T77 as J19. All the locomotives of class J19 were rebuilt in a similar style to the D16/3 and B12/3 classes, commencing in 1934. The un-rebuilt locomotives were classified J19/1 and the rebuilt locomotives J19/2. The locomotives of class J18 were rebuilt to class J19/2 in 1935 and 1936. The last members were withdrawn in 1962.

Class D81 consisted of twenty-five 0-6-0 locomotives built by the GER in 1920 and 1922. The LNER classified them J20 and they were rebuilt in the same manner as the D16/3, B12/3 and J19/2 classes. No 64699 'originally GER No 1294' worked the last steam goods train over the Southminster line on 26 August 1960. One is recorded as working an excursion train to Southend in the 1950s whilst another is known to have worked a Shenfield to Southend local during the 1950s.

The first locomotives of class L77 (and what was later LNER class N7) first appeared in 1915. This very useful class of 0-6-2 tank locomotives eventually numbered 134 locomotives. Twelve were built by the GER. Two in 1915 and ten in 1921. Ten were built by the LNER at the GE's Stratford works in 1923 and 1924. The remaining 112 were built between 1925 and 1928 at the former Great Central Railway (GCR) works at Gorton in Manchester, at the former Great

**Rochford station** in 1956 with J20 No 64693 on a goods train. (*R.C. Riley/Transport Treasury*)

**J20 64694** on up Southend line goods approaching Shenfield in July 1959. (*R.F. Roberts SLS Collection*)

Northern Railway(GNR) works at Doncaster, Robert Stephenson's and William Beardmore. The original locomotives had Belpaire fireboxes, as did most of the later locomotives, but those built at Doncaster had round topped fireboxes. Some of the locomotives with Belpaire fireboxes were later rebuilt with round-topped fireboxes. The last survivors of the class were withdrawn in 1962. One locomotive, No 69621, which was the last locomotive built at Stratford, has been preserved and was at the Southend centenary celebrations in 1989.

Following its formation, the LNER renumbered all the GER's locomotives by adding 7,000 to their old number e g. No 1 became No 7001 and No 1900 became No 8900. In 1946 there was another renumbering of LNER locomotives.

Following the Grouping of the GER into the LNER in 1923, a number of classes of locomotives from the other constituent companies appeared on the New Essex Lines. These were mainly

**LNER built** N7 No 69630 at Southminster on a Wickford train in the last days of steam working. (*Author's collection*)

ex-GNR locomotives. There were also a number of new classes that were built under the Chief Mechanical Engineers Nigel Gresley, Edward Thompson (1941-6) and Arthur Peppercorn (1946-7). It was the class that *wasn't* built that is of most interest. In 1927, the use of tender locomotives on the Liverpool Street to Southend services was deemed by the LNER as wasteful. The Southern and the London, Midland and Scottish railways used large tank locomotives for similar or longer distances. A tank locomotive of the 2-6-4 wheel arrangement was designed for the Southend services, but as mentioned earlier the Sevenoaks accident on the Southern Railway involving one of that company's River class 2-6-4 tank locomotives caused the LNER to abandon the proposed L2 class 2-6-4 tank locomotive. With the current projects for new build locomotives, I can't help but wish one of these locomotives which potentially had so much promise could be built.

The first main former GNR classes to see service on the GE were classes K1 and K2 2-6-0s. Class K1 first appeared in 1912 and comprised ten locomotives. Class K2 first appeared in 1914 and comprised sixty-five locomotives. Between 1920 and 1937, the ten members of class K1 were rebuilt to class K2. K1s had first appeared on the former GE lines in 1923 and the K2 class in 1924. The last member of the class was withdrawn in 1961. Whilst photographic evidence exists for class K2 working a service to Southend, it is not known if a K1 ever proceeded this far. According to the *Railway Magazine* of March 1928, two K2s had recently been stationed at Southend.

The K3 class was a three cylinder 2-6-0 which first appeared on the GNR in 1920 and ultimately consisted of 193 locomotives. They first saw service on the former GE in the 1930s. They were used on amongst other things, the Southend passenger services. In 1945, one of the locomotives was rebuilt with two cylinders. This is also known to have worked to Southend. It was classified K5. The class K5 was withdrawn in 1959. The last class K3 was withdrawn in 1961. Plans exist for a new K3 to be built.

Other locomotive classes of GNR origin that are known to have worked on the New Essex Lines, were the N2 0-6-2 tank locomotives, which numbered 107 locomotives The class had first appeared in 1920. Photographic evidence exists of one at Southend in the late 1920s. They are known to have been occasionally allocated to Southend and were used on Southend to Shenfield

K3 No 61921 between Hockley and Rochford in 1956. (*Brian Pask*)

local trains. One was, for a time the shed pilot at Southend in the 1950s. The last member of the class was withdrawn in 1962. One, No 69523 (originally GNR No 1744), has been preserved.

When the Southend line was being electrified, a Class C12 4-4-2 tank locomotive worked on the Southminster branch. Class C12 were built for the GNR under the locomotive superintendentship of Henry Alfred Ivatt (1895-1911).

A number of GNR classes are reported to have worked to Southend on excursions. There is photographic evidence of a class D2 4-4-0 at Southend and J3 0-6-0s are also known to have worked to Southend on excursions. The D2 class originated in 1897 under Ivatt and the J3 in 1892 under the locomotive superintendentship of Patrick Stirling (1866-95). There were 293 members of the J3 class and seventy-two members of the D2 class. The last member of the D2 class was withdrawn in 1951 and the last member of the J3 class in 1954.

The J6 class 0-6-0s are known also to have worked excursions to Southend. The J6 class consisting of 110 locomotives had first appeared in 1911. The last member was withdrawn in 1962.

A number of locomotives whose origins go back to the former GCR or, as it was called up until 1897, the Manchester, Sheffield and Lincolnshire Railway, are known to have visited the New Essex Lines.

During the period of the electrification of the Southend line, an N5 0-6-2 tank locomotive was allocated to the New Essex Lines and worked on the Southminster branch. The N5 class comprised 131 members and had first appeared in 1891 under the locomotive superintendentship of Thomas Parker (1886-93). The last member of the class was withdrawn in 1960.

During the rebuilding of the turntable at Liverpool Street in the spring of 1951 to allow its use by the new Britannia Class 4-6-2 locomotives, some A5 4-6-2 tank locomotives appeared on the Southend services. The A5 class comprised of forty-four locomotives built between 1911 and 1925 and had first appeared under the locomotive superintendentship of John Robinson (1900-22). Those that appeared on the Southend services had been built in 1925 (to the LNER's composite loading gauge) rather than the GC loading gauge. As mentioned earlier, they were not popular during their time on the Southend services; either with engine crews or passengers. The last member of the class was withdrawn in 1960.

The B17 class 4-6-0s comprised seventy-three locomotives built between 1928 and 1937. The reason that they were built was the shortage of express passenger locomotives on the GE section, which by the mid-1920s had become chronic, exacerbated by an increase in traffic and the introduction of standard LNER carriage trains which themselves had become heavier. The loading gauge of the GE section was smaller than that of most of the other constituents of the LNER. There were also restrictions on the axle load of a locomotive that could be used on the GE section, in particular into its London termini of Liverpool Street and Fenchurch Street. The K2 class had been sent to the GE lines in 1924. The only modification required had been the shortening of their chimneys. Whilst the K2s had been more powerful than the B12s, they had not really been suitable for heavy passenger work. Things came to a head in 1926 in the aftermath of the General Strike, when, as mentioned earlier, there was a shortage of coal which led to appalling engine performances and the virtual failure of stopping services on the Southend line. The management of the LNER ordered Nigel Gresley to do something, which was how the design for the 2-6-4 tank locomotive for the Southend services came about. He was also ordered to arrange for a new three cylinder 4-6-0 express locomotive for the longer distance main line services. Owing to the weight restrictions on bridges and the length of the turntables on the GE section (which caused problems for the Doncaster drawing office), Gresley handed the design over to the North British Locomotive Company who came up with a satisfactory design of locomotive.

Two members of the class were streamlined in 1937 for the 'East Anglian' service from London to Norwich. This was rather more of a cosmetic exercise as the average speed of the train was less than 60 miles per hour. The streamlining was removed in 1951. The class was all named. The first one was named *Sandringham* after the royal residence in Norfolk. Later ones were named after football clubs. These locomotives originally worked on the GC section. A few were named after regiments associated with the east of England. The two locomotives that were streamlined were given names associated with the service; *East Anglian* and *City of London*. Nine of the locomotives were rebuilt from 1944 with two cylinders and were classed B2. Both the B17s and the B2s worked to Southend. A B17 is known to have worked a Southminster branch passenger train on at least one occasion and the train was photographed by Brian Pask. The last B17 was withdrawn in 1960 and the last B2 in 1959. The last B17, No 61668 *Bradford City*, was stored at Southend before scrapping. There are plans to build two new members of the class. One named *Spirit of Sandringham* and the other named *Manchester United*.

The J39 class of 0-6-0s originally appeared in 1926 and consisted of 289 locomotives. They were used on the New Essex Lines on both passenger and goods services to Southend and goods services to Southminster. The last one was withdrawn in 1962.

**B17 No** 61612 *Houghton Hall* on a down train between Prittlewell and Southend. (*Kidderminster Railway Museum*)

**A J39 arriving**
at Wickford on
a goods train.
(*Brian Pask*)

The V1 class three cylinder 2-6-2 tank locomotives first appeared in 1930 and a total of eighty-one were built. In addition, ten locomotives which had their boiler pressure increased from 180 pounds per square inch to 200 pounds per square inch were classed V3 appearing in 1939, plus seventy-one of the V1s were rebuilt to class V3. Although they were mainly allocated to sheds in the north of England and Scotland, some did work in the east of England from 1939 to the early 1950s. The V1 class is known to have worked both to Southend and to Southminster. The V1s were all withdrawn by the end of 1962. Three of the V3s which had been rebuilt from V1s were allocated to Stratford on 31 December 1947. Although I have not found any record of them having reached Southend, I don't discount it as often the commonplace does not appear in magazines such as *Trains Illustrated*. In any event, unless one was very knowledgeable, one could not distinguish a V3 from a V1. According to David Butcher, although of higher route availability than the published figure for the Southminster line, they were still permitted to run over the line by special dispensation. The V3s were all withdrawn by 1964. There are plans for a new V3 to be built.

The V4 class three-cylinder 2-6-2 locomotives comprised two locomotives which were introduced in 1941. Although the class worked in Scotland for most of their life, in the early days, the first member of the class was based in London and worked to Southend. They were good engines and were well liked by engine crews. They were withdrawn in 1957. The reason that no more were built was that shortly after their completion, Sir Nigel Gresley died and was succeeded as Chief Mechanical Engineer of the LNER by Edward Thompson who had different ideas on locomotives. At the time of Gresley's death, a further eight V4s were on order. Thompson cancelled the order. Had the class appeared a few months earlier, more would have been built. It was a case of the class appearing at the wrong time. There are plans for a new V4 to be built.

In late 1939, Gresley designed a 2-6-4T for outer suburban services. There were two versions of the design. One with two cylinders and one with three cylinders. Unfortunately nothing came of the proposal.

The new class B1 two cylinder 4-6-0s first appeared in 1942. A total of 410 B1s were built. They were used all over the LNER system including the Southend line. No 61335 hauled the last steam passenger train from Southend to Liverpool Street on 30 December 1956. No 61156 worked a ballast train on the Southminster branch on 29 August 1961. This was the last steam working on the Southminster branch and the New Essex Lines. The last members of the class survived until 1967. Two have been preserved – Nos 61264 and 61306 *Mayflower*. They were good engines, but rough riders when they were run down.

The first member of the new class L1 2-6-4 tank locomotives appeared in 1945 and further members of the class started appearing in 1948. In total one hundred were built. They saw service on the Southend line on passenger and parcels trains. Because the class had an LNER Route Availability of 7 and the Southminster branch had a Route Availability of 6, the engines were not supposed to work to Southminster, but they occasionally did. A member of the class, No 67729, worked the last proven steam train into and out of Southend (Victoria) on 18 May 1961. The last member of the class was withdrawn in 1962. The locomotives had a mixed reception.

**B1 No** 61363 leaving Rochford in October 1956. (*R.C. Riley/Transport Treasury*)

**L1 No** 67729 departing Shenfield for Southend in the early 1950s. The leading coach is ex-GER. (*On-Line Transport Archive*)

The new K1 class 2-6-0 first appeared in 1945 when one of the six three cylinder K4 2-6-0s which had first appeared in 1937 was rebuilt with two cylinders. A batch of seventy new locomotives, but modified from the prototype by Arthur Peppercorn, appeared in 1949. Some of them worked to Southend. The last member of the class (No 62005) was withdrawn in 1967 and was preserved.

The new O1 class of 2-8-0s had first appeared in 1944. (The original GNR O1s were reclassed O3.) The class which consisted of fifty locomotives was rebuilt from the former GCR O4 class which first appeared in 1911 and which ultimately comprised 126 locomotives. However, a further 511 locomotives were built for the British government for use by the army in the First World War and to keep British industry going during the post-war run-down in military manufacturing. Additionally nineteen locomotives were rebuilt to class O4 from the O5 class of 2-8-0s, which had first appeared in 1918. An O1 is known to have visited Southend in 1958. The last O1 was withdrawn in 1965.

Two of what can be termed wartime classes made appearances on the New Essex Lines. The WD 2-8-0s (or later LNER O7 class) originated in 1943 to the design of Robin Riddles who was later

**L1 No** 67726 at Southminster on a Wickford train composed entirely of Thompson carriages. *(W.A. Camwell/SLS Collection)*

**K1 No** 62040
at Rochford on
a parcels train.
(*Brian Pask*)

the Chief Mechanical Engineer of British Railways from 1948 to
1953. The class totalled 935 locomotives and were based on the
class 8F 2-8-0s of the LMSR which had first appeared in 1935
under that railway's Chief Mechanical Engineer William Stanier.
(1932-44). Between 1935 and 1946, 852 of the locomotives were built
including 208 for the War Department, 331 for the LMSR, 68 for the
LNER and 145 for the wartime Railway Executive Committee. The
LNER locomotives were classed O6. It is not known if one reached
Mountnessing siding on an oil train. The WDs certainly did. From
a remark about members of the class being used on goods trains
to Southend in the immediate aftermath of the East Coast floods
in 1953, it is clear that the WDs also reached Southend during the
Second World War. In 1946, the LNER purchased 200 of the WD
locomotives and classed them O7. The O6 Class was sold to the
LMSR. British Railways purchased a further 533 WD locomotives.
During BR days, the class worked to Southend on goods trains and
apparently, sometimes on excursion trains, although I have found
no printed evidence of their use on passenger services. Allegedly,
if Stratford shed in East London wanted an engine for an excursion
to Southend it would book a WD off a goods train which had come

down from March as having dropped its firebars and send it off to Southend on an excursion! The last WD was withdrawn in 1967 and the last 8F in 1968. Examples of both classes have been preserved.

The S160 class 2-8-0s comprised a total of 2,120 locomotives of which 400 worked on Britain's railways. The class was first built in 1942 and was constructed to the overall design of Major J.W. Marsh for the Railway Branch of the Corps of Engineers of the American Army. 168 locomotives saw service on the LNER. They are known to have worked oil trains to Mountnessing and one was seen by David Collins in Billericay yard with a cracked frame. Given that WD 2-8-0s are known to have worked to Southend, it is not disproven that class 160s also worked to Southend, although I have not found any evidence of them having done so. Following the Allied invasion of Europe in 1944, the S160 class left the LNER and the British railways as a whole for the continent. Some have been preserved and several have been brought back to this country.

Following its formation, British Railways renumbered all its locomotives other than those of the former Great Western Railway. The locomotives of the former LNER had 60,000 added to their number and the former LMSR 40,000 to their number e.g. LNER No 1000

**An unidentified** ex-WD 2-8-0 passing a pair of class 307 emus at Rochford. (*Brian Pask*)

became BR No 61000 and LMSR No 5000 became BR No 45000. Former Southern Railway locomotives had 30,000 added to their number.

After the formation of British Railways, a number of former LMSR locomotives appeared on the New Essex Lines. During the 1950s the most common ones were the former MR locomotives. The MR version of the LTSR 79 class 4-4-2 tank locomotives had been ordered by the MR in 1922 just before the grouping, but the first members of the class did not appear until after the grouping in 1923. The original 79 class had consisted of 4 locomotives built for the LTSR in 1909 under the locomotive superintendentship of Thomas Whitelegg (1880-1910) who was the father of Robert Harben Whitelegg (1910-12). The GER would not however allow Robert Whitelegg's 4-6-4 tank engines into Fenchurch Street station. The MR version of the 79 class were built because the MR got to the point where it decided that the GER wouldn't allow anything bigger into Fenchurch Street and electrification was going to take some time. In total, thirty-five locomotives were built. They first appeared on the GE section in 1954. They were used in passenger and parcels service on both the Southend and Southminster lines. The last one was withdrawn in 1960.

On two occasions, three cylinder 2-6-4 tank locomotives that had been built for the LTS line in 1934 worked to Southend (Victoria). This happened once with an inspection saloon and once with a breakdown crane. There were thirty-six of these and they survived until the end of steam on the LTS line in 1962. The first member of the class No 42500 is preserved.

**An unidentified** former LMS built 79 class locomotive on a parcels train near Warners Bridge, Rochford, in 1957. (*Brian Pask*)

**Southminster station** about 1953 with an unidentified former LMS built 79 class locomotive on a Wickford train awaiting departure. (*Kidderminster Railway Museum*)

**ex-LMS** Stanier class 4MT 3 cylinder 2-6-4T No 42525 at Southend GE shed on a breakdown train in 1955 on one of the only two times that a member of the class visited Southend GE. (*HMRS*)

The class 4MT or class 4 Mixed Traffic locomotives had first appeared on the LMSR in 1947. 162 were built and they were designed under the direction of Henry Ivatt who was the Chief Mechanical Engineer of the LMSR in 1946 and 1947. There are references in *Trains Illustrated* in the 1950s to them working to Southend. The last member of the class was withdrawn in 1968. One is preserved.

Other locomotives of LMSR origin that reached Southend on excursions were the class 5MT 4-6-0s which originated in 1934. There were 842 locomotives in the class and some lasted until 1968. Also the class 5MT 2-6-0s which originated in 1926 and comprised 244 locomotives, of which some lasted until 1967.

According to the *Railway Observer* of November 1959, on 2 October of that year one of the class 2MT 2-6-0s which originated in 1946 worked to Southend on goods duties. Some of the class lasted until 1967 and a few are preserved. British Railways Standard locomotives also appeared on the Southend line.

**An ex-LMS** 5MT 4-6-0 entering Prittlewell on an excursion from the London Midland Region in 1957. (*Brian Pask*)

The Britannia Class 7MT 4-6-2s which first appeared in 1951 and numbered fifty-five locomotives were the largest engines ever to work a passenger or a goods train to Southend. Their most famous

appearances were made during the 1955 footplatemen's strike, but they also appeared sporadically at other times. The first instance seems to have been on 21 June 1953 when No 70037 *Hereward the Wake* was observed at Brentwood on a Southend semi-fast. No 70002 *Geoffrey Chaucer* worked an evening rush hour train in April 1955. After the strike, there were occasions they appeared at Southend, including some goods workings. The late Dennis Swindale in *Branch Line to Southminster* mentions the legend that one of the class visited the Southminster branch. Having too high a route availability for the branch, they would not have been allowed on it. It is not impossible though that at some time for some reason one ventured a very short way up the branch and so the legend started. There again somehow someone may have confused the Standard Class 4 2-6-0s which did work to Southminster with the Britannias. Some Britannias survived until 1968. Two have been preserved.

Rather more down to earth were the class 4 2-6-0s which first appeared in 1953. Five of the class of 115 were allocated to Stratford and sometimes worked on Southend and Southminster trains. The last members of the class were withdrawn in 1967. Some are preserved. In 2002 a Class 4 and an ex ex-LMS class 5 4-6-0 visited the Southend and Southminster lines on a railtour.

**BR Standard** 7MT 4-6-2 No 70009 *Alfred the Great* leaving Southend on a return excursion to Norwich in 1957. In the background is an L1. (*HMRS*)

**Preserved 7MT** No 70000 *Britannia* at Southend Airport station on a special train. (*Dr Ian Scotchman*)

**An unidentified** Standard 4 2-6-0 leaving Southend for Liverpool Street. (*Brian Pask*)

## Electric multiple units/traction

We now come to the electric multiple units. In British Railways days practically everything worked to Southend.

The oldest units were the ninety-two members of class 306 three-car units which been built for the Shenfield electrification of 1949. The original intended electrification date was 1941. According to Ernst Birchler, one time Area Mechanical and Electrical Engineer at Ilford Depot prior to the cessation of work for the duration of the war, the first six units had been built but not fitted with traction motors, motor generator sets and other electrical equipment and were stored at various places around the country, including Epping according to Dave Brennand who was told this by an old driver. Construction of the remaining eighty-six units did not start until 1946. These units worked to Southend whether in 1500 volt direct current mode or when converted to alternating current at 6,250/25,000 volts. When they were designed, the middle trailer carriage was going to be a First and Third Class composite carriage, but in 1940, First Class accomodation on local trains in the London Transport area was withdrawn and the carriage became all Third Class. The original livery of the first six units was blue and cream. The livery was altered at the beginning of the Second World War from red and cream as the livery for the LNER's electric multiple units was too easily visible to enemy aircraft. It is not known whether any of the units, other than the first six, were painted blue and cream. Prior to their delivery, any units previously painted blue and cream were repainted BR multiple unit/railcar green. The reason that we know that the first six units were painted blue and cream is that according to Ernst Birchler, the driving trailer of unit 06 was damaged in Ilford Car Sheds in a collision with a concrete buffer stop and it was then that the blue and white livery was discovered. Units 04, 29 and 69 formed the first electric train to reach Southend on 11 December 1956. The class was introduced into service in 1949 and lasted until 1981. They were not the most comfortable units to ride in, but they could certainly convey huge passenger loadings, being of sliding door open stock. On conversion to alternating current the motor coach with the pantograph was re-positioned from one of the end carriages to the middle carriage and their numbers were prefixed by an additional 0. No 017 has since been preserved.

The following four classes were originally mixed compartment and open stock. The thirty-two members of class 307 four-car

**Class 306** emu No 062 converted in preparation for alternating current but working on direct current leads a Southend train at Shenfield in 1960. *(Frank Church/Essex Bus Enthusiasts Group)*

units appeared in 1956. Unit No 02s was exhibited at the Southend Centenary exhibition in March 1956 and units 15s and 16s worked the special train carrying dignitaries from Southend to London on 28 December 1956. As mentioned earlier, following the conversion from direct current to alternating current, there was a plan to send some of the units to the Manchester to Sheffield line which was still operating on 1,500 volts direct current and use them to replace locomotive hauled trains on some services. This never happened, and all the units were eventually converted to alternating current. After conversion from direct current to alternating current, the carriage with the pantograph was re-positioned from an intermediate carriage to one of the end carriages. The suffix 's' was dropped and their numbers were prefixed with a 1. In the early 1980s the class was completely refurbished. All compartments were taken out and the trains were made open plan with gangways between carriages within the set. Unit No 307104 formed with unit No 305510 part of the first electric test train on the Southminster branch on 23 March 1986. They survived until 1990 on the former GE lines, but four were sent to Leeds in Yorkshire where they worked until 1993.

Class 302 comprised 112 four-car units which were introduced in 1959 and first saw service on the Tendring Hundred lines following the electrification of the section from Colchester to Clacton and Walton in that year. They were alternating current units from the start and were used on both the GE and LTS lines. Some, but not all in the early 1980s had their compartments removed and some but not all were refurbished in the manner of the class 307 units. Some were converted to three-car postal units by the removal of the composite trailer carriage and the removal of all seats from the other carriages plus the sealing of doors and the provision of large folding shutters. The class lasted into privatisation days and the last members were withdrawn by LTS Rail which was re-branded c2c in 1999.

The class 305 and class 308 four-car units were similar to the class 307 and class 302 units, except that instead of having flat ends of the driving carriages they had partially sloping ends which were termed 'piano fronts'. They were all refurbished like class 307. Class 305 survived into the 1990s, but class 308 as late as 2001. By the time of their final withdrawal, they had been moved away from the GE area and some of the class 305 had been converted to three-car units by removing the intermediate trailer carriage. To slightly confuse matters, there were also versions of the two classes that were built as three-car open carriage units. These were mainly used on the Enfield and Chingford lines, but like most electric multiple units, ended up on the Southend line. The three-car units disappeared in the late 1980s. For a time in the 1980s, some of the three-car units had an intermediate composite trailer carriage added making them four-car units. All three classes were introduced into service in 1960. However for the boat train traffic to Tilbury that existed when the LTS line was electrified, a variant of the four-car units which had a luggage van in the formation was provided for the line. With the decline and eventual demise of the boat train traffic from Tilbury in 1971, the luggage van in some was fitted up for passenger accommodation. Of those that remained, three were converted to parcels units by removing the intermediate trailer car. All variants of these ended up at Southend. These lasted until the late 1980s and early 1990s. In total there were thirty-three class 308 four-car Great Eastern line units, nineteen class 305 four-car units, fifty-two class 305 three-car units, three class 308 three-car units and nine LTS line class 308 four-car units. The difference between a class 305 and a class 308 unit was that the former had GEC motors and the later English Electric motors. It was in un-refurbished class 308 unit No 154 that I had my only cab ride in the spring of 1985. Unit No 305510 formed with unit No 307104 part of the first electric test train on the Southminster branch on 23 March 1986.

Classes 302, 305, 307 and 308 worked to Southminster after the electrification of the line. In the early 1960s, whilst the class 306 and class 307 units were being rebuilt to alternating current, some class 304 four-car units built from 1960 onwards for the Manchester,

**Class 305** emu
No 510 and a class
307 await departure
from Southend in
1976. (*R.F. Roberts/
SLS Collection*)

Liverpool and Crewe services, were loaned to the GE lines, and ended up at Southend. This class had forty-five members and latterly converted to three- car units by dispensing with the trailer composite carriage.

From the late 1970s onwards members of class 312 started appearing on the Southend line. Initially in off-peak hours, but later in the peak hours. The class comprised forty-nine four-car units and first appeared in 1975, but did not go into traffic until 1976. They were gangwayed within sets. On the Southminster line they appeared on peak hour workings to and from London until the end of June 2004, when the last one was withdrawn. The reason for their long usage on the Southminster peak hour services was that, until selective door opening could be fitted to class 321 units, the Department of Transport would not allow the use of twelve carriage trains with sliding doors on lines where there were platforms only capable of taking eight carriages.

During the mid-1980s, some class 310 car units appeared on the Southend line. These comprised fifty units, which had been introduced in 1965 for local services out of Euston. Initially they were gangwayed between the first and second and third and fourth carriages within a unit, but not throughout the whole unit. In the mid-1980s they were refurbished and gangwayed throughout the whole set. They operated to Southend in both their original and refurbished versions. The refurbished versions are also known to have worked to Southminster. They left the former GE lines during the early 1990s, but the last in service was on what is now c2c in 2004.

The sixty-one class 315 four-car units first appeared in 1980 and withdrawal is now taking place. They have worked to both Southend and Southminster, but since 2015, work only on London Overground and TFL Rail services. They are open stock with sliding doors.

Class 321 is comprised of ninety-four four-car units and was introduced in 1988. They are open stock with sliding doors and have virtually monopolised the Southend services and latterly also the Southminster services. At the end of 2013 Abellio Greater Anglia, the current holders of the Greater Anglia franchise in conjunction with Eversholt Rail Group, refitted class 321 unit No 321448 as a demonstrator to show what they planned to do with their class 321 fleet. The refurbishment involved completely refitting the interior resulting in two variations of seating arrangements. The upgrade offered two plus two and two plus three seating and a new First Class area, air conditioning and fixed panel windows to replace opening windows, an overhauled traction system as well as a new livery. Passengers were asked to provide their comments on the two new types of train interior. In mid-2015 Webtec were awarded a contract to refurbish and overhaul an initial batch of thirty units. These were due to return to service between spring 2016 and late 2017. The first ones have now entered service.

Class 322 four- car units which comprised five members were introduced in 1989 originally used for services to Stansted Airport

**Class 321** emu No 321 327 at Southminster in 1994. (*RCTS*)

appeared and on the New Essex Lines in 2004 and 2005. These were similar to class 321, but had slightly more luggage space.

In 2004 and 2005 four class 357 four- car units from c2c were loaned to'One' railway as it was then. The class consists of seventy four units, which are open stock with sliding doors.

Class 309 were the units built in 1962 for the Liverpool Street to Clacton and Walton services. The class comprised twenty-seven units. Of these, eight were originally two- car units, eight were four-car griddle (buffet) units and seven four-car units. Later there was some reformation of the units which resulted in two-car, three-car and four-car units. As mentioned earlier in April 1972 during an industrial dispute a Southend line train is known to have been worked by some of these units. Other than that lone example, the only other workings to Southend that I am aware of was one appearing at the Southend centenary celebrations in 1989 plus two rail tours – one in 1978 and one in 1994. In 1994, some units were transferred to north-west England where some remained in service until 2000. Two units have been preserved.

As part of Abellio's £1.4bn investment programme, twenty-two ten-car emus of class 720/1 and eighty-nine five-car units emus of class 720/5 are to be introduced on suburban services on the West Anglia and Great Eastern lines in 2020. These will replace the class 321 emus on the New Essex Lines.

Class 86/2 Bo-Bo electric locomotives had been introduced in 1965. They first appeared on the lines of the former GER in 1985 for use mainly on the London to Norwich services and London to Harwich boat trains. They also appeared on a few other services including from the summer 1985 timetable the newspaper and mail services to Southend. Owing to the lack of an electrified crossover at Southend their appearance was the exception rather than the rule. From the summer 1986 timetable electric haulage of the service was discontinued. One is known to have worked to Southminster after the electrification of the line. Some are still in service mainly on Freightliner services.

A number of other emus have visited the New Essex Lines, but not in regular passenger service. These were class 317 which visited Southend Victoria on excursions to the Southend Airshow, a railtour in 1992 and the centenary exhibition in 1989. There was the out-of-hours test of the class 379 electric multiple unit on the Southminster line in October 2014. Both class 360 and class 345 (CrossRail Elizabeth line) emus that have been tested on the Southend line but not in traffic.

# Diesel multiple units

Various diesel multiple units operated over the New Essex Lines, mainly to Southminster including the section of the Southend line from Shenfield to Wickford. They were occasionally seen on the Southend line when engineering work was taking place before rail replacement buses became the norm. Diesel multiple units were also used on some Southend services during the 1982 footplatemens'strike. In the summer 1962 timetable there is shown a working from Shenfield to Southend and return on Saturday night/Sunday morning, as specifically being worked by a diesel unit.

The first diesel unit to appear on the lines was the ACV/BUT lightweight three- car dmu which was built in 1952 running trials on the Southminster branch from 21 September to 9 October 1953. As related elsewhere, prior to going into service on the Southminster line, the train is known to have reached Southend (Victoria), but without carrying passengers. It would seem that the train was refuelled at Southminster and Wickford by a road tanker.

Early units on the Southminster line were Derby Lightweight two-car dmus first introduced in 1954, first appearing on the New Essex lines in 1956. There were 219 of these units and they lasted until 1969.

Another class was the Wickham two-car dmus which comprised five units. They were introduced in 1957. They had a chequered career. The last unit surviving until the early 1980s albeit in departmental use. British Rail classed this class 109.

The Craven two-car and three-car dmus of classes 105 and 106 were in service from 1959 to 1988.

The Metro-Cammell class 101 units could be used in two-car, three-car or four-car formations. They first appeared in 1956 and lasted until 2003.

The Derby built Lea Valley Class 125 three-car units had been introduced in 1958 for use on the Lea Valley line out of Liverpool Street, which was not electrified until 1969. They also saw service on other lines including the Southminster line.

The class 116 Derby suburban units also saw service on the Southminster line. The class was used on the line as three-car units. class 116 was introduced in 1957 and survived until 1990. Some have been preserved.

A class 201 six-car diesel electric multiple unit visited Southend and Southminster on a railtour in 2002.

## Diesel locomotives

The Class 08 diesel-electric shunters of 0-6-0 wheel arrangement, which date back to 1953, are known on rare occasions to have visited the New Essex Lines. This class which boasted 996 members was used all over the British network and some are still in service. This class and the following class 03 had their cab at one end of the locomotive. All diesel shunters were essentially diesel versions of steam locomotives. Although they did some light goods work as well as shunting, normally they did not haul passenger trains. James Jolly photographed one on an electrification works train at Southminster in 1985.

Class 03 diesel-mechanical shunters of 0-6-0 wheel arrangement first appeared in 1957 and comprised 230 members. One – D2184 – was used at Southend coal depot. All except one have been withdrawn. A number have been preserved including five examples at Mangapps Farm Railway Museum.

Class 15 Bo-Bo diesel-electric locomotives first appeared in 1957. The class comprised of forty- four locomotives and were mostly used on local freight and empty stock workings. Their main use on the New Essex Lines was on freight, as well as one notable occasion hauling class 302 emus to Southend prior to the conversion of the line from direct to alternating current. Some of them worked summer excursion trains to Southend (Victoria). As they were not fitted for train heating they could not undertake passenger work in the winter. With the closure of goods yards, there was less work for them and they were all withdrawn by the end of 1971. Four were kept as non-powered electric train pre-heating units and one has survived into preservation. class15 and the following class 16 were very similar to an American road switcher in that they had a long hood on one side of their cab and a short hood on the other side. This necessitated a crew of two, which did not quite fit in with British Rail's ideas for single-manning of locomotives.

The ten locomotives of class 16 were introduced in 1958 for local freight working and only lasted until 1968. Their demise can again be attributed to the widespread closure of goods yards. Like class 15, they were not fitted for train heating. Although intended for freight work the class is known to have worked summer excursion trains to Southend.

Class 20 originally consisted of 228 locomotives of the Bo-Bo wheel arrangement introduced in 1957. They were mainly used

on freight work including the nuclear flask trains to and from Southminster. On 31 August 2006, Nos 20306 and 20309 worked the final nuclear flask train. They also worked summer excursion trains to Southend, but like classes 15 and 16 they are not fitted for train heating. Some of class 20 are still in service and some have been preserved. Class 20 has the cab at one end of the locomotive.

The class 31 A1A-A1A diesel-electric locomotives first appeared at the end of 1957. Eventually 263 were in service. Some of their trials were conducted on the Southend line. They were used on goods and passenger workings on the Southend line, including excursions and parcels workings. As mentioned earlier, during industrial disputes, they occasionally worked scheduled passenger services on the Southend line such as the working in the industrial dispute in 1974 and during the ban on overtime and Sunday working by maintenance supervisors in the spring of 1975. On the Southminster branch they were used on goods workings including the nuclear flask train and the Sunday through passenger train in the late 1950s at least. These, and all subsequent diesels, were doubled ended. The last one in traffic was withdrawn in 2018.

**An unidentified** class 16 arriving at Southend on an excursion in 1959. (*HMRS*)

**An unidentified** class 20 arriving at Southend on an excursion in 1959. (*HMRS*)

**Class 31** No D5506 on an excursion train at Billericay in 1960. (*Frank Church/ Essex Bus Enthusiasts Group*)

The 309 class 37 Co-Co diesel-electric locomotives first appeared in 1961. They saw similar duties on the New Essex Lines to class 31 including sand trains and flask trains from Southminster as well as excursion trains and service passenger trains during the ban on overtime and Sunday working by maintenance supervisors in the spring of 1975. Some are still in service and some have been preserved.

**Class 31** No D5519 heads a ballast train through Burnham-on-Crouch in 1968. *(R.F. Roberts/SLS Collection)*

Class 47 Co-Co locomotives first appeared in 1962 and a total of 512 were built. Although used on passenger work on the main lines to Norwich and Kings Lynn as well as goods and parcels work, their use on the New Essex Lines was on parcels trains to Southend and sand trains to Southminster plus excursions. Thirty-seven have been modified to class 57 by having their British Sulzer engines replaced by Canadian General Motors engines. Several class 47s are still in service although many have now passed into preservation. One example is 47793 *James Nightall,* which is located at Mangapps.

Class 66 Co-Co diesel-electric locomotives were introduced in 1998 and unlike the other diesel and electric locomotives were built in Canada by the Electro Motive Division of General Motors. They have been observed on engineering trains on the Southend and Southminster lines and a rail tour on the latter. These locomotives may be found in Britain as well as the continent.

**A class** 26 in Southend carriage sidings with the stock of an excursion. (*Brian Pask*)

A number of classes have made infrequent visits to the line. A class 40 1-Co-Co-1 diesel-electric locomotive visited Southend for the first time in 1958. Class 40 comprised 200 locomotives and were first introduced in 1958. The class survived until 1988. Some have been preserved.

On a couple of occasions, class 50 Co-Co locomotives have visited the New Essex Lines. On one occasion on a sand train to Southminster. Class 50 comprised fifty locomotives introduced in 1967 with a Co Co wheel arrangement. They survived in service until 1994. Some have been preserved.

In 1997 a High Speed Train whose power cars are classed 43 visited the Southend and Southminster lines.

Other locomotive classes known to have visited the New Essex Lines are classes 24, 26, 27, 33, 60 and 67 diesel locomotives and class 86/0, 87 and 90 electric locomotives.

At the 1933 Southend exhibition the following locomotives were on display. A1 'later A10 and later still A3 class' 4-6-2 *Flying Scotsman* and the W1 class 4-6-4 No 10000, B12/3 No 8516, B17 No 2800 *Sandringham*, D16/3 No 8900 *Claud Hamilton* and Y5 class 0-4-0S(addle)T(ank) No 7230.

At the Southend centenary exhibition the following locomotives were on display: 08833, 20088, 20187, 31250, 31294, 37138, 37892, 47054, 47581, 58019,59004, 86401, 86410, 91006, Deltic D9000

**Class 37** No 247 on a ballast train at Southminster in 1976. A class 104 dmu is in the platform. (*R. F. Roberts/SLS Collection*)

(Class 55), 309623, 317334, 302991(parcels unit) and of course N7 69621 whilst the Southminster branch that day was worked by green- liveried class 302 302 200 and green livered class 306 306 017.

CHAPTER NINE

# Dates of Opening and Closing and Distances

## Part 1: Lines

Shenfield to Southend: opened Shenfield to Wickford 19 November 1888 for Goods and 1 January 1889 for Passengers. Opened Wickford to Southend 1 October 1889 for Goods and Passengers. Closed for goods circa 1983. Last appearance of goods train to Southend in 1983 working timetable. Closed for mail trains 4 October 1993. The final mail working was on the night of 1/2 October 1993.

Wickford to Southminster: opened Wickford to Southminster 1 June 1889 for Goods and 1 July 1889 for Passengers. Closed to goods on 4 October 1965 except for some private sidings at Battlesbridge, which were closed 5 June 1967, ballast trains to and from Southminster which ceased in November 1978, resumed spring 1979 and ceased November 1979. Nuclear flask trains to and from Southminster: last recorded nuclear flask train running on Thursday 31 August 2006. Since then there have been a number of workings over the line in connection with Decommissioning the power station.

Woodham Ferrers to Maldon East: opened October 1889 for Goods and Passengers. Closed 11 September 1939 for Passengers. Timetabled working for Goods traffic between Cold Norton and Woodham Ferrers ceased on 26 October 1940. Workings over that section of the line by special traffic notice until at least the spring of 1942. Officially Closed for Goods between Maldon West and Woodham Ferrers 1 April 1953. Maldon East to Maldon West Closed for Goods 1 September 1954, Reopened for Goods 3 January 1957. Closed again for Goods 31 January 1959. An enthusiasts' special ran over the section from Maldon East to Maldon West on 6 April 1957.

Fanton Junction to Belchamp Junction and Maldon West Junction to Langford Junction: opened for Goods and Passengers 1 October 1889. Closed for Goods and Passengers 28 February 1895. Apart from the weekly Southend to Colchester and return market train, public excursions to Southend were run from Colchester on 1 October, Harwich and Brightlingsea on 2 October and Walton and Clacton on 3 October 1889. They were poorly patronised.

There were also other occasions prior to their closure when the curves were used by special trains.

Shenfield to Mountnessing: opened for Goods and Passengers 1 January 1934. Down direction only. Became bi-directional in the latter part of 1961. Exact date not known.

## Part 2: Stations and Public Sidings in Alphabetical Order

Althorne: opened 1 June 1889 for Goods and 1 July 1889 for Passengers. Closed 19 December 1960 for Goods.

Barons Lane Public Siding: opened 1 October 1889 for Goods. Closed 1 April 1953 for Goods.

Barons Lane Halt: opened 1 May 1922 for Passengers. Closed 11 September 1939 for passengers.

Battlesbridge: opened 1 June 1889 for Goods and 1 July 1889 for Passengers. Closed 4 October 1965 for Public Goods, but some Private sidings remained open. These closed 5 June 1967 (Not shown in WTT commencing this date).

Billericay: opened 19 November 1888 for Goods and 1 January 1889 for Passengers. Closed 5 June 1967 for Goods.

Bridge 774: Private Halt Opened 1 May 1922 for Passengers and Closed 1 May 1925 for Passengers.

Burnham: opened 1 June 1889 for Goods and 1 July 1889 for Passengers. Closed 4 October 1965 for Goods.

Cold Norton:opened 1 October 1889 for Goods and for Passengers. Closed 11 September 1939 for Passengers and 1 April 1953 for Goods.

Creeksea Ferry Public Siding: opened 1 June 1889 for Goods and Closed 6 October 1947 for Goods.

Down Hall Halt: this was a proposed Passenger Halt which was never built, although trial runs of an auto train were carried out in 1913. The siding here was a Private Siding and not a Public Siding.

Fambridge: opened 1 June 1889 for Goods and 1 July 1889 for Passengers. Closed 4 October 1965 for Goods. Renamed North Fambridge 20 May 2007.

Hawkwell Public Siding: opened for Goods on 1 October 1889 and Closed for Goods on 1 March 1901.

Hawkwell Halt: this was a proposed Passenger Halt which was never built, although trial runs of an auto train were carried out in 1913.

Hockley: opened 1 October 1889 for Goods and Passengers. Closed 5 June 1967 for Goods.

Hogwell Public Siding: opened some time between 12 September and 1 October 1889 for Goods and Closed 6 October 1947 for Goods. Reopened for Goods 5 June 1950 and closed 24 September 1950 for Goods, according to information available.

Maldon East: opened for Goods 15 August 1848 and Passengers 2 October 1848. Closed for Passengers 6 September 1964 and for Goods 15 April 1966.

Maldon West: opened for Goods and Passengers 1 October 1889. Closed for Passengers 22 May 1916. Re-Opened for Passengers 1 August 1919. Closed for Passengers 10 September 1939. Closed for Goods 1 September 1954, Reopened for Goods 3 January 1957, Closed again for Goods 31 January 1959.

Mountnessing Public Siding: opened for Goods 19 November 1888. Closed 9 August 1965 for Goods but some Private sidings remained open. These closed 5 June 1967.

Mountnessing Halt: this was a proposed Passenger Halt which was never built, although trial runs of an auto train were carried out in 1913.

Prittlewell: opened for Goods and Passengers 1 October 1889. Closed 5 June 1967 for Goods.

Ramsden Bellhouse Public Siding: opened for Goods 19 November 1888. Closed 22 August 1960 for Goods.

Ramsden Bellhouse Halt: this was a proposed Passenger Halt which was never built, although trial runs of an auto train were carried out in 1913.

Rayleigh: opened for Goods and Passengers 1 October 1889. Closed 5 June 1967 for Goods.

Rochford: opened for Goods and Passengers 1 October 1889. Closed 5 June 1967 for Goods.

Shenfield: First station opened for Goods and Passenger traffic 1 October 1847 and closed for both 31 March 1850 according to information available. New station opened for Goods and Passengers 1 January 1887. Closed for Goods 4 May 1964.

Southend: opened for Goods and Passengers 1 October 1889. Closed for Public Goods 5 June 1967 but some Private sidings remained open. These closed in the early 1980s. They are last shown in 1983 working timetable. Southend was renamed Southend-on-Sea (Victoria) on 1 May 1949 and renamed Southend (Victoria) on 20 February 1969.

Southend Airport: opened for Passengers on 18 July 2011.

Southminster: opened 1 June 1889 for Goods and 1 July 1889 for Passengers. Closed 4 October 1965 for Goods, except for Ballast Siding and Nuclear Flask Siding. Early November 1978 Ballast Siding Closed. Re-Opened Spring 1979 Goods Ballast Siding. Closed again 3 November 1979. Nuclear Flask Siding officially closed 31 August 2006, but some use has been made of it since that date.

Stow St Mary's Halt: opened for Passengers and Milk Traffic 3 September 1928. Closed for Passengers and Milk Traffic 11 September 1939.

Wickford: opened 19 November 1888 for Goods and 1 January 1889 for Passengers. Closed 5 June 1967 for Goods.

Woodham Ferrers: opened 1 June 1889 for Goods and 1 July 1889 for Passengers. Closed 4 October 1965 for Goods. Renamed South Woodham Ferrers 20 May 2007.

## Part 3: Electification, Diesel Passenger and Final steam

First electric trains on Southend line: 30 November 1956 to Rayleigh, 11 December 1956 to Southend. Trial runs. Public service 31 December 1956 with partial working on 30 December 1956. All at 1,500 volts direct current Shenfield to Southend converted to 6,250 volts alternating current 5 November 1960 and 25,000 volts alternating current 22 January 1979.

First electric train on Southminster line: First test run over line on 23 March 1986. Public service 12 May 1986 with some partial working from 14 April 1986.

First use of diesel traction: 21 September to 9 October 1953 – Wickford to Southminster. Some trial trips before that including one to Southend on 18 September 1953. A special ran from Liverpool Street to Southend on 3 March 1956. Shenfield to Southend. A non-stop relief train operated by a diesel multiple unit 9 to 17 August 1956.

Dieselisation Wickford to Southminster line: 17 September 1956 with one Saturday return working to Shenfield from 22 September to 29 December 1956.

Last known steam working to and from Southend - 18 May 1961.

Last known steam working to and from Southminster - 26 August 1960.

Last known steam working of all on the New Essex Lines – 29 August 1961 Shenfield to/from Burnham

## Distances from Shenfield

| | |
|---|---|
| Shenfield | 0 miles |
| Mountnessing | 1¼ miles |
| Billericay | 4¼ miles |
| Ramsden Bellhouse | 7 miles |
| Wickford | 8¾ miles |
| Rayleigh | 12¾ miles |
| Hockley | 15¾ miles |
| Hawkwell | 17¼ miles |
| Rochford | 18¼ miles |
| Southend Airport | 18¾ miles |
| Prittlewell | 20½ miles |
| Southend | 21¼ miles |

## Distances from Wickford

| | |
|---|---|
| Wickford | 0 miles |
| Battlesbridge | 2½ miles |
| Woodham Ferrers | 5 miles |
| Hogwell | 6¼ miles |
| Fambridge | 8¼ miles |
| Althorne | 11¼ miles |
| Creeksea Ferry | 13 miles |
| Burnham | 14¼ miles |
| Southminster | 16½ miles |

## Distances from Woodham Ferrers

| | |
|---|---|
| Woodham Ferrers | 0 miles |
| Stow St Mary's Halt | 2¼ miles |
| Cold Norton | 3½ miles |
| Barons Lane Siding and Halt | 5 miles |
| Maldon West | 7¼ miles |
| Maldon East | 8¾ miles |

## Modern Day Distances from London Liverpool Street

| | M Ch |
|---|---|
| Shenfield | 20.16 |
| Mountnessing Jn | 21.32 |
| Billericay | 24.28 |
| Wickford | 29.02 |
| Wickford Jn | 29.13 |
| Rayleigh | 33.09 |

| | |
|---|---|
| Hockley | 36.10 |
| Rochford | 38.54 |
| Southend Airport | 39.44 |
| Prittlewell | 40.67 |
| Southend Victoria | 41.42 |
| Wickford | 29.02 |
| Wickford Jn | 29.13 |
| Battlesbridge | 31.40 |
| South Woodham Ferrers | 34.00 |
| North Fambridge | 37.23 |
| Althorne | 40.27 |
| Burnham-on-Crouch | 43.24 |
| Southminster Ground Frame | 45.30 |
| Southminster | 45.42 |

# Sources and Acknowledgements

I would like to thank the following persons for their assistance:

Ernst Birchler; Beryl Board; Nigel Bowdidge; Dave and Belinda Brennand for checking the manuscript; David Butcher; Ken Butcher; Richard Casserley; the late David Collins; Richard Delahoy; Sue Garnham; Rodger Green; David Holden; Barry Jackson; John Jolly for writing the foreword; Peter Kay; Graham Kenworthy; Bill King; the late Paddy Lacey; John Lodge; Vic Mitchell; Myles Munsey for proofreading; Alan Osborne; Brian Pask; the late John Plume; Stephen Potter; John Scott-Morgan of Pen and Sword; John Shelley; Mike Stanbury; Alan Watkins; John Watling. I also wish to thank the following organizations for their assistance:

British Newspaper Library; Essex Bus Enthusiasts Group; Essex County Libraries; Essex Record Office; Great Eastern Railway Society and its members; National Archives; The Omnibus Society.

The following publications were consulted during the research for this book:

*Bradshaw's Railway Guide*
*British Railways (Eastern Region) Magazine*
*Cold Norton Parish Magazine*
*Essex Chronicle*
*Essex Newsman*
*Essex Standard*
*Essex Weekly News*
*Great Eastern Journal*
*Great Eastern Railway Magazine*
*Gloucester Citizen*
*Guardian/Manchester Guardian*
*Ipswich Journal*
*LNER Magazine*
*Railway Magazine*
*Railway and Travel Monthly*
*Railway World*
*Southend Standard*

*The Times*

*Trains Illustrated*

Kelly's, Pigot's and White's directories

Public Timetables of the Great Eastern Railway; London and North Eastern Railway; British Railways; National Omnibus Company; Eastern National; Omnibus Company; City Coach Company and Westcliff-on-Sea Motor Services Limited

Working Timetables of the Great Eastern Railway; London and North Eastern Railway; and British Railways

*The London and North Eastern Railway* – Cecil J. Allen (Ian Allan 1966)

*A History of the LNER* –Michael Bonavia Vol 1 (Allen and Unwin 1982)

*Great British Tramway Networks* - Wingate H. Bett and John C. Gilham (LRTA 1962)

*A History of the LNER* - Michael Bonavia Vol 2 (Allen and Unwin 1982

*A History of the LNER* - Michael Bonavia Vol 3 (Allen and Unwin 1983)

*Echoes of the Great War: The diary of the Reverend Andrew Clark 1914-1919* – Andrew Clark, James Munson, Asa Briggs (eds) (OUP 1985)

*The Westcliff-on-Sea Motor Services Limited. A Company History* Peter F. Clark (Omnibus Society 2014)

*The Years Between Vol 1* R.J.Crawley, D.R. MacGregor and F.D.Simpson Simpson (D. R. MacGregor 1979)

*The Years Between Vol 2* R.J.Crawley, D.R. MacGregor and F.D.Simpson Simpson (OPC 1984)

*By Rail to Victory* - Norman Crump (LNER 1947)

*Southend Corporation: Trams, Trackless and Buses* – Richard Delahoy (Yarnacott 1986)

*Fields of the First: a history of aircraft landing grounds in Essex used during the First World War* – Paul A. Doyle (Forward Airfield Research Publishing 1997)

*A History of the Diocese of Brentwood 1917-1992* – Stewart M. Foster (Diocese of Brentwood 1994)

*South Woodham Ferrers: A Pictorial History.* John Frankland ( Phillimore 1992)

*Anglia East: The Transformation of a Railway.* Ian Cowley (David and Charles 1987)

*Eastern Electric* – John Glover (Ian Allan 2003)

*The Network South East Story 1982-2014* Chris Green and Mike Vincent (OPC 2014)

*Great Eastern Railway Engine Sheds Part 1-* Chris Hawkins and George Reeve (Wild Swan 1986)

*Great Eastern Railway Engine Sheds Part 2-* Chris Hawkins and George Reeve (Wild Swan 1987)

*Thoughts on Ramsden: a brief history of village life.* Isabel Johnson (Author 1993)

*The London, Tilbury and Southend Railway Vols 1, 2, 3 and 4 -* Peter Kay (Peter Kay 1996, 1997, 2010, 2014)

*Essex Railway Heritage and Supplement* – Peter Kay (Peter Kay 2006 and 2007)

*The City Coach Company – An Illustrated History* Alan Osborne and Peter Snell (South Anglia 1988 )

*City Fact File* – Alan Osborne (Essex Bus Enthusiast Group 2002)

*Westcliff-on-Sea Motor Services Limited: An Outline History.* Alan Osborne and J.R. Young (Farley 2011)

*Branch Lines to Maldon* Peter Paye (Lightmoor 2016)

*Shenfield to Southend Line* –Charles Phillips (Oakwood 1984)

*The Story of Stock and Buttsbury* – Charles Phillips (Ian Henry 2002)

*The Story of Billericay -* Charles Phillips (History Press 2013)

*Thompson and Peppercorn Locomotive Engineers -* Col H.C.B. Rogers (Ian Allan 1979)

*Essex Airfields in the Second World War* – Graham Smith (Countryside 1996)

*Essex and Its Race For The Skies 1900-1939* – Graham Smith (Countryside 2007)

*Branch Lines to Maldon* – Dennis Swindale (East Anglian Railway Museum 1978)

*Branch Line to Southminster* – Dennis Swindale (East Anglian Railway Museum 1981)

*Industrial Railways and Locomotives of Essex* – Robin Waywell and Frank Jux (Industrial Railway Society 2011)

*Wickford: A History.* Judith Williams (Phillimore 2008)

*Trackmaps Book 2 Eastern 4th Edition* November 2016

Digital copies on cds of the following magazines are available from the Great Eastern Railway Society:

*British Railways Magazine – Eastern Region,* which was published between 1948 and 1963

*The Great Eastern Railway Magazine,* which was published between 1911 and 1926

*The LNER Magazine,* which was published between 1927 and 1947

*Railway and Travel Monthly* which was published between May 1910 and March 1920 and continued between April 1920 and December 1922 under the revised title of *Travel and Transport Monthly.*

They are a very useful source of information for research and worth purchasing.

For more information please see the Great Eastern Railway Society website: www.gers.org.uk

# Index

## A

Accidents 36-7, 44, 56, 78, 80, 108-9,
  114-6, 155, 157-8, 163-4, 166
Adams, William 61, 207
Air raids 78-81, 107-10
Althorne 32-3, 44-5, 122, 158-9, 162-3,
  165, 171,197-8, 245, 248-9

## B

Barking 12, 17, 21-2,27-8, 59-60, 69, 76,
  128-30, 134, 153
Barons Lane 8, 38, 53, 84-6, 124, 179,
  203, 248
Battery traction 161-163, 181
Battlesbridge 14, 16, 18, 34-5, 44-6,48,
  52-3,108, 159, 163-4, 180, 192-4, 197,
  244-5, 248-9
Benfleet 16,20, 87, 120-1
Billericay 9, 11, 14, 16-20, 22, 25-7,
  29-34, 37-43, 50-2, 75, 79-80, 83,
  93-4, 96, 98, 102, 107-8, 110, 127,136-
  8,145,147-8,150-1, 155, 158, 166-7,
  173, 184-5, 225, 240, 245, 248,
Birchler, Ernst 231
Bird, Charles Kellem 119, 127-9
Bonavia, Michael 129-31
Bradwell 14, 23, 33, 44-5, 49-50, 65,
  87,103, 106, 153, 159, 161, 177-8,
  182, 192
Brentwood 10-11, 14, 17-18, 24, 27, 39,
  41-2, 53, 71, 81, 93, 102, 109-10, 125,
  153, 229
Bromley, Massey 207
Burnham on Crouch 13, 15-6, 19, 24-5,
  30, 36, 42, 44-51, 58, 63, 65-66, 75, 79,
  83, 106, 111, 115, 140-1, 151, 157, 159,
  161-5, 174, 181, 195, 197-9, 241,
  245, 247-9

## C

Canals actual and proposed 11, 16
Canvey 86-7
Chelmsford 10-11, 19, 24,34-6, 53, 64,
  81-3, 96, 102, 110,113, 119-20, 124-8,
  130-1, 133-5, 139-40, 147, 149, 157
City Coach Company 93-4, 102,
  108-10,120, 147, 174
Colchester 7, 10, 13, 23-4, 43, 52-3, 56,
  61, 63-6, 96, 104, 109-10, 119-20, 154,
  207, 244
Cold Norton 13-4, 32, 34, 36, 43, 49-50,
  53, 68, 75, 79, 85, 88, 91, 96, 102-5,
  109-14, 122-4, 165, 173, 179, 201-3,
  244-5, 248
Creeksea Ferry 46-7, 49, 115, 197, 245, 248

## D

Diesel traction 100, 131-3, 139-42, 150-2,
  154-7, 162, 167, 170-1, 174, 181,
  237-43, 247
Down Hall 77, 187, 245

## E

Ealing 69, 73
Eastern National Omnibus Company
  82-3, 90, 93, 96, 99, 108-10, 120, 149, 165.
Electrification 76-7,97, 110, 116-20, 124-40,
  143-50, 154-157, 167-8, 170-2, 247
Electric traction 69, 117, 121, 130, 134,
  139, 142, 149, 155-7, 169, 173,175,
  180-2, 225, 231-6, 242-3, 247
Elliot John 120, 127-9, 131

Emmerson H. J. 17, 25, 42

Essex Chronicle 17-18, 21, 23-5, 27,
    29-33, 37-42, 44, 46-7, 50-3, 60, 71,
    75-6, 78, 81-2, 85, 99-100, 107, 109-11,
    131, 135, 140

Essex Iron Railway 7, 10

Exhibitions 97, 139, 174, 181, 242-3


F

Fambridge 10, 14-5, 44-7, 49, 104,
    108, 114-5, 141, 159, 162, 165, 168,
    171,178, 180, 195-7, 245, 248-9

Fenchurch Street 12, 27, 58-62, 64, 67,
    76, 97, 107, 110, 118, 121, 128, 134,
    143, 153, 156, 158, 218, 226, 228

First World War 77-81

Floods 63, 120-122


G

Galleywood 83

Gresley, Nigel 90, 211, 216, 218, 222


H

Harris, Rev Beresford 17, 25, 27, 39

Hawkwell 34, 28, 52, 64, 77, 189,245, 248

Hill, Alfred 208,

Hockley 10, 13, 20, 22, 25, 34,51-3, 64,
    75, 77, 115, 147, 150, 155, 187, 189,
    212-3,217, 245, 248-9,

Hogwell 47, 115, 119, 195, 246, 248,

Holden, James 57, 206, 209,

Holden, Stephen 208,


I

Ilford 10, 78, 81, 90, 117, 125-6, 128, 130,
    147, 155-6, 231

Ingatestone 17-8, 20-3, 39, 108-9, 131, 167


J

Jolly, John 7, 9, 174,181

Johnson, Sir John 25

Johnson, Samuel 56, 206, 208

L

Leech, Kenneth 76

London and Blackwall Railway 12

London, Tilbury and Southend Railway
    10-18, 20-5, 27-8, 34, 50, 58- 60, 62, 65,
    69-73,75-77, 82, 86, 88,-9, 117, 121-2,
    135-6, 139, 146,170, 182, 206, 226,


M

Maldon 7-8, 10-11, 13-17, 19-20, 22-25,
    28-34, 36-38, 41-44, 47, 50-9, 61, 63-4,
    68, 71, 75, 78-86, 88-91, 96, 99-114, 119,
    122-4, 152-3,159, 164, 168, 174, 179,
    181-2,201-5, 207, 210-12, 244, 246, 248

Mangapps Railway Museum 174,
    181-2, 197, 238, 241

Metropolitan District Railway 69

Mid Essex Junction Railway 20-3, 25

Midland Railway 62, 73, 76

Mountnessing 20, 40, 42, 68-9, 77-9,96,
    106, 124, 137, 158-9, 183-4, 224-5,
    245-6, 248


N

Navvies 30-9, 43-4


P

Paddle steamers 13, 58-9

Peppercorn, Arthur 216, 223

Prittlwell 11,15-16, 20,24, 52-3, 58, 64-5,
    93, 121, 138-9, 144-5, 187, 189-90,
    119, 228, 246, 248-9


R

Rayleigh 11, 13-14, 16-17, 19-22, 25,
    27-8, 51-3, 55-6, 61, 64-5, 75, 77, 80-1,
    83, 86, 89, 93, 96, 99,107, 115, 121,
    138, 142, 144, 150, 155, 186-8, 246-8

Riddles, Robin 223

Rochford 11, 13-17, 19-20, 22, 24-5,
    27-30, 33-4, 38-9, 42, 51-5, 64-7, 71,
    75, 79-80, 83, 87, 95, 105-7, 126, 139,

144-5, 150, 179, 187, 189-90, 210, 214, 217, 222, 224-6, 246, 248-9

Romford 10, 18, 20-2, 25, 27-8, 38, 89, 115, 125, 147, 152, 170, 178

S

Second World War 101-10

Shenfield 8,10-11, 13-14, 17-25, 27-34, 36-44,47, 49-54, 56-7, 59-60,63, 74-5, 77, 79, 82, 84, 87, 96-7, 105, 107-8, 110, 112, 116-21, 124-142, 144-7, 149, 153-9, 167-8, 173-4, 178, 183-4, 213-4, 216, 222, 231-2,237, 244-8

Snow 107, 114-5

Southend 7-8,10-25, 27-30, 32, 34, 38-9, 42, 44, 47, 50,-4, 56-84, 86-90, 93-9, 102, 104-10, 115-22, 124-59, 163-9, 173-76, 178-85, 187, 191-2, 206-42, 244, 246-9

Southend Airport 105, 132, 139, 145, 149, 157-8, 179-81, 189, 230, 246,248-9

Southend and District, Bradwell-on-Sea and Colchester Light Railways 65-6

Southminster 7-8,10, 14-16, 19-20, 22-5, 28-30, 32-3, 36, 42-54, 57-65, 71, 74-5, 78, 82-4, 87, 89-90, 96-7, 102-3, 105-8, 110-11, 113-6, 118-20, 122, 125-6, 131-3, 136, 140-3, 147-53, 157-75, 178-82, 187, 192, 199-201, 206, 209, 211, 213, 215, 217-21, 223, 226-7, 229, 232-9, 241-4, 247-9

Stanier, William 224, 227

Steam navvies 31-5

Steam traction 40, 56-7, 67-9, 76-8, 81, 88-91, 94-8, 104-5, 107-9,114-5, 117-22, 127, 136-9, 142-3, 145-6, 151-3, 155, 157, 174-5, 177-8, 182, 185-6, 189, 191, 194, 199-200, 203-4, 206-30, 242-3, 247

Stock 22-3, 38, 83

Stow Maries/ Stow St Mary's 8-9, 53, 68, 79, 89, 91-3, 96, 99, 104-5, 111, 113, 124-5, 165, 173, 179, 201, 247-8,

Storm 153, 173

Strikes and industrial actions 75-6, 81-2, 88-90, 135-6, 167-8, 237

Stride, Arthur Lewis 22, 25- 7, 59, 70,

Surrey Iron Railway 10

Swindale, Dennis 168, 178, 229

T

Thompson, Edward 216, 221, 223

Tilbury 12-13, 17, 20-2, 25, 27-8, 76, 121, 153, 233

Tilbury, Maldon and Colchester Railway 13

Tramways 24, 64-66

W

Westcliff-on-Sea Motor Services 83, 90, 93-4, 120

Whitelegg, Robert Harben 76, 226

Whitelegg, Thomas 226

Wickford 7-8, 10-11, 13-14, 17, 20, 22-5, 28-34, 37-60, 62-4, 67, 75, 79, 83, 86, 89-90, 93-4, 96-7, 103, 105, 108, 112, 125, 132, 136, 138, 140-5, 148, 150, 152, 155, 158, 161, 163, 165-6, 170-4, 178-9, 181, 184, 186-7, 192, 208, 220, 237, 244, 247-9

Witham 7, 14-15, 23, 23, 36, 43, 52-3 61, 63, 86, 96, 102, 105, 108, 112, 122-3, 159, 182, 203

Woodham Ferrers 7-8, 10, 14, 22, 25, 29-30, 32, 25, 43-7, 52-4, 56-7, 59, 62-3, 68, 75, 83, 85-6, 88-9, 91, 96, 99-105, 107-115, 119, 122-3, 151, 159,162, 165, 167, 170-2, 178-9,181-2, 192, 194-5, 201, 244, 247-9

Worsdell, Thomas 207

Z

Zeppelins 78-80